Dress 'Em Out

Dress 'Em Out

by
Captain James A. Smith

Illustrations
by
Susan Gilbert

Stoeger Publishing Company

Stoeger Publishing.
Great Outdoor Books & More Since 1924

STOEGER PUBLISHING COMPANY
is a division of Benelli U.S.A.

Benelli U.S.A.
Vice President and General Manager:
  Stephen Otway
Vice President of Marketing and Communications:
  Stephen McKelvain

Stoeger Publishing Company
President: Jeffrey Reh
Publisher: Jay Langston
Managing Editor: Harris J. Andrews
Design & Production Director:
  Cynthia T. Richardson
Photography Director: Alex Bowers
Imaging Specialist: William Graves
National Sales Manager: Jennifer Thomas
Special Accounts Manager: Julie Brownlee
Publishing Assistants:
  Christine Lawton and Tina Talmadge
Administrative Assistant: Shannon McWilliams
Cover Photographs and Design: Ray Wells

Published by Stoeger Publishing Company
17603 Indian Head Highway, Suite 200
Accokeek, Maryland 20607

BK6123
ISBN: 0-88317-107-4
Library of Congress Control Number: 83-051865

Manufactured in the United States of America.
Distributed to the book trade and
to the sporting goods trade by:
Stoeger Industries
17603 Indian Head Highway, Suite 200
Accokeek, Maryland 20607
301-283-6300   Fax: 301-283-6986
www.stoegerpublishing.com

OTHER PUBLICATIONS:
Shooter's Bible
  The World's Standard Firearms
  Reference Book
Gun Trader's Guide
  Complete Fully Illustrated
  Guide to Modern Firearms with
  Current Market Values

Hunting & Shooting:
Advanced Black Powder Hunting
Archer's Bible
Complete Book of Whitetail
Hunting
Cowboy Action Shooting
Elk Hunter's Bible
Great Shooters of the World
High Performance Muzzleloading
  Big Game Rifles
Hounds of the World
Hunt Club Management Guide
Hunting America's Wild Turkey
Hunting and Shooting
  with the Modern Bow
Hunting the Whitetail Rut
Hunting Whitetails East & West
Labrador Retrievers
The Pocket Survival Guide
Shotgunning for Deer
Taxidermy Guide
Tennessee Whitetails
Trailing the Hunter's Moon
The Turkey Hunter's Tool Kit:
  Shooting Savvy
The Ultimate in Rifle Accuracy
Whitetail Strategies

Collecting Books:
The Lore of Spices
Sporting Collectibles
The Working Folding Knife

Firearms:
Antique Guns
Complete Guide to Modern Rifles
Complete Guide to Service
Handguns
Firearms Disassembly
  with Exploded Views

FN Browning Armorer to the World
Gunsmithing at Home
Heckler & Koch:
  Armorers of the Free World
How to Buy & Sell Used Guns
Modern Beretta Firearms
Spanish Handguns
The Ultimate in Rifle Accuracy
The Walther Handgun Story

Reloading:
Complete Reloading Guide
The Handloader's Manual of
  Cartridge Conversions 3rd Ed.
Modern Sporting Rifle Cartridges

Fishing:
Bassing Bible
Catfishing: Beyond the Basics
The Complete Book of Flyfishing
Deceiving Trout
Fishing Made Easy
Fishing Online: 1,000 Best Web Sites
The Fly Fisherman's Entomological
  Pattern Book
Flyfishing for Trout A-Z
The Flytier's Companion
The Flytier's Manual
Handbook of Fly Tying
Ultimate Bass Boats

Cooking Game:
The Complete Book of
  Dutch Oven Cooking
Fish & Shellfish Care & Cookery
Game Cookbook
Wild About Freshwater Fish
Wild About Game Birds
Wild About Seafood
Wild About Venison
Wild About Waterfowl
World's Best Catfish Cookbook

Wildlife Photography:
Conserving Wild America
Freedom Matters
Wild About Babies

Fiction:
Wounded Moon

Dedication

For Jay—who was taken too soon from a world he loved so much, who so loved animals and people that by the age of 20, he had earned the respect of both. I once asked him if he knew what love was. He said, "Love is that that is endless." He left this world because of an animal and a human, but his love for both, even at the end, was endless. I dedicate this book to Jay, my son, who so loved the world.

—J.A.S.

Acknowledgments

Many people have spent tireless hours contributing to what at last has become a book. While I have personally thanked each one throughout the progress of this project, I would like to express my gratitude to those individuals and organizations who have put forth outstanding effort.

First, I would like to acknowledge the Fish and Game Departments of each of the 50 states of the United States and of the provinces of Canada for the fine service they provide the sportsman, and for the excellent wildlife management programs they have instituted for the benefit and protection of the great natural resources of North America.

Specifically, I would like to thank:

Nick Pinell, Wildlife Technician, of the Colorado Division of Wildlife; Allen Woodward, Statewide Coordinator of the Alligator Management Program of the Florida Game and Freshwater Fish Commission; Don Ashley, Executive Director, Pam Ashley, Administrative Assistant, and Rick Schutz, of the National Alligator Association of Florida; John Tarver of the Louisiana Department of Wildlife and Fisheries; Ellie Horwitz of the Massachusetts Division of Fisheries and Wildlife; the New Mexico Department of Game and Fish; the New York Department of Wildlife; the Ohio Division of Wildlife; Bruce Stomp of the Oklahoma Department of Wildlife Conservation; and Steven A. Wilson, Superintendent, State of West Virginia Department of Natural Resources.

Special contributors Chris Belden, Wildlife Biologist, of the Wildlife Research Laboratory of the Division of Game and Freshwater Fish Commission in Gainesville, Florida; Art Belsom of Lafayette, Louisiana; Rolland Fuller and Bill Greenway of Indian Rocks Beach, Florida; and Chief John Harvey of the Bellefontaine, Ohio, Police Department.

The Denver Department of Natural Resources for permission to reprint "How to Pack a Horse" by Archie Pendergraft; The Louisiana State University Cooperative Extension Service for permission to reprint excerpts and recipes from "The Alligator Production Handbook," compiled by Michael W. Moody, Associate Specialist, and Paul D. Coreil, Assistant Marine Agent, and recipes by Jean J. Picou and Windell A. Curole; and Dr. Thomas G. Glass Jr. for tips from his book *Snakebite First Aid* (© 1974 by Thomas G. Glass Jr., M.D.).

Artist/researcher Susan Gilbert and researcher Pat Finch, for their endless efforts in researching and interviewing. My deep appreciation to Susan, especially, for rendering and meticulously refining all the illustrations.

Project Editor Charlene Cruson; Jay Cassell, Senior Editor of Sports Afield Magazine, and editors Tucker Spirito and Bill Jarrett. Also, Lottie Nielsen, who retyped the entire manuscript.

About the Author

Captain James Atkinson Smith loves the outdoors—and always has. Born in Connecticut, a state rich in wildlife, Smith learned how to hunt, fish and trap by age 12. Through trial and error and the coaching of his father and grandfather, he perfected his skills at field dressing, skinning and preparing all the species of animals and birds he bagged.

Smith travels worldwide in search of hunting adventures. He has combed the U.S. and Canada in pursuit of nearly all the big game and game birds he discusses in this book; and he has fished off the coasts of Japan, South America and Mexico, where he once landed a trophy-sized sailfish.

Being an accomplished marksman has of course helped his hunting endeavors. As a U.S. marine during the Korean conflict, he earned the Expert Rifleman's Badge and became an instructor in the use of small arms. In the mid-50's he was a certified rifle instructor with the National Rifle Association, an organization in which he continues membership.

The title "Captain" comes from Smith's 30 plus years in law enforcement. He began his career in 1952 as Chief Constable in his home state and later became Deputy Chief of Police. In 1959 he moved to El Paso County, Colorado, where he was swiftly promoted from Special Deputy Sheriff to Deputy Sheriff to Captain. For years he maintained the rank of Captain-Consultant for El Paso County as well as for Logan County in Ohio. In

addition, he is an active member of the International Association of Chiefs of Police, the National Association of Chiefs of Police and many other law enforcement organizations throughout the nation.

The Captain is deeply commited to law enforcement, particularly defensive tactics that will assist the uniformed officer and the pedestrian on the street. Holder of a sixth degree black belt in judo and karate, he has taught defense procedures at various police academies and has written articles on using handcuffs as defensive weapons. He was recently named Assistant Chief of Police, Director of Training for the Lake Charles (Louisiana) Police Department. Smith also invented "The Source," a non-lethal electronic defense weapon/flashlight for use by police and security personnel. He is the director of the International Non-lethal Weapons Association and serves as a staff instructor for the Justice System Training Association. To help women combat the ever lurking crime of rape, he even wrote the book, *Rapist Beware*, which has been revised and published by Stoeger Publishing under the title *Rape: Fight Back and Win*.

His helping hand does not stop there. He was one of the first Hunter Safety Instructors while in Connecticut, then in Colorado, he became Special Wildlife Officer, an American Red Cross-rated instructor and a medical and rescue officer with the rank of major for the Emergency Services Squadron of CAP (Civil Air Patrol). In this capacity, he headed numerous search and rescue missions in the five-state Rocky Mountain region. Additionally, he co-authored, for the auxiliary Air Force, a manual, "Search and Rescue," the procedures of which are still employed by the military today. Needless to say, he is aptly qualified to impart and discuss the survival techniques and hunting precautions you will read in the following chapters.

Smith has appeared on national television, radio talk shows and is constantly asked to conduct seminars and demonstrations at colleges, police academies and civic and convention centers. In recognition of his public service and social contributions, he received the Human Resources Award in 1976, recorded in the Library of Human Resources, Washington, D.C.

Now in this book, Captain Smith has produced a service-oriented guide for hunters that combines his love of the outdoors with his vast and varied experiences, many of which he relates with humor and the wisdom of the years. Not surprisingly, those experiences include his dabbling—in a serious way—in the kitchen, concocting recipes and new taste combinations that always send his dinner guests home raving.

We at Stoeger Publishing think that DRESS 'EM OUT is at once informative, instructive and interesting to read, and we hope all of you will benefit from the Captain's efforts and expertise.

—*The Editor*

Introduction

In response to my request for information for this book, an officer of the Texas Wildlife Division wrote:

"We all assume that the hunters or fishermen who go into the fields or waterways are familiar with the proper methods of handling their kill or catch. Yet time and time again, the overwhelming amount of mishandled and wasted game found each year proves otherwise."

He went on to say that, although he could send me some pamphlets on the laws and methods of hunting, he had very little or nothing at all on the subjects of field dressing, skinning, butchering and cooking. From state to state the replies were strikingly similar: It was generally assumed that the hunter or fisherman already understood the do's and don'ts of his sport.

In my studies over the years, another obvious and unfortunate fact has emerged—that too many sportsmen, geared up, licensed and eager to take the trophy of a lifetime, are loathe to ask questions for fear of being labeled a novice or a know-nothing. Consequently, it is their taxidermists or butchers who must tell them—all too late—that their skinning techniques have spoiled the mount or their field dressing methods have ruined the meat. This is assuming that the poorly handled game even gets that far. Many times the product of the sportsman's error simply ends up in the trash bin or wasted in the field.

This need for information is the prime motivation for my writing DRESS 'EM OUT. I know there are experts in the field of hunting who do almost everything right and enjoy their sport to the fullest, but their numbers are small. This book is written for the millions of North American sportsmen and women who are finding more time to hunt, specifically big game, upland birds and waterfowl, but who are not always sure of the proper post-kill techniques. (*Editor's note:* Methods for handling small game, saltwater fish and freshwater fish will follow in the next volume of this series.)

In addition, this book is intended for the millions for whom the taking of a trophy is only a small part of the total outdoor experience. The world of nature is open to all who wish to be master of their own thoughts and dreams, in a place where age has little importance, where the frenzy of urban living melts away, where a free, peaceful mind can revel in a joy that defies all definition. Nothing compares, for example, to the camaraderie that develops around a campfire where tales of the hunt are told against the majesty of the setting sun. So that lack of know-how will not detract from the magnificent outdoor experience, so that every person will obtain the best results and deepest satisfaction from his hunting endeavors, I have created this book with the assistance of many knowledgeable sportsmen and the Wildlife Divisions of the United States and Canada.

In the following chapters, I will explain in step-by-step fashion the full range of procedures: from how to determine if your animal is dead to transporting it back to camp; hunting tips you will find helpful when you are stalking your elk, mountain lion or woodcock; survival techniques and what to do in the case of certain emergencies; why to carry a thermometer and two knives; how to eviscerate a big game animal in half an hour; what's the best way to pack something as large as a moose rack, for example; how to retrieve the cape area undamaged for your trophy mount; how to skin and salt the hide; plus a special detailed chapter on butchering cuts—why you should do your own butchering and really how easy it is, as well as freezing, preserving and storing techniques.

I will also discuss bird hunting in depth. Many people don't realize it is one of the single greatest sports. Fifteen million pheasant hunters take to the fields every year and five million or more quail hunters harvest 20 million birds annually and don't even make a dent in their population. Duck hunters? Their duck stamp purchases alone have brought in over two-and-one-half billion dollars that's gone right back into game preservation and upkeep.

In addition to the basic methods of handling game and birds, I've included some of my favorite recipes. These will provide new and savory experiences for your taste buds and will dispel, unquestionably, your previous notions about the alleged gamy taste and toughness of wild meat and fowl.

To prove the point, my wife and I gave a fondue party for six couples who swore they did not like and would not eat wild game. I had arranged six small platters on which I placed six different types of meat, cut into one-inch cubes. Below each dish was a number, 1 through 6, corresponding to the different meats. I had the usual sauce dips of chutney, mustard mayonnaise, and the like, in which to dip the meat after each person cooked his own cubes in the hot oil of the fondue pot.

I told everyone we were going to try an experiment. I asked each person to sample cubes from each platter, then rate them on a scale of one to six, one being their favorite and six being the meat they liked least. Well, my guests enjoyed themselves immensely, not knowing they were eating moose, antelope, bear, elk, deer and sirloin steak. How did they rate the meat? Moose took first place; elk was number two; deer, three; antelope, four; bear, five; and, to their surprise, good old Black Angus beef came in last.

"How could it be?" they asked in amazement. "Fat," I answered. The fat is what carries the gamy taste. While domestic cattle contain about 30 to 35 percent fat, wild game has only 8 to 12 percent. If you remove the fat and cook the meat properly, wild game makes an exceptional meal. You don't have to scorch it till it's black or boil it till it's tasteless or marinate it for days either. Its own taste is delicious. You wouldn't take a filet mignon and burn it to a crisp to try to remove the flavor. You'd have shoe leather. And that, unfortunately, is exactly what happens to wild game when the cook does not understand how to prepare it. With fondue, you dip the meat into hot oil and usually cook it only until it is rare or medium rare. That is why the fondue was such a gastronomic success to our unsuspecting guests. Now they eagerly look forward to dinner invitations to our home and have even become interested in obtaining their own cuts of venison and such.

Well, I have tried to cover a lot of ground in DRESS 'EM OUT by including some general information about the animals, hunting and survival tips, field dressing procedures, skinning and butchering methods, and cooking and preserving techniques. I think there's enough in here to satisfy every person who enjoys the world of hunting and the steps that take your game from the field to the table. I hope you profit in many ways from using this book. And, don't forget, for those of you who lean more toward small game and fish, Volume 2 will discuss those in detail.

Good hunting and Bon Appétit!

Captain James A. Smith

Contents

section 1

section 1

Preparing for the Hunt

A successful hunt—one in which you return safely with game or birds in hand—depends on many factors: your equipment, your hunting skills, your familiarity with the wilderness and, perhaps most important, your ability to anticipate and cope with unexpected dangers. Most hunters take to the field with weapons and ammunition matched to the animals they are after, and they know how to use the weapons to best advantage. They usually wear clothes that are suitable to the climate and terrain they will be hunting in and most often know something about the area. Where they fall short, however, is in the face of a crisis by not being prepared—mentally or otherwise—for a sudden storm, a knife cut, hypothermia or getting lost. Remember that while the animal's No. 1 enemy is man, man's No. 1 enemy is the elements. But there *are* things you can do to plan for exigencies and increase your chances of survival.

All hunters—whether in pursuit of a mountain lion or a mallard—should become familiar with the following points *before* the hunt begins. In addition to the standard gear you usually bring along to set up a base camp or just hunt for the day, be mindful of the equipment needs I've listed to ensure a safe,

comfortable trip; then read on to review the survival procedures in case you do run into trouble.

Equipment Needs

1. The type of *clothing* you wear is very important.

• A *hat* is imperative; many a hunter has been saved from hypothermia by using a warm head covering (more on hypothermia later). Your head should never be exposed to the elements, especially to cold or wet rainy weather. This is particularly true if you become lost and are under stress.

• Wear clothing that can be worn in *layers* and removed or added with ease. Keep in mind that weather can change drastically, even though it might be ideal when you begin your hunting or fishing expedition. Wet clothing is not only uncomfortable, but can lead to many other problems. While down-filled clothing is both comfortable and light, if it becomes wet, in most cases it will lose its insulating qualities.

• Always carry *gloves and mittens* with you, even if the weather is not cold. Gloves will provide ample protection for your hands on temperate days. The mittens will protect you against extreme cold or during a snowstorm and will be much warmer than gloves under these conditions.

- Always carry a few extra pairs of *dry socks*, preferably made of wool. If you are active, your feet usually will perspire a great deal and, depending upon the terrain, you can lose as much as a cup or more of body water through your feet during an eight-hour period. Wear only one pair of socks at a time, because if you wear two, water can become trapped between the two layers and freeze during cold weather.

- The *boots* you wear should be matched to the terrain over which you will be traveling. Sturdy leather boots are an excellent choice, particularly if they are waterproofed, as this allows the boots to breathe. If your boots become wet, allow them to dry slowly. I do not recommend boot liners, because in cold weather they become saturated with perspiration and tend to dry out too slowly. I would suggest that you check with your guide, if you will be using one, a sporting goods store, or with people familiar with the area you are going to hunt. They are the most knowledgeable in regard to the correct clothing and footwear that should be worn.

2. Insofar as *sleeping bags* are concerned, they should be insulated and suitable for all types of weather and not chosen on the basis of being lightweight. I would also suggest that you bring along a foam rubber pad to be placed under the sleeping bag. An air mattress is much more inconvenient to use, as it has to be blown up every time you use it.

3. I strongly recommend that you at all times carry *two knives* as well as a small sharpener or whetstone and honing oil. If you lose one knife or break it, you will always have another one available to you. Also, with many big game animals, two knives are always used in dressing out: one for removing the glands and the other for gutting and skinning. I usually carry one four- to five-inch single blade as well as a folding knife with several blades that is also equipped with a can opener. The folding knife is small and doesn't take up much room, but can prove to be invaluable when you need it (*See Figure 1-1*).

It is very important to learn how to sharpen your knives properly. Purchase a small but good *whetstone* and it will last for years. Take the whetstone and moisten it with fine honing oil which will prevent the blade from becoming worn down. (You can carry the oil in a small eyedropper bottle that takes up little space.) Keep the stone "wet" during the sharpening, but use water *only* in emergency situations. To sharpen the knife, stroke one side of the blade on the stone in the same direction at about a 20-degree angle. You can push in a circular motion or straight away from you approximately eight times. Then do the reverse side of the blade in the same way with the exact same number of strokes. (See "Some Notes on Knives.")

4. Assuming you are going to field dress the game you bag, you will need, in addition to two knives, the following *dressing-out tools* (*See Figure 1-2*):

For big game—

- a small axe and/or folding saw or bone saw for splitting the pelvis and sternum as well as quartering the meat;
- string, twine or shoelaces of at least 10 inches long for tying the urethral and rectal tubes;
- plastic bags for transporting such organs as the heart, liver and kidneys;
- optional plastic skinning gloves;
- clean cloths or paper towels for wiping out the body cavity;
- strong rope or nylon cord for transporting (dragging) and/or hanging the carcass;
- block-and-tackle gear for hoisting, if you have a very large animal;
- cheesecloth, meat sacks and/or a tarpaulin for transporting sections of meat.

For birds—

- game shears for clipping the wings
- optional plastic skinning gloves
- clean cloths or paper towels
- rope or nylon cord for tying the birds together for carrying

5. Even if you are not planning to field dress, at least carry with you a couple of pieces of *strong cord* approximately 24 inches long. They may prove helpful in trapping small game animals if you become lost and find yourself without provisions.

6. Carry a *compass* and wear a *watch*. Both of these can be used to help you find your bearings, should you lose your way. Take a reading with your compass before you start out so you know where you should wind up if you are not that familiar with the area. To determine north with the watch, point the hour hand toward the sun with your wrist in front of you. Halfway between the hour hand and 12 o'clock will be south, so directly behind you will be north.

7. Be sure to carry in your pocket *wooden safety matches* in a small watertight metal container designed for this purpose (available in sporting goods stores). Book matches can easily become wet and will not provide you with the insurance you need to light a fire at night to keep warm or even light a distress signal if you need to.

8. Bring along several *firestarters* that you have

(Continued on page 22)

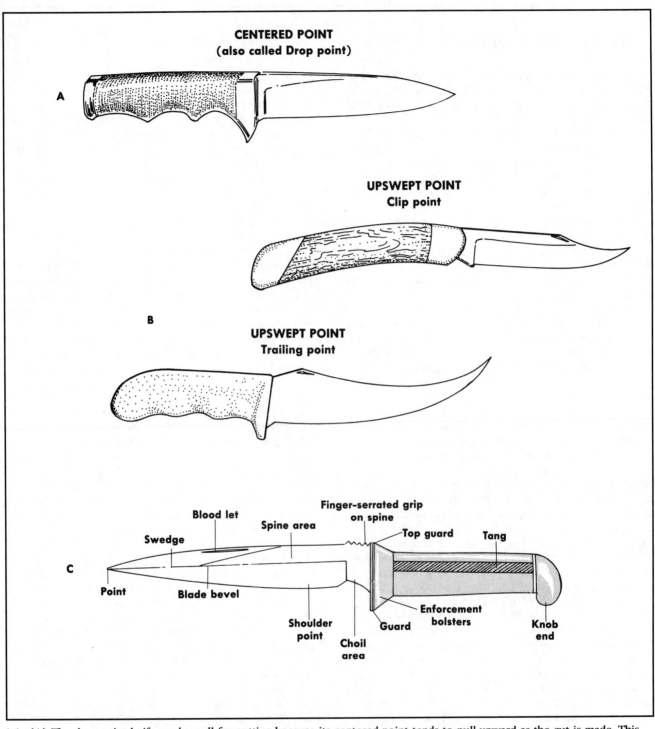

CENTERED POINT
(also called Drop point)

A

UPSWEPT POINT
Clip point

B

UPSWEPT POINT
Trailing point

C

Blood let
Swedge
Spine area
Finger-serrated grip
on spine
Top guard
Tang
Point
Blade bevel
Shoulder
point
Choil
area
Guard
Enforcement
bolsters
Knob
end

1-1. (A) The drop-point knife works well for gutting because its centered point tends to pull upward as the cut is made. This prevents accidental rupture of the underlying viscera. The broad curve also makes this knife effective in skinning out the large areas of a hide. (B) The upswept blades have extremely sharp points, making them effective for cutting into small areas, such as working the hide off the base of an antler, or cutting through a gambrel joint to hang a carcass. The clip point is good for gutting an animal, but is not advised for skinning, as it does not have enough curve to do the job smoothly. (C) Prototype of knife. All these knives come in fixed or folding blade designs. For fixed blades, the length should be 3 to 5 inches for maximum manageability. If you are choosing a folding style, be sure that the blade is at least 2½ inches long, and locks in place when opened.

SOME NOTES ON KNIVES

Although most hunters believe that the best knife is one that is lightweight, easy to handle, durable and multifunctional, it is my opinion that a knife should be carried for the job you intend to use it for.

If you are hunting big game, for example, you should have a knife that:

- you can field dress and skin with properly;
- is wide enough at the swedge and pointed in the direction that will facilitate the task at hand (See Figure 1-1);
- will not easily slip in your hands so you wind up with an injury;
- is strong enough to take lateral pressure and not break during use, and;
- can be sharpened easily without a great deal of effort or fear of breakage.

If you are a fisherman, you will no doubt want a knife made of stainless steel and one that has an edge sharp enough to fillet with. Or, if you are a camper, you will need a knife for cutting not only branches but one that will meet other demands, such as opening canned goods; in this case, you'd certainly want a knife that is strong, sufficiently wide, and can be sharpened frequently. A dull knife can injure you when you start to apply extra pressure (or it slips) because you cannot get through whatever it is you are trying to cut.

At this point you will ask, "What should I buy?"

There are thousands of knives on the market all designed for different uses, some for combination uses. Sportsmen are very jealous of their knives, and price is often no object. And there are so many combinations of steel, some that are extremely hard—over C60—and others in the lower C40 range. "C" is a Rockwell standard used to measure the hardness of steel when a diamond is drilled into it. Other types of scales exist also, which may confuse you. The usual alloys combined with steel contain carbon and various percentages of nickel, molybdenum or other metals. The combinations and heat treatments are preciously guarded secrets and even custom knife makers will stop a conversation when questioned about their formulas and processes. Certain blades are too hard for work such as skinning a moose or elk and take a long time to sharpen. Others are too soft and require too much sharpening. So, it is a must that you choose a knife for the job it is intended to do.

When looking to purchase a knife, I strongly suggest that you consult with someone at your local sporting goods store or with an expert on the subject. Don't talk to just one source, but compare the advice of several people. Then make up your own mind based on what is best suited to your needs.

I prefer a knife about four to five inches long with a hardness of C58 to C59, one that has a wide swedge and a good guard. In fact, I recommend that you always carry two knives: one straight knife and one folding knife. This is in case you lose or break your one-and-only knife. There are also many things you can do with a folding knife that you might not with a straight knife—which is not to say that a folding knife is preferred over a straight knife.

Carry a whetstone with you in the field or you could end up in a mess. I use a soft Arkansas stone, preferred by most knifesmiths, to sharpen my blades. I have a large stone at home and carry a much smaller one in a knife sheath when I'm hunting. Never use the whetstone dry. A small plastic eyedropper bottle filled with Bear, Gerbers, Russells or any other top brand of honing oil should always be carried with you. In an emergency, you can use water, but this will cause excessive wear of both your knife and the stone. The object of the oil is to help the blade actually float across the top of the stone in one direction or the other. If magnified, the oil would show floating in it small steel filings moving directly in front of your blade.

To sharpen the blade properly, hold the knife at a 20-degree angle and move it away from you in straight strokes. The number of strokes usually depends on how dull the knife is to begin with, but at least 8 to 10 strokes in the same direction is recommended. Then reverse the blade and come back the same way. Make sure that when you sharpen the blade, you follow it on the stone all the way up to the tip. Not doing this is a common mistake made by most beginners. It will take time to get the feel of it, but after a little practice you will improve. You can use a leather strop, the palm of your hand, or a piece of corrugated cardboard to wipe off and put the final touch to your blade.

A word about sheaths: not only for safety, but for the good of the blade, don't buy a cheap one. Buy a good one that is designed for your knife. Even folding knives have sheaths today. And remember this extra point when you return from the field: always remove your knife from the sheath, as the tannic acid in leather can cause damage to the steel if left for long periods of time. Clean your blade, dry it completely, add a light preservative coat of oil, wrap it in wax paper or dry cloth, and put it away until next time. This will keep one of your most important tools in good condition and will help make you a more professional sportsman.

temporary splint. In the following section on survival tips, I discuss how you can use these cravats in various other situations.

11. There are three basic types of *packs,* each designed for various cargoes and functions:

- *Frame pack.* Designed for heavy-duty loads, the best type of frame pack comes with padded straps around the shoulders and hips. This is good for carrying a rack or large quarter of game meat, because the weight of the load is evenly distributed over the body. In certain cases, the pack enclosure may be removed in order to strap larger loads to the bare frame (*See Figure 1-3*).

- *Day pack.* A day pack is usually strapped to the body in the same manner as the frame pack. This pack is soft and designed to carry lighter objects on your back. Some are made with several compartments which are useful for separating various hunting and camping items.

- *Fanny pack.* Similar in function to the day pack, this is also designed to carry light objects. It is worn around the waist and rests just over the fanny, hence the name. Although this pack will not carry as much as the frame or day pack, it is still a convenient item to have in the field, as what it does carry is conveniently out of your way, and easy to reach. Choose the right pack to meet your hunting needs.

Survival Procedures

Many people panic when they realize they have become lost or the weather has turned so awful they cannot return to their camp or car. They have no prior experience with these situations and their emotions overtake them. No two emergencies are exactly alike, but you can do something about all of them. Be smart. Be alert to your changing environment. And, above all, be mindful of the following points when you are planning your trip so you will be prepared for the unexpected. Know what to do and how to do it, because someday it may save your life or the lives of those who are searching for you.

1. Know how to read a map and how to use a compass. Don't, however, rely only on verbal instruction; learn by taking a trip into the field with friends and making actual use of both the map and compass. Learn by doing.

2. Never hunt alone in an area with which you are not familiar.

3. If you don't know the area, make sure you study a map carefully so you will be able to establish your location. Indicate with a pencil or colored pen various points on the map so you will be able to locate your approximate position.

4. If you decide you want to take a hunting trip alone, be sure to let someone know where you will be and, if possible, provide him with a map of your approximate location and your expected time of return.

5. If you are not hunting alone, set up a code or alarm system with your hunting partner that will signal an emergency; for instance, a whistle blown three times or a gun fired three times at specified intervals or three flashes of a flat mirror reflecting off the sun. Also, a signal-back, so you will know your companion has heard you.

6. Under no circumstances should you travel during the nighttime hours in unfamiliar territory or woods; it could only lead to more problems, i.e., getting lost, injuries and the like. Stay put.

7. If the weather conditions turn bad or you are lost, both of which situations would prevent you from returning to camp or car before dark—seeking *shelter* is the first and most important thing you should do.

- Search for a spot that is protected from both wind and snow.

- Never build a shelter next to a river bed or wash, because a sudden downpour could cause a dam to break above you.

- Be sure your shelter is not underneath any large trees with broken or split branches. High winds could cause them to fall, bringing with them the good possibility of your sustaining an injury.

In building a shelter, use whatever material is available to you—a strong log or branches you can lean against a limb of equal size or a rock wall. Cover the ground with dry branches and boughs. If none are available, take a leaf-covered branch and with it brush away any snow that may be on the ground. If you have cause to worry about water or rain accumulation in your shelter, run the end of a sharp-tipped branch around the shelter, creating a runoff trench.

8. In the emergency situation mentioned in 7 above, it is crucial that you *do not panic.* Although it is perfectly normal to feel confused and afraid initially, it is essential to your survival that you stop and calm yourself down so you can think rationally. If you have kept others informed of your approximate whereabouts and arrival time, they will soon begin to search for you. But you will probably have to spend a long, lonesome night waiting, for few search parties are active in the dark. So prepare yourself for the ordeal, maintain your composure and, once you have set up a shelter, build a fire.

9. As Greek mythology tells it, Prometheus risked his life to bring the benefits of *fire* to mankind. And

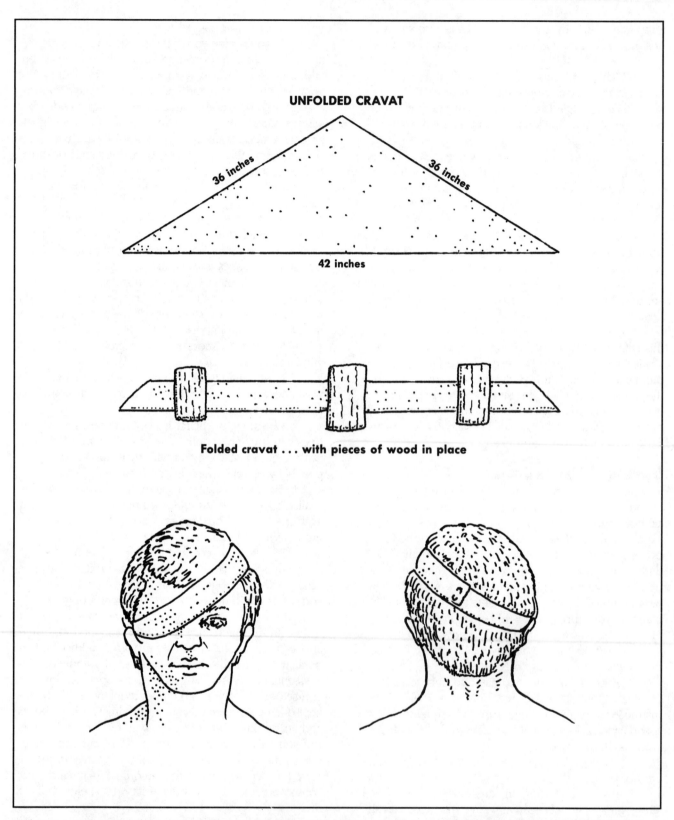

UNFOLDED CRAVAT

36 inches

36 inches

42 inches

Folded cravat ... with pieces of wood in place

1-4. For an injury to the eye, use one of your cravats folded into a band. Wrap it around the injured area, then tie or pin it in back of the head. This will prevent exposure to the elements and hopefully further injury until you have it treated properly.

benefits there are many, especially in an emergency situation in the wilds. There is nothing more comforting on a cold black night than nestling next to a crackling fire. Not only does it provide warmth, but heat for cooking, light to see by, protection from the elements and a distress signal to those who may be searching for you. Once you've got your fire going, you should be in good shape until your rescue arrives.

There are several ways to build a fire, depending on the weather conditions. When it is windy, dig a hole in the ground 12 to 15 inches deep and surround the top of the hole with stones. You can then build your fire at the bottom of the hole where it is protected from the wind. Never take stones from the water, however, for use in constructing a fireplace or to be placed near a hot fire. When cold water is poured on hot porous rocks or stones that have been rounded and smoothed by water, like the kind you find at a lake or river bottom, there is a great probability they will explode and you will be injured.

Under no circumstances should you ever build a fire under tree branches or in a tree stump, as this could develop into a forest fire.

Remember that you don't need a large fire during the nighttime hours. It is a waste of wood that should be saved for a distress signal during the daylight hours. You only want to radiate the heat toward your shelter during the night. Pile large logs or rocks at the back of the fire, i.e., the side farthest away from you; this will radiate the heat toward you and help prevent sparks or flames from blowing in your direction. You should gather twice as much firewood as you think is necessary. What you are not using at the moment should be covered with boughs to keep it dry should rain or snow develop.

If it is wet outside, you still have the trusty firestarters and dry wooden safety matches you've been carrying in your pocket. You can also make firesticks by taking pieces of hardwood and cutting into them at an angle so a fuzzy effect is produced at the ends. Four to six inches of small slices cut many times at the ends should be sufficient to serve as kindling to get the fire started.

One final point to file away regarding fires: Always have at least three stacked signal fires ready to go. Be sure to have green leaves nearby, as these will cause a great deal of smoke. In making an emergency fire, start with small kindling, then add larger branches and finally good-sized logs, if possible. A hardwood fire will burn longer, but a pine fire will produce more smoke,

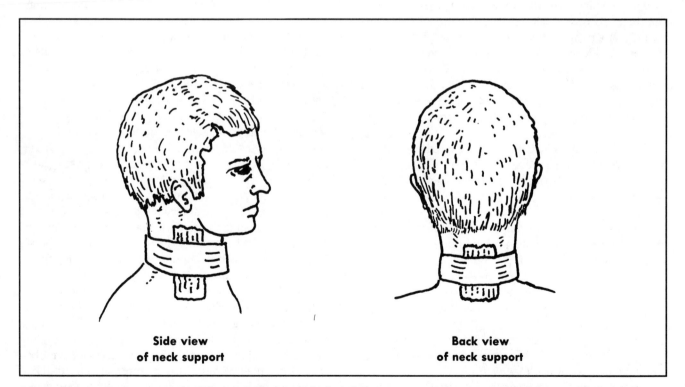

**Side view
of neck support**

**Back view
of neck support**

1-5. Should you sprain your neck while in a remote area far from help, you can construct a temporary brace with three pieces of wood (one longer for the back) tied around the neck with two cravats for support (knots should fall at back and sides only).

which is essential for a distress signal.

While the area and terrain will determine what type of materials you can gather for a fire, your mental and physical shape as well as the weather will dictate how well you assemble those materials and cause them to burn.

10. Although *food and water* are necessary for survival, you can live without them for a short while. Your No. 1 enemy is the elements, remember, not lack of food.

This is when the beef jerky and hard candy you have carried in your pocket will come in handy (if you haven't eaten them already); they will keep up your energy level and the citrus-flavored suckers will keep your mouth from becoming dry. The sweeter types will only make you thirsty.

If, after a while, your rescue does not arrive and your stomach starts growling, your own resourcefulness should aid you in finding food. Use whatever weapon you have to hit a squirrel or rabbit, or the 24-inch cord tucked in your pack to trap small game. You can also jerry-rig a spear out of knife and cord or set up a small net with a cravat tied between two poles to catch fish if you are near a stream.

You could survive a few days without water once you finish the contents in your thermos, although you may suffer somewhat from dehydration. There is water out there, however, waiting to be found. In the summer months, stones are always wet on the back side in the morning and leaves have some moisture on them (*in* them, too, if you know which ones are edible). In the winter months, when you need plenty of fluids, there is usually snow or ice available. Of course, the ideal situation would be if you were near a stream, lake or river.

Again, a survival situation is the supreme test of your endurance, your preparedness, your resourcefulness and your ability to cope with nature's contingencies. The more you know, the more secure you'll be.

11. It often happens that in a survival situation a person becomes confused and starts running. If that occurs in a wooded area, it is very easy to run into a branch, or trip and have a branch strike the eye. For this kind of *injury,* and many others, your orange-colored cravats will serve as your first aid.

For an injury to the:

• Eye—you can place a cravat directly over it, or if water is available, wash the eye out first, then place a moistened cravat over it (*See Figure 1-4*).

• Neck—if you have sprained it and it is in pain and swollen, carefully (so you do not jostle the neck

and spine) gather three pieces of bark or take a dry branch and break it into three pieces, roughly the length of your neck. Two pieces should be shorter, one for each side of the neck, and a longer one for the back. Fold both cravats separately so they are 2 to 3 inches wide. Take one cravat and loosely tie it around your neck, then place the two shorter sticks under the cravat, one on each side. Gently tighten the cravat so the sticks stay in place. Then insert under the cravat the third longer piece of wood behind your neck. Place the second cravat over the first, wrapping it around so the overlapping and knots fall at the sides and back of the neck, not at the front. This should provide you with excellent protection against further injury and will allow you to trudge short distances without too much pain (*See Figure 1-5*).

• Wrist and shoulder sprains are common injuries to people who, in a survival situation, panic and run—and inevitably fall. The cravat can be used as a sling to relieve the pressure, while still enabling the use of both hands.

• For any broken bones, you can fold one cravat into a two-inch-wide band and tie it around the broken area and a temporary splint you have made from a branch or your gun, if you have one (*See Figure 1-6*).

• If you cut yourself while field dressing, for example, you can use one cravat as a pressure bandage or compress and the other one to hold it in place.

• If you become caught in a trap, the cravats are particularly useful. You can free yourself easily by first moving the snared foot as close as possible to the trap. Place your free foot on the back side of the trap, while tying one end of a cravat securely to the stake pole. If the pole is flush with the ground, place the cravat through the chain link closest to the stake. Run the other end of the cravat through the opening where the foot is caught. Bring the cravat around the pole again, pull toward you and the trap jaws should open so you can remove your foot. If any injury has resulted to the foot, use the other cravat to wrap around the wound. One of the main reasons not to travel in unfamiliar territory, particularly where fur-bearing animals abound, is the danger of becoming trapped during the nighttime hours when you cannot see the traps.

• The primary reason for using the bright orange color, rather than white, is that it can be easily sighted. If you are injured and are dragging yourself through the underbrush, the blazing color will hopefully prevent your getting shot at. As a distress signal, it can even be seen from small planes if tied to a tree or laid out flat on the ground. So use the orange, it is truly a survival color. (*Editor's note:* "The Hunter's Cravat Kit,"

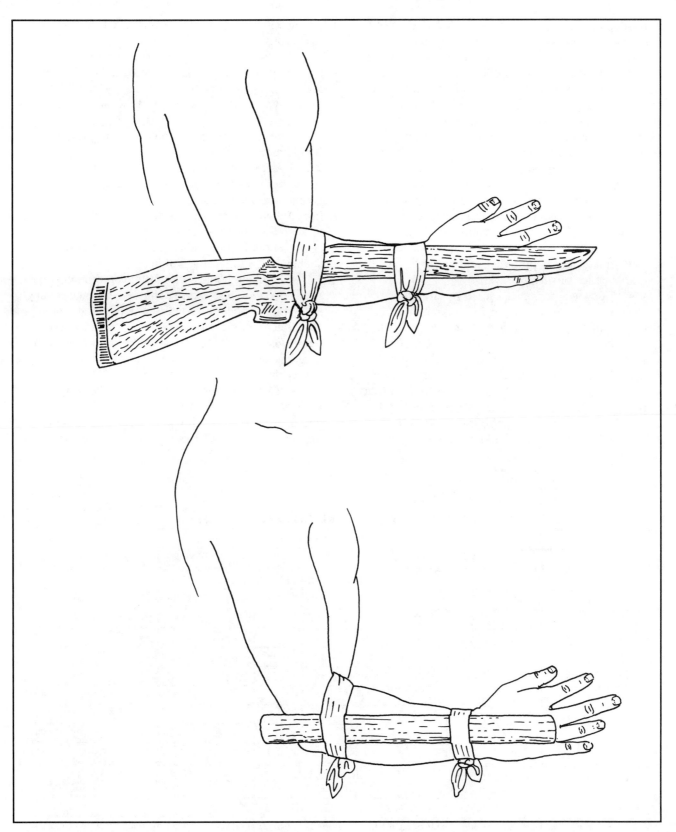

1-6. For a broken limb, you can again tie the cravats around the injured part, using as a splint a tree branch or a long gun.

consisting of two large cravats, a plastic bag in which to carry water, and instructions for the many uses of cravats, will soon be available in sporting goods stores.)

12. *Hypothermia,* often called the silent killer, strikes in many ways and under various conditions. It is characterized by the lowering of heat in the central, or inner, core of the body, producing abnormally low body temperatures. The telltale signs of hypothermia, or exposure, as it is often mistakenly labeled, are loss of coordination and uncontrollable shivering. When an individual cannot stop shivering, he soon begins to lose judgment and to slur his words. The next phase is lapsing into semiconsciousness and finally total unconsciousness, sometimes resulting in death.

The factors contributing to hypothermia are:

• An individual's physical condition, age, injuries and knowledge of survival.

• How wet a person is, caused by any of the following—rain, snow, perspiration or immersion in water from falling through thin ice or out of a boat.

• The wind is a common adversary. Although temperatures may be above freezing, with a strong wind of 20 to 30 miles an hour, which is common in the mountains or on an open lake, the wind chill factor may produce temperatures of anywhere from −2° F. (−19 C.) downward. See the accompanying chart (*Figure 1-7*) indicating how cold it can become when a strong wind blows and the levels at which it becomes dangerous.

The fourth factor is not knowing how or when to treat hypothermia. This lack of knowledge is shared by a great many hunters, fishermen, campers and hikers. This is why hypothermia is called the silent killer of the unprepared.

Here are some things you can do to prevent hypothermia:

• As I mentioned, one of the most important parts of the body to keep covered and warm is the head; this is one area that demands a great deal of inner core heat. When you are in the field do everything possible to keep your head warm and dry.

• Should bad weather ensue, find immediate shelter and get into dry clothing.

• Drinking liquids is a must. Even though you may be low on water, don't conserve it by just taking sips. You are better off to take a mouthful at a time. Under no conditions drink anything of an alcoholic nature, as this will cause your body to burn up sugar very quickly and within a matter of minutes you will be extremely cold again.

• If your clothes are wet, remove them and dry them by the fire. You may have to do it piece by piece, and if you do, start with your socks first. It is very important to keep your clothes dry, as water will

COOLING POWER OF WIND ON EXPOSED FLESH

ESTIMATED WIND SPEED (MPH)	ACTUAL THERMOMETER READING (°F)											
	50	40	30	20	10	0	−10	−20	−30	−40	−50	−60
	EQUIVALENT TEMPERATURE (°F)											
	50	40	30	20	10	0	−10	−20	−30	−40	−50	−60
5	48	37	27	16	6	−5	−15	−26	−36	−47	−57	−68
10	40	28	16	4	−9	−21	−33	−46	−58	−70	−83	−95
15	36	22	9	−5	−18	−36	−45	−58	−72	−85	−99	−112
20	32	18	4	−10	−25	−39	−53	−67	−82	−96	−110	−124
25	30	16	0	−15	−29	−44	−59	−74	−88	−104	−118	−133
30	28	13	−2	−18	−33	−48	−63	−79	−94	−109	−125	−140
35	27	11	−4	−20	−35	−50	−67	−82	−98	−113	−129	−145
40	26	10	−6	−21	−37	−53	−69	−85	−100	−116	−132	−148
	LITTLE DANGER (for properly clothed person)				INCREASING DANGER				GREAT DANGER			
	DANGER FROM FREEZING OF EXPOSED FLESH											

1-7. The wind is a crucial factor to consider when dressing for the outdoors. The stronger it blows, the colder the temperature will seem, and the more danger you will be exposed to, especially if you are not properly clothed.

conduct heat away from the body 27 times faster than dry air does.

• Should you fall out of a boat or the boat overturns in water of 50° F. (10° C.) or below, which it normally is from late September on in most places, do not attempt to swim to shore. Hang onto the overturned boat and try to get as much of your body out of the water and onto the boat as possible. Under no circumstances should you kick your legs, as hypothermia can set in in 10 to 15 minutes and in many cases an even shorter period of time. Kicking your legs only burns up energy and body heat. If necessary, get under the boat and keep your head in the trapped air space, using as little body movement as possible.

13. *Snakes* can be a threat in some hunting areas. Should you ever be bitten by one, especially one of a poisonous variety, keep these points in mind. They are recommended by Thomas G. Glass Jr., M.D., F.A.C.S., Clinical Professor of Surgery at the University of Texas Medical School at San Antonio in his book, *Snakebite First Aid:*

• The venom and swelling spread up and down the arm and leg at the same rate. The venom does not travel just toward the heart of the victim.

• The venom is affected by gravity as is the swelling. Therefore elevation of an arm or leg will hasten the spread of the venom and swelling toward the body.

• Cooling the venom (even that injected into the muscle) will rapidly and effectively inactivate the venom. Warm the venom and it is reactivated.

• The back of the hands and fingers and the back of the feet and toes are very sensitive to the venom, and efforts should be made to prevent the spread of venom to these areas.

• It is rare that a person dies from snakebite within the first 24 hours even if no first aid or treatment is given.

• In 10 percent of rattlesnake bites, the blood will not clot as early as two hours after the bite. Any type of cuts in the field may cause a large loss of blood.

• Tourniquets applied too tight can cut off the blood supply to the bite area and this enhances the action of the venom. Tourniquets applied just tight enough to compress the tissues and not obstruct the blood supply above and below the bite site will effectively prevent the spread of the swelling.

The following are the most practical first-aid measures for all snake bites:

• Immediately after the bite, apply a light tourniquet (a simple rubber band will do) directly above and below the bite, if possible.

• Apply crushed ice in plastic bags widely around the bite area.

• Remove the snakebite victim and, if possible, the snake to a medical facility in a rapid and safe manner and do not harm the victim.

• A bite by a large rattlesnake (four feet or more) may kill a small person within several hours. When hospital care is not available, the bite area should be immediately excised (surgically removed by medically trained personnel only), then the victim taken to a medical facility as soon as possible.

• Don't skin test or give antivenin (horse serum) in the field. It is unwise to do either unless adequate facilities are available to care for an immediate severe reaction to the horse serum.

• Don't waste time at the scene trying to start a difficult intravenous injection.

• Don't inject Xylocaine (Lidocaine) in severe bites regardless of heart irregularity. Lidocaine may precipitate a convulsion in a victim with a severe bite.

However, there are times when for various reasons your hunting party may be away from medical care for many hours. If you travel in an area where a bite by a very large rattlesnake may occur, you should be prepared to do more than apply tourniquets or ice. Carry a snakebite kit with you and learn the proper procedure for treating a bite before you leave on your trip.

The kit includes: 2,000 mg. hydrocortisone sodium succinate (Solu-Cortef); syringe and needle to inject the cortisone I.V.; two tourniquets; 20 cc. vial of Xylocaine (1 percent) without adrenalin; syringe and needle to inject Xylocaine; sterile scalpel; sterile gauze dressings; Ace elastic bandage (4 inches wide); and alcohol (70 percent) antiseptic solution.

Prior to going into the field, any person planning to attempt the procedure should be instructed by a qualified physician or first-aid person. The procedure is:

• Apply tourniquets immediately above and below the bite site.

• Cleanse bite site with alcohol.

• Inject Xylocaine under skin around bite site.

• With sterile scalpel, excise a circle of skin and fat which includes both fang marks. Excise down to bone or muscle, opening fascia (covering of muscle).

• Apply sterile dressings and Ace bandage.

• Give 1,000 mg. of Solu-Cortef I.V. and repeat if necessary to eliminate symptoms of nausea and vomiting.

• Transport the victim to a hospital.

Fortunately (or unfortunately) most bites occur

GROUND–AIR VISUAL CODE FOR USE BY SURVIVORS

REQUIRE DOCTOR SERIOUS INJURIES	**I**	REQUIRE SIGNAL LAMP WITH BATTERY AND RADIO	**I̵**	*REQUIRE FUEL AND OIL	**L**
REQUIRE MEDICAL SUPPLIES	**II**	INDICATE DIRECTION TO PROCEED	**K**	ALL WELL	**LL**
UNABLE TO PROCEED	**X**	AM PROCEEDING IN THIS DIRECTION	**↑**	NO	**N**
REQUIRE FOOD AND WATER	**F**	WILL ATTEMPT TAKE-OFF	**▷**	YES	**Y**
REQUIRE FIREARMS AND AMMUNITION	**V**	AIRCRAFT SERIOUSLY DAMAGED	**L⌐**	NOT UNDERSTOOD	**JL**
REQUIRE MAP AND COMPASS	**☐**	PROBABLY SAFE TO LAND HERE	**△**	REQUIRE MECHANIC	**W**

IF IN DOUBT, USE INTERNATIONAL SYMBOL **S O S**

GROUND–AIR VISUAL CODE FOR USE BY GROUND SEARCH PARTIES		
NO.	MESSAGE	CODE SYMBOL
1	Operation completed.	**L L L**
2	We have found all personnel.	**L̲L̲**
3	We have found only some personnel.	**╫**
4	We are not able to continue. Returning to base.	**X X**
5	Have divided into two groups. Each proceeding in direction indicated.	**⚡**
6	Information received that aircraft is in this direction.	**– →**
7	Nothing found. Will continue search.	**N N**

1-8. The above symbols are generally used if you are a survivor anticipating a search, or are directly involved in a search by air. When you are on the ground, lay out symbols by using strips of fabric, such as the orange cravats if you have enough, pieces of wood, stones or any available material; provide as much color contrast as possible between material used for symbols and background against which symbols are exposed; symbols should be at least 10 feet high or larger and care should be taken to lay them out exactly as shown; in addition to using symbols, every effort should be made to attract attention by means of radio, flares, smoke or other available means; on snow-covered ground, signals can be made by dragging, shoveling or tramping, with the depressed areas that form the symbols appearing black from the air; pilot should acknowledge message by rocking wings from side to side.

between the knee and ankle. Excision in this area is not likely to cause any great problems. Cuts around or near the wrist or ankle should be avoided. When necessary great care should be exercised to avoid large nerves and arteries.

14. In *Figure 1-8* I have included *air visual codes* which you may find helpful if you are in a remote area and a search is conducted by air.

I realize I have included many points to ensure your preparedness for a hunt. But they are all important and it is essential to your safety and the success of your hunt to absorb them all. Once you do, you'll be able to go anywhere with the security that you can cope in almost any emergency. Good hunting.

section 2

section 2

Big Game

DEER

Deer are the most hunted antlered animals in North America—for the meat as much as for the sport. Pursuing them is the kind of experience that, no matter how often you take to the field, it is always thrilling to watch them bound through a forest or silently graze in a meadow. And of course those who enjoy a good venison roast will always hanker for more.

Deer are members of the biological family called *Cervidae* (pronounced *serv*-id-ī) that bear solid-boned antlers (unlike bighorn sheep, for example, that grow hollow horns). Along with a few other game animals, deer nearly became extinct at the turn of the century because of unconscionable slaughtering. This was prompted by the Victorian Era's conspicuous consumption of exotic goods and unusual foods, including such delicacies as moose and buffalo tongue, deer liver and the like—not to mention the display of various hides as rugs or wall coverings.

Today, with more stringent state regulations and wildlife management, the deer population reaches well into the millions. The white-tailed variety, a very adaptable subspecies, inhabits almost every part of the United States and has multiplied in the largest numbers. The mule deer, which roams the area from the plains states westward, and its smaller cousin, the black-tailed deer, which roves the Pacific coastal mountains, make up a smaller percentage. Other sought-after cervid game include elk, moose and caribou and are discussed in separate chapters.

White-tailed Deer. This reddish-brown-colored mammal ranges in weight from 50 to 200 pounds and grows to a height of approximately 32 inches at the shoulders. The border and underside of its tail, often a foot long in larger deer, is completely white, a distinguishing feature you can readily see when the animal is alarmed or running. Individually, the whitetail usually occupies and maintains a range space of about one square mile; but when faced with the lack of available herbage, the deer will expand its natural boundary in search of food.

Mule Deer. This large deer got its name from its ears, which are long like a mule's—but that's where the similarity stops. It is fleet, runs with a jumping stride and is one of the most clever four-footed creatures you'll ever hunt. While the doe weighs a relatively moderate 160 pounds, the buck averages 220 pounds, some having been recorded at over 300 pounds. And think about this: a mule deer of 170 pounds yields about 100 pounds of edible meat when fully dressed out. That's a lot of food for the freezer. It is not

Mule deer

uncommon for a novice hunter to report mistakenly having seen an elk, when in reality it was a sizable muley.

All deer usually molt twice a year: in the spring when they replace their thick grey winter coat with thinner, shorter tawny-colored pelage; and again in the fall when they prepare for the rigors of winter.

Another changing characteristic, experienced only by the male, is the annual shedding and regrowing of antlers. While the white-tailed buck sprouts antlers with a single tine emerging from a main stem, the muley grows tines that are forked and long (*See Figure 2-1*).

Antler development begins sometime after the buck reaches nine months of age. The increasing daylight in the spring signals the pituitary gland to stimulate the release of testosterone in the blood stream. This hormone is responsible for antler growth

and maintenance. The buck enters a stage called "in velvet" when the antlers are covered with a thin velvety-textured skin filled with tiny capillaries. These nourish the bony structure. If struck, scraped or in any way damaged while in velvet, the antlers will bleed profusely. When antler growth reaches its peak, the velvet simply dries up and becomes nonfunctional. At this point, the buck begins scraping his antlers against trees and other hard objects to remove vestiges of the membrane. This practice also helps to sharpen the tines of his rack. (Between shedding and regrowth, the deer is without antlers for a period of about four to six weeks.) Although the diameter of the antler base tends to increase with age, the size of the rack is also a function of the animal's diet. While in velvet, protein is a necessary nutriment and later calcium, found in many plants, is the key mineral that contributes to the size

White-tailed deer

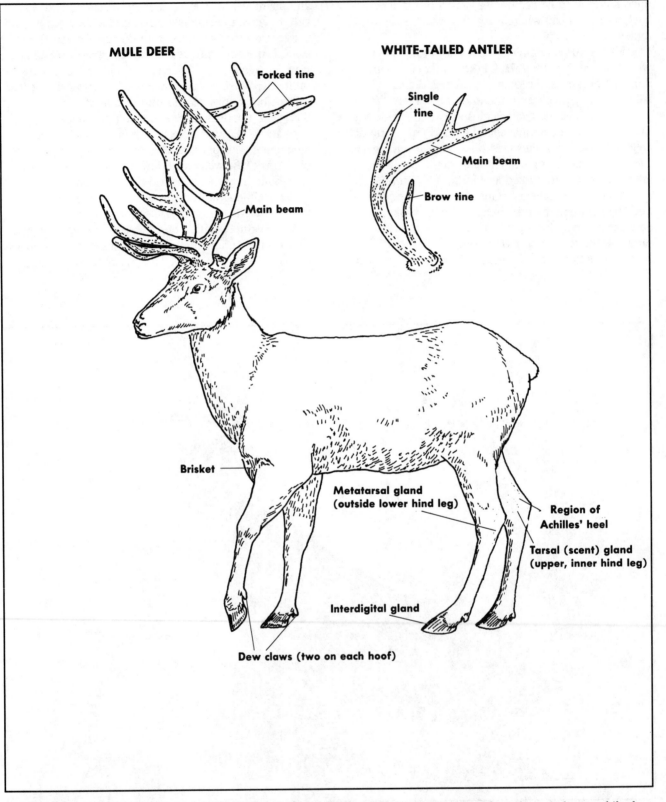

MULE DEER

Forked tine

Main beam

WHITE-TAILED ANTLER

Single tine

Main beam

Brow tine

Brisket

Metatarsal gland
(outside lower hind leg)

Region of
Achilles' heel

Tarsal (scent) gland
(upper, inner hind leg)

Interdigital gland

Dew claws (two on each hoof)

2-1. General physical anatomy of the deer. Note that the mule deer has forked tines branching from the main beam, while the whitetail has only single tines.

and proper formation of the bone.

As ruminants, deer have four-sectioned stomachs and chew their cud like cows. They are herbivorous, feeding on herbaceous plants, grasses, moss, lichens, tree leaves, bark, and the like. Many prize—and good eating—deer have been taken from farming areas where the main diet consists of corn, soy beans and wheat.

Hunting Tips/deer

Whether your aim is a cache for your freezer or a trophy mount, keep in mind these tips when you hunt deer. • The whitetail's color perception is extremely limited, although studies at Montana State University have revealed that it can perceive bright colors, such as blaze orange (which some states require hunters to wear as a safety regulation). Fortunately, showing this color has reduced hunting accidents significantly.
• Most important is the deer's awareness of motion and sound. Even if you are dressed in bright hues, but you are still and quiet, you should remain undetected. Patience and endurance are your strongest allies while you wait for a good shot. • The deer's sense of smell is incredibly acute. To help camouflage their own human scents, some hunters wear strips of cloth dabbed with apple, grape or skunk scents (don't use too much). If you do this, look carefully into what you are using, because the deer's olfactory sense is so sharp it can often distinguish between natural scents and those manufactured with chemicals. • Try to make a "clean" kill—i.e., aim for a vital area, like the brisket or behind the shoulder joint. A shot in the rear may only cripple the deer and cause unnecessary suffering, while a hit in the gut may puncture the internal organs and contaminate the surrounding meat. • The meat from an animal killed during or after a prolonged period of stressful running will most likely be tough and taste gamy. The chemicals released in the bloodstream during the animal's fright and flight cause the buildup of metabolic wastes in the muscles, affecting the texture and taste of the meat. So if tender, good-eating meat is what you're after, a well-placed shot in a young deer will yield the best results.

Some other hunting tips came out of one of my most memorable deer hunting experiences. My two sons—Jay, who was 16, and Bob, who was 14 at the time—and I went to Meeker, Colorado, in the Seven Lakes area, a favorite spot for many sportsmen. Even Teddy Roosevelt used to hunt there often. While the fishing is great, the area is considered the "back door" to great elk and bear hunting. In recent years, moose have become more populous in the Colorado area and the Wildlife Division will soon initiate a permit draw, just as they do for antelope.

Deer season was about to open, and my sons wanted to learn some new hunting tips. We had about two days before the start of the season. We had already been lucky with the fishing, so we decided to make the next few days a learning experience for them. We went up a couple of miles west of our camp, where we walked along a crystal clear stream. I told the boys to watch for signs of any animal prints. The sun had only been up about an hour and soon we hit some coyote tracks. There were some smaller animal tracks, also, and then we spotted deer tracks, both large and small. I pointed out to the boys that the ones farthest from the stream were beginning to dry up on one corner and that some of the prints had leaves and other debris in them, which no doubt had blown in on the wind from the night before. I showed them that the tracks nearest to the water were still moist, but the edges were starting to curl over. This meant that the deer had probably been there at least four hours earlier. Farther up the stream, we came upon tracks that were far apart. This was a sure sign that something had scared the animals and they were running for cover. Sure enough, we found bear tracks nearby.

The beavers in the area had built their dens in the middle of the streams and ponds, which also confirmed that bear were in the vicinity. Beavers will usually build their dens alongside the stream, unless their number one enemy, the bear, is close by.

A major point in hunting game anywhere is to know all the water sources. Most all wounded animals will head for the nearest water hole. If the hunter waits a few minutes and then starts to track them, he will usually find them heading in that direction. When wounded, shock begins to set in and once an animal lies down it is almost impossible for it to get up. If you immediately chase after a wounded animal, it can and will go for miles, and most likely you'll wind up losing it.

At this point, Bob asked why all the deer prints were in a circle. We were about a mile away from the nearest water and on the side of a draw that went up to some quakies. I told him that the deer were looking for a place to bed down. They wanted a good place where they could see, as a deer's eyesight is pretty sharp.

Then I did what the boys had been wanting me to do. I picked up two smooth hardwood branches and told the boys to sit very still. I got into some deep cover and started to strike the branches together. It made a sound just like two bucks fighting over an area. After about 20 minutes of this, off and on at intervals of about every three minutes, Bob's eyes nearly popped out. There at the edge of the quakie clearing were two does. Bob couldn't contain himself. He jumped up and pointed to about six does and a buck running downhill. Naturally, the other two does broke. I had only hoped that one deer might appear, but this was a real treat, not only for the boys, but for me, too.

On this same trip, I also pointed out the rutting signs that deer make before mating and how the droppings would begin to harden and change color, and as the sun grew higher during the day, how grass would straighten upward, all of which are extra points for hunting any animal.

Well, it took the boys and me three days to get our fill, but they had a chance to learn some additional information that every father should teach his sons or daughters if they are to take their hunting seriously.

Field Dressing/deer

Let's assume you've bagged a deer. Now what do you do? If you've read "Preparing for the Hunt," you've come equipped to field dress, skin and perhaps quarter your deer before you return home, and you are carrying the following gear:

- two knives—one skinning knife and one pocketknife
- a small axe, folding saw or bone saw
- string, twine or shoelaces of at least 10 inches long; and some strong rope or nylon cord
- optional plastic skinning gloves
- clean cloths or paper towels
- plastic bags
- thermometer for gauging outdoor temperature

Before you begin, check the deer to make certain it is dead. Approach from behind since it's probably your safest direction in the event it rears up. Keep your weapon pointed at its head in case you have to finish the job there. Check the eyes for a glassy, blank look. A deer dies with its eyes open, so don't think you'll have to lift the lids to perform this test. Then you can proceed.

Time and temperature are two very important considerations when field dressing any animal. The warmer it is outside, the quicker you must dress and cool your game. The thermometer you've brought with you will give you an indication of how fast you must work. As a rule of thumb, at 45° F. (7° C.), spoilage occurs rapidly, so field dressing must be begun immediately and finished quickly.

The entire field dressing procedure should be completed within 30 minutes, but many seasoned hunters can do the job in 10. Practice is all it really requires and of course knowing what you're doing.

And, as with many things in life, there is no one correct way to field dress. Hunters argue the pros and cons of various techniques which tend to change through the years. I'll give you some idea of these methods and you can decide for yourself, based on your beliefs, preferences and what you basically feel comfortable with.

Bleeding. If the deer was alive for some time following the shot, chances are internal bleeding was massive. If this is the case, sticking your knife in one of the main arteries of the circulatory system, which is advised by some hunters, will only expel the blood remaining in the system, provided clotting has not occurred. You must also consider that once the heart has stopped beating, the pumping action of the blood will also cease. Rather than spend the time it takes to bleed a deer, I begin field dressing immediately. A good deal of blood is eliminated during the dressing itself.

1. The first step in field dressing is to position the animal on its back with the head higher than the torso. Make sure it is stable by tying a rope around one of its legs to a tree or by placing large rocks around the body.

2. Some hunters believe it is essential to remove the scent, or tarsal glands, one located on the inside of each hind leg alongside the Achilles' tendon (*See Figure 2-1*). The glands are encased in a thin protective membrane, but messing with them could lead to trouble. The odor of the secretion is pungent and will permeate the meat if allowed to come in contact with it. Also, if you puncture the gland itself, you could accidentally make your much-wanted venison very unpalatable.

However, if you are of the mind that these glands should be removed, use your pocketknife and slice deeply around these protrusions (the whitetail's glands are about one-inch long; the muley's, four to five inches). Keep a wide margin on all sides so as not to puncture the glands themselves.

Once you have removed the glands, be sure to wash your hands with water, if available, or otherwise clean them some way before you handle the rest of the animal. In addition, never use the same knife for field dressing that you've used for gland removal; carry two knives. I find that a good jackknife with a can opener and saw blade is a very useful second knife to have on a hunting trip. Also, should one knife get lost, you'll always have a backup. Remember to clean your blades with a clean, dry cloth; using water on them may lead to corrosion, so use water sparingly, if you must.

Sitting in your favorite chair reading about field dressing and actually doing it in the wilds on a chilly

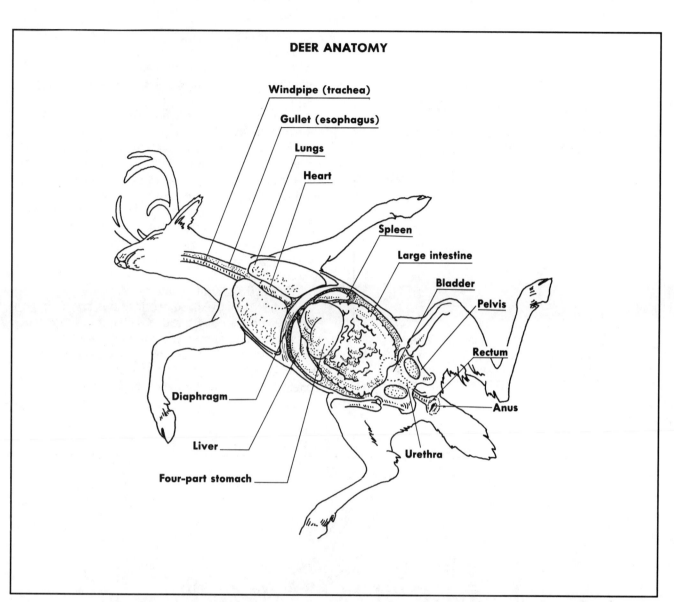

DEER ANATOMY

Windpipe (trachea)

Gullet (esophagus)

Lungs

Heart

Spleen

Large intestine

Bladder

Pelvis

Rectum

Anus

Diaphragm

Liver

Urethra

Four-part stomach

2-2. Internal anatomy of the deer. As a ruminant, or cud-chewing animal, the deer has a large four-chambered stomach to aid digestion of the grasses and plants it feeds on. Also note that the deer has no gall bladder.

morning are two vastly different experiences. With the illustrations that follow we have tried to show what you will encounter when you cut open a deer. It is difficult because, regardless of the detail in the drawings, it's tough identifying the various organs during the actual gutting. And, while these illustrations appear in black and white, remember that the task you will eventually perform will be in bloody living color. Before you leave for the hunt, familiarize yourself with deer anatomy by studying *Figure 2-2*.

3. Now, with a clean knife, beginning just below the breastbone, or sternum, and midway between the two front legs, cut away a small section of hide. It should be just large enough to slip your index and middle fingers underneath. Form a "V" as shown in *Figure 2-3*, and lift the hide as you cut *blade up* from underneath.

This initial cutting technique is important for two reasons: You do not want to cut deeply on the first incision or you may rupture some internal organs that

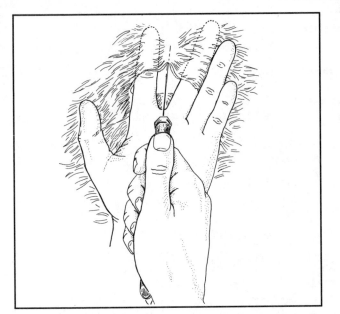

2-3. It is important to use the "V" formation with the knife blade up and placed between your index and middle fingers (palm facing up). This facilitates control of the knife, prevents dulling, and helps keep the hair of the hide away from the meat.

could contaminate the meat; and by approaching from underneath, you will not only avoid cutting directly through the hide from above—which will dull your knife—you will also prevent the hairs from mingling with the meat.

Now cut until you reach the genital region, as shown in *Figure 2-4.*

4. Pull the hide away on both sides to expose the underlying muscles of the belly (*See Figure 2-5*). Then cut through the muscle layer as you did with the hide, starting below the sternum and stopping when you reach the genitals. Again, be careful not to puncture any of the inner organs, such as the stomach or spleen. Should this happen, however, cut away the section of meat that has been tainted and wipe the surrounding area so the rest of the meat does not become contaminated and foul-tasting.

So far you have made two incisions: one through the hide and the other through the layer of muscle. If you are a novice hunter, you will find that cutting through the hide first, then the muscle layer in two steps may help you get the feel of using a knife and better acquaint you with the deer's anatomy. However,

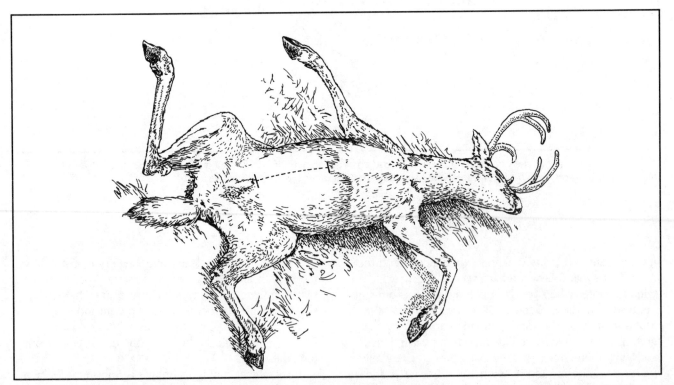

2-4. In field dressing your deer, the first incision is made at the sternum, or breastbone, and continues until you reach the genital area. If you are new at this, cut only through the hide first.

many experienced hunters cut straight through to the inner cavity on the first cut, thus saving time (especially on a warm day). *This saves time only if it is done carefully.* I recommend making two cuts, regardless of how much experience you have—particularly if you plan to take a nice chunk of venison home to your family. But, as I mentioned before, you do whatever is most comfortable for you. Remember, however, whichever technique you choose, always begin with the first incision through the hide forming a "V" (*Step 3*) to help guide your cutting. And *always* be watchful about puncturing the digestive organs you will eventually remove.

5. Tying off the bladder and anal openings (tubes) takes only a few minutes and is important in preventing the waste matter of the bladder and rectum from spoiling the meat when these organs are pulled under the pelvic bone and emptied on the ground with the other entrails. It is another step in field dressing that is often neglected or completely eliminated by many rushed, modern hunters. I still advocate that it be done, however, because if it is not, you may wind up with one miserable mess on your hands, literally, especially

if you are not wearing gloves. So tie the tubes—you'll be glad you did. Here's how to do it.

In the *buck,* both the penis and the rectum should be tied off. The penis is attached to the outer surface, while the tube inside it, the urethra, curves around under the pelvic arch and attaches to the bladder (*See Figure 2-6A*). Hold the penis in one hand while you cut with the other down to the base of attachment; do not cut it or the scrotum off completely. Cut a deep circle around the anus; pull it out gently until you can see the rectum. Then simply tie a strong piece of twine around both the urethra and rectum, as shown in *Figure 2-6B*.

In the *doe,* the urethra ends at the vagina and does not curve around the pelvic bone as in the buck. To locate the tubes of the urethra and rectum, cut one big circle around the vagina and anus, as indicated in *Figure 2-6C*. Then gently pull out and loosen the circle of flesh until you can see the urethra and rectum. Tie the two together as shown in *Figure 2-6D*.

6. Split the pelvic bone and empty the lower cavity. To do this, cut through the thighs (rounds—upper inner legs) which will expose the pelvic or aitch bone. Using a good knife or a small axe, cut through

2-5. Pull away the hide, revealing a layer of muscle underneath. Then make a similar cut through the muscle—carefully—so as not to puncture any of the digestive organs. If you are more skilled with a knife, you can cut through hide and muscle in one procedure.

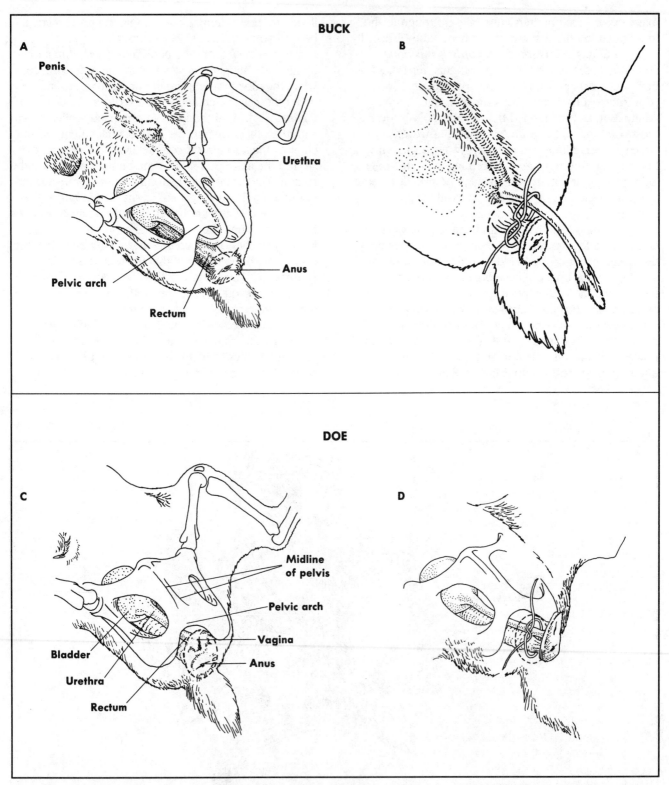

BUCK

A

Penis

Urethra

Pelvic arch

Anus

Rectum

B

DOE

C

Midline
of pelvis

Pelvic arch

Vagina

Bladder

Anus

Urethra

Rectum

D

2-6. Tying off the bladder and anal tubes is necessary in preventing the contents of the bladder and rectum from spoiling the meat. In the buck, (A) cut the penis down to its base of attachment, then encircle the anus; (B) gently pull the two organs until you can see the rectal sac (the urethra which connects to the bladder is not visible in the male). Tie the two tubes as shown. In the doe, (C) simply cut a large circle around the vagina and anus; (D) gently pull out and tie together.

the pelvis along the midline (*See Figure 2-6C*). Be careful that you do not rupture any of the viscera located beneath it. After cutting the bone, spread it apart. This will expose the bladder and small intestines and free the way for removal of the organs. Now turn the deer on its side and empty the contents, being especially careful when pulling out the bladder and intestines. Now the body temperature of the meat will begin to cool down.

7. The chest cavity is emptied next. The diaphragm is a wall of muscle that separates the upper chest cavity from the lower abdominal cavity. Like the skin of a drum, it stretches around the perimeter of the torso. The gullet and several major arteries and veins pass through openings in the diaphragm to connect with the contents of the lower torso (*See Figure 2-2*).

Reach up into the belly and encircle the inner perimeter of the rib cage with a sharp knife. This will separate the diaphragm from the walls of the chest.

With the diaphragm severed, you will be able to reach high up into the throat of the deer and cut the windpipe and gullet. Use both hands for this—one to grasp the tubes, the other to cut them off as high up as you can reach. Once cut, pull down on the windpipe and gullet; this will also loosen the heart and lungs. Pull all the contents out of the chest cavity. Essentially you're done with the field dressing.

(Many hunters prefer to cut the testicles off first and lay back the penis at the same time or remove, depending on state laws, and then cut upward toward the brisket. This method is fine, but I prefer the downward method, as do many of my friends, for several reasons. First, you are cutting with the hair and you can dull your knife very quickly and waste a lot of time later on sharpening your blade, thus risking the possibility of spoiling some of the meat, depending upon the weather conditions. Second, there is more space because the rib cage and intestines are pressing against the lower wall and will slip out easier when cutting downward and will not spill all over you and your feet.)

Incidentally, if you are wondering what to do now with the entrails that are all over the ground, don't worry. Leave them where they lie. Nature and her animals will take care of them.

If you have decided to save the heart, liver and kidneys (kidneys are attached to the back wall of the body, about halfway down the spinal column), trim off all connecting blood vessels and place the organs in a plastic bag with a small amount of water. This will keep them moist. (Since these particular organs are usually eaten right away, it is the only time water should be

used this way). The bag can later be placed inside the carcass for convenient storage during transporting of the deer.

If blood has pooled in the now-empty carcass, turn it over to drain for a few minutes. Then return the deer to its back and wipe the inside with a clean dry cloth. The most important thing now is to cool the meat of the animal. Prop the body cavity open with one or two appropriately sized sticks and hang the deer for additional cooling and ventilation when you get back to camp or home. See accompanying chart (*Figure 2-7*) for average cooling times.

One tip to remember before transporting your deer is that if you're going to drag him, a few stitches in the body cavity with a large needle and heavy thread will prevent unwanted dirt from getting inside.

Transporting/deer

Before moving your deer anywhere, keep in mind that skinning him can wait till you get back to camp or home, but field dressing cannot. It must be done immediately and as quickly as possible.

Once that's accomplished, the most common way of getting your deer from the field to the camp or car is dragging, shown in *Figure 2-8*. An alternate method requires two men to carry a pole onto which the deer has been securely tied down. Two people can also transport a deer by simply grabbing an antler each and dragging once again.

Whichever way you transport your deer, make sure you have tied a piece of brightly colored, preferably hunter orange, cloth or a scarf around the part of the deer that will most readily be seen by fellow hunters. This will protect you from getting shot at.

If you intend to bring your field-dressed, unskinned deer home for further processing, tag him, if that is required in your state. Push a wire through the edge of his ear; affix the tag; fold in that section of the ear, then overlap the top, securing it by wrapping the wire around the entire ear (*See Figure 2-9*).

Also take care to shield the carcass from any unnecessary heat. Never carry your deer on the hood of a car or in a closed trunk where the temperature may rise to dangerously high levels. You may transport the deer on the roof of your vehicle, but remember to cover it properly with the head out, tie it down securely and make sure the tag will not blow off during the drive.

Once you arrive at home with your catch, hang it, skin it—if you haven't already done so—and prepare for butchering.

COOLING GAME

AVERAGE COOLING AND HANGING TIME

Animal	8-hour inner meat temperature after death at 42°F. (6°C.) external temperature	Cooling time at 42°F. (6°C.) (skinned)	Animal	8-hour inner meat temperature after death at 42°F. (6°C.) external temperature	Cooling time at 42°F. (6°C.) (skinned)
DEER	65°–70°F. (18°–21°C.)	18–20 HOURS	MT. GOAT	68°–70°F. (20°–21°C.)	20 HOURS
ELK	75°–76°F. (24°C.)	24 HOURS	BEAR	76°–77°F. (24°–25°C.)	30 HOURS
MOOSE	76°–77°F. (24°–25°C.)	30 HOURS	MT. LION	70°–72°F. (21°–22°C.)	20 HOURS
CARIBOU	75°–76°F. (24°C.)	24 HOURS	*JAVELINA	68°–69°F. (20°–21°C.)	10–12 HOURS
PRONGHORN	69°–72°F. (21°–22°C.)	18 HOURS	*WILD PIG	68°–70°F. (20°–21°C.)	10–12 HOURS
SHEEP	70°–71F. (21°–22°C.)	18 HOURS	*ALLIGATOR	N/A	N/A

*The temperature is usually well above 40°F. (4°C.) where and when these animals are hunted. If possible, most hunters should get their game to the cooler the same day they are shot. The alligator is controlled and must be butchered in a cooler; by law, it cannot be hung to cool.

2-7. Cooling an animal after field dressing is essential before you butcher, package and freeze the meat. The No. 1 enemy of all hides and meat is heat, both external—the sun and exposure to high temperatures—and internal—the inner body core of the animal itself. When the external temperature gets into the above 45° F. (7° C.) range, it could mean trouble—and spoilage. The body fat and weight of the animal also determines how long it will keep its high temperature. An elk, for example, after field dressing and hanging for eight hours, will still have an inner body temperature of about 75 degrees, so longer cooling time is necessary to lower the body temperature to a recommended 40 degrees.

(The temperature can be taken at the upper hind leg directly through the meat to the rump or spinal area.)

There are two schools of thought on cooling game—with the hide left on and with it removed. If the game is large and the temperature stays in the 30's, you can cool the animal with the skin on. This protects it from dust, dirt and insects. However, if the temperature is well into the 40's, depending on the size of the animal, it should be skinned and hung to cool. The chart shows average cooling time for *skinned* animals and the internal temperature after eight hours of cooling at 42° F. (6° C.).

Hanging and Skinning/deer

If you don't intend to use the head for a trophy mount, you can tie a rope around the deer's neck and suspend the carcass from a sturdy tree branch or a beam in your garage. This allows for additional blood drainage as well as for cooling.

To skin, remove the lower portion of all four legs, cutting through at the center joint of each. Then completely encircle the neck just below the jaw, being careful to cut through the hide only, as shown in *Figure 2-10.* Begin to pull down with your hands on

the hide; you should be able to remove it in virtually one piece this way. You may need the aid of a sharp knife in spots, but generally speaking, your own knuckles should be sufficient if you are careful. When you reach the tail, sever only the soft inner cartilage, the tailbone, which is attached to the skeletal structure much like the ear is to the skull. Once severed, continue pulling downward, but do not cut the tail away from the hide itself.

If you are interested in saving the hide, extra care should be taken when skinning. You want to work

2-8. In transporting your deer, one relatively easy way, if you are alone, is to tie a rope around the front legs and head and drag it along with a hand pull. Whichever way you choose to remove your deer from the hunting site, be sure both you *and* your deer are wearing regulation blaze orange so you are not mistakenly shot at by other hunters.

2-10. To skin a deer not intended for a trophy mount, hang it head up. Carefully cut a circle around its neck through the hide only and pull the hide down with your hands, using a knife only for the tough-to-handle spots.

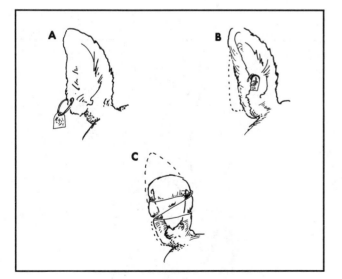

2-9. A properly tagged carcass leaves no doubt in a game warden's mind that you are licensed by your state to take home the deer you've just bagged (provided you're in a regulation wildlife or private hunting area). Push a wire (A) through the edge of the deer's ear and affix the tag; (B) fold in that section of the ear, then overlap the top; (C) secure it by wrapping the wire around the entire ear.

only in the thin membrane layer that separates the muscle from the hide and you want to remove the hide with no cuts and no meat or fat left on it.

Trophy Mount. Hang the deer head down, as shown in *Figure 2-11,* if you are planning for a trophy mount. To do this, insert a strong piece of wood that has been sharpened at the ends into the gambrel joints of the hind legs (*See Figure 2-12*). Note that all four legs have been cut off between the mid-joint and the hoof. A rope or block-and-tackle arrangement with a pulley can then be set up and used to hoist the carcass.

Before you begin removal of the hide, you must make several cuts into it as the dotted lines in *Figure 2-11* indicate: cut around the lower joints of the legs and up the middle of their inner sides; across the pelvis; and around the entire upper torso, where the cape actually starts. You want to save as much of the cape as possible to give the taxidermist enough area to work with. Remove the hide from the torso area first by simply pulling down from the legs where you have already cut through the hide.

Skinning the Cape. Before skinning the cape, with a sharp knife cut a straight line down to the base of the skull, then cut down to each antler in an inverted "Y" position, as shown in *Figure 2-13*. Pull the hide down to expose the complete length of the neck.

At this time, it is best to remove the head from the body to facilitate skinning the delicate areas of the face. Starting at the front of the neck just under the lower jaw, cut through to the base of the skull where it joins the spinal column and twist the head to free it (*See Figure 2-14*).

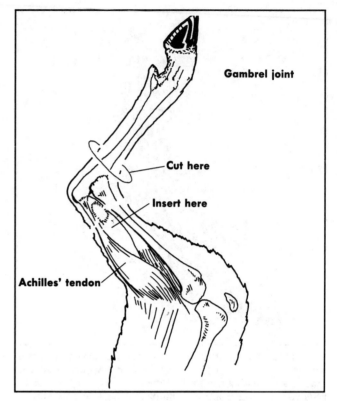

2-12. To ensure that the carcass is hung securely during the skinning, insert a sturdy length of wood into the gambrel joints of the hind legs or set up a block-and-tackle arrangement that will facilitate hoisting.

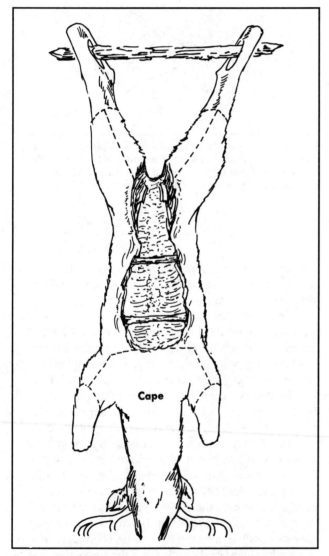

2-11. Hang the deer head down if you are planning for a trophy mount. Cut off the legs below the mid-joints and make cuts into the hide along the dotted-line areas as shown. Then skin the torso first by pulling down from the leg cuts.

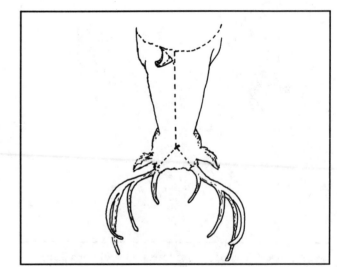

2-13. Removal of the cape begins after you have cut a straight line down to the base of the skull, then branched out to the base of each antler, like an inverted "Y".

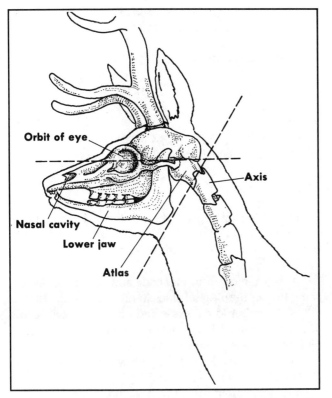

2-14. To remove the head, cut through the base of the skull between the atlas and axis, the first two vertebrae of the spinal column, then twist off. To detach the rack, saw through the skull at eye level, below the antlers, starting from the back.

Now you can peel the hide to the base of the antlers, using a dull flat implement, such as a screwdriver, to work the hide loose. Then use a knife to cut under the ears, and keeping the knife close to the skull, free the ears. The cartilage remaining in them may be kept inside until you have finished the skinning and have more time to clean them out. The chief point to bear in mind when skinning the face is to keep your skinning implement as close to the skull as possible, especially when you are cutting through the connective tissue of the ears, nose and lips. It can be a tricky process. Also, follow the contours of the skull; it will make your task easier.

Whether you need it to complete your mount or if the rack is your main concern, removing the antlers is the last thing you'll need to do during the skinning phase. For this you'll need a saw to cut through the skull below the antlers, as indicated in *Figure 2-14.*

Cooking/deer

Since many big game with similar anatomy are butchered in the same manner, a separate chapter on

"Butchering and Preserving Game" discusses the various and most successful methods of processing meat, beginning on page 142.

Deer meat is very tasty as well as healthful and has great versatility in the kitchen. The following are my favorite deer recipes.

Venison-Stuffed Zucchini Squash
(Serves 4 to 6)

6 zucchini squash	salt and black pepper to
2 pounds ground venison	taste
½ cup vegetable or	2 cups rice, cooked
peanut oil	1 large onion, diced
	1 green pepper, chopped

Parboil or steam zucchini until crisp-tender. Scrape out the seeds and hollow out the centers.

Crumble the venison and brown it in oil, salting and peppering to taste. When meat is browned, remove from heat and mix together with rice, diced onion and green pepper. Stuff the hollowed-out squash with this mixture and place on baking sheet. Bake in preheated oven at 325° F. for 30 minutes.

Oriental Venison Pepper Steak
(Serves 2)

1 pound venison flank	2 medium green peppers
steak, well trimmed	cut into half-inch
3 tablespoons soy sauce	squares
1 tablespoon dry sherry	¼ cup vegetable oil
1 teaspoon sugar	4 slices peeled fresh
3 teaspoons cornstarch	ginger, 1-inch long and
	⅛-inch thick

Cut steak lengthwise into 1½-inch-wide strips and crosswise into ¼-inch slices. Mix soy sauce, sherry, sugar and cornstarch in large bowl. Add meat strips and toss to coat evenly. Marinate 4 to 6 hours.

Heat 12-inch wok or 10-inch frying pan over high heat for about 30 seconds. Pour in 1 tablespoon oil and swirl in pan; heat for 30 seconds. Add green peppers and cook until tender. Remove peppers from pan and reserve. Add remaining oil to pan and heat. Add ginger and cook for several seconds, then add meat and marinade. Stir and cook for several minutes until meat is browned. Return green peppers to pan and cook a few minutes more. Discard ginger. Transfer to serving platter and serve with rice.

Venison Stew
(Serves 4 to 6)

1½ pounds venison shoulder, cut into 1½-inch cubes
2 pounds venison shin, cut into 1½-inch cubes
flour
⅓ cup vegetable or peanut oil
2 cups onion, coarsely chopped
2 teaspoons salt
whole peppercorns to taste
3 teaspoons paprika
1 clove garlic, minced
1 pound tomatoes, coarsely chopped
1 to 2 dashes hot pepper sauce
1 bay leaf
2 cups hot water
2 cups green bell pepper, cut into thin strips
½ cup dry sherry
1 teaspoon Worcestershire sauce
1½ tablespoons parsley, chopped
2 teaspoons sugar
1 6-ounce can tomato paste

Dredge meat in flour and coat evenly. Heat oil in heavy skillet and brown meat well on all sides. Add onion, salt, peppercorns, paprika, garlic, tomatoes, hot pepper sauce, bay leaf and water. Simmer about 40 minutes, then add green pepper strips, sherry, Worcestershire sauce, parsley, sugar and tomato paste.

Cover and simmer over very low heat until meat is fork-tender, about 2 to 3 hours.

Venison Sauerbraten
(Serves 6 to 8)

4-pound venison rump roast
¼ cup vegetable or peanut oil
salt to taste

Marinade:
3 cups water
1½ cups red wine vinegar
2 bay leaves
12 peppercorns
2 whole cloves
1 carrot, sliced
1 onion, sliced
2 stalks celery, sliced

Place roast in a large glass or ceramic bowl. Combine all ingredients for marinade in a large saucepan and boil 5 minutes; pour over meat. Refrigerate 3 to 4 days, turning frequently.

Remove meat from marinade and pat dry. In Dutch oven, brown meat on all sides in oil and season with salt, if desired. Add marinade and bring to a boil. Lower heat and simmer 3 hours. When meat is fork-tender, remove and keep warm.

To the marinade, add the following:
12 gingersnaps, crushed
2 tablespoons flour mixed with ¼ cup water
3 to 4 tablespoons sour cream

Bring mixture to a boil again, stirring until thickened. Serve with potato pancakes and applesauce.

Burgundy Venison
(Serves 4)

1½ pound cubed venison, all fat removed
flour
vegetable oil
2 cups fresh mushrooms, sliced
1 clove garlic, minced
1 12-ounce can tomato paste
1 10½-ounce can beef consommé
1 tablespoon Worcestershire sauce
½ cup red Burgundy wine
½ cup sour cream

Dredge meat in flour. Heat oil in large skillet over medium-hot heat; add meat and brown. Add mushrooms and stir well. Add remaining ingredients except for Burgundy and sour cream. Reduce heat to low, stir well and cook for approximately 1½ hours, or until meat is tender. About 20 minutes before serving add Burgundy and sour cream. Serve over noodles or rice.

Pot Roast of Venison, Hungarian Style
(Serves 8)

1 4-pound venison rump or shoulder roast
2 tablespoons bacon fat or butter
salt and freshly ground black pepper to taste
1 tablespoon paprika
¼ teaspoon thyme
1 bay leaf
1 cup sherry
1 cup beef stock
1 large onion, sliced
2 carrots, sliced into thin strips
2 stalks celery, coarsely chopped
1 cup sour cream

In a large Dutch oven, brown the meat in bacon fat or butter.

Season meat with salt, pepper and paprika. Add thyme, bay leaf, sherry, stock, onion, carrots and celery. Bring liquid to a boil, reduce to simmer and cook for 2 hours.

Remove roast to a heated platter and keep warm. Strain sauce and return to Dutch oven along with meat.

Simmer over low heat until tender, about 45 minutes. Remove meat and gradually stir in sour cream until well blended. Serve sauce over meat.

Rock Salt Roast
(Serves 3 to 4)

This centuries-old method of roasting venison in a thick mound of rock salt is little used by modern-day cooks; however, the delicious advantages of the method are reasons enough for repopularizing this technique. The meat, though seared in a very hot oven, does not shrink, nor does it lose any of its juiciness because of its protective "armor" of rock salt. Venison cooked in this offbeat manner will even please people who shun salt because rock salt has no salty taste.

3 strips bacon, chopped
1 2- to 3-pound venison
   roast, trimmed of all fat
black pepper to taste

3 pounds rock salt, or
   more as needed
apple slices, marinated
   pears, parsley sprigs
   (garnish)

With a thin knife or skewer, force bacon into roast about 1½ inches apart (it is not necessary to completely embed bacon into roast). Pepper meat all over.

Cover bottom of a large roasting pan with one inch of rock salt. Place roast in pan and encase in a mound of rock salt, using a little warm water where necessary to hold rock salt together.

Preheat oven to 500° F.; place roast in oven and immediately reduce temperature to 450° F. Cook 15 minutes per pound for medium meat; 13 minutes per pound for medium-rare meat. Remove roast from oven. The rock salt will have hardened to a black-and-white mound. Wearing an oven mitt, hit a hammer and chisel or a large screwdriver against the rock salt. Large pieces will break off. Use two large forks to lift roast off rock salt base onto platter and wipe off excess particles of salt. Garnish with a ring of parsley and stick apple slices and pears into sides of roast, securing with toothpicks. Pour some brandy over roast, ignite, then serve.

Elk

ELK

To the American hunter, one of the most seemingly impossible and difficult animals to hunt and take down is a member of the solid-antlered deer family known as the American elk or wapiti. (The European elk is equivalent to the American moose.) The elusive 700- to 900-pound bull elk, which is about the average trophy size, can test any man's strength, nerves and endurance. Consider the ruggedness of the Colorado or Wyoming terrain the Rocky Mountain elk inhabits and add to that the challenge of climbing to altitudes necessary to find him and you will begin to wonder how any hunter fells an elk.

Your first sight of the elk may be a blurred image of this beast in motion, out of range and on a distant ridge. Perhaps, if you are fortunate, you will find him feeding quietly at the edge of a park. Inevitably, on the narrowest ledge with the worst footing imaginable is the spot you'll find this magnificent animal with its rack stretching a good five feet or more from tip to tip. You will marvel at how the bull elk throws its huge head and rack back over its shoulders and runs with the grace of a small deer. You will be alarmed if you hear its bugle when you least expect to hear a sound.

The bull elk can grow to a length of 9½ feet, a shoulder height of 5 feet and a weight of more than 1,000 pounds. It is the second largest member of the deer family, although as in many species, the female is smaller. The cow weighs only from 500 to 650 pounds. Only? The average whitetail buck weighs far less. In some states the cow can be hunted by permit only, but she is sought after because the meat, especially that of a young cow, is very tender eating. Elk usually travel in herds and are often seen in winter in the valleys foraging for twigs and whatever herbaceous growth they can find; in the summer they move to the mountains, where the bulls usually separate from the group. Like other deer, the male sheds its antlers annually and, as its rack expands with age, so does its status, setting up a well-defined social order among the herd.

Many conservation programs have been instituted to protect and maintain the elk population in several states. During one severe winter in Colorado, the elk came down into some of the smaller towns in search of food. The Wildlife Division spent over three-quarters of a million dollars airlifting tons of bales of hay to them. Many elk perished in spite of these provisions and others fell prey to coyotes, dogs and other animals. Yet the herds still flourish with the present population of over one million in the high country states alone (primarily Colorado, Montana, Washington, Wyoming, Utah and New Mexico).

One time I was hunting the western slopes of Colorado, near Salida, a small town that has become the center for many hunters. This is the place where, if you have forgotten any supplies, you can get them— such as when you leave your sleeping bag at home, or when you're so careful with your ammunition that you leave it in that special place on the back porch.

On this particular hunt, Dick Anderson and several other friends of mine (including Nick Pinell of the Colorado Wildlife Division) drove our jeeps and four-wheel vehicles about 40 miles northwest of Salida. We followed a wash and a jeep trail for several hours until we came to a small stream, which was an excellent site for our base camp.

After setting up camp, cutting and hauling wood and all the other necessities, Dick and I went over the map of the area. We discussed how we could hunt and what signals we'd use if we became lost or brought some meat down. This may sound amateurish to some of you, but having been on many search parties and bringing out dead or injured people, I feel that all hunters should share information with each other, not only for safety's sake, but to help make a good hunt. Many injuries are caused by hunters not doing this or not listening to their guides. This is particularly true when hunting big game.

We were after elk and a couple of guys in our party had cow permits. We were going to hunt in some of the area "parks," which were just a little above the timber line, about 9-10,000 feet. The elk would not be down this year, at least not at the first snow. The skies, however, looked like we might be getting some soon. The next morning we started up some pretty rough trails. Normally, we'd have horses, but this time we were going to "hoof" it. Dick and I had decided to cross through a draw and end up on the west side of the lake. We knew that if we were lucky, a jeep could be brought around to at least a mile from the area.

About three hours after we had started from the camp and were working our way out of the aspen-filled woods, we came upon a grassy area, one of the parks I mentioned. We searched the area with our binoculars, but saw nothing. We decided to sit down for a rest. Just as we got comfortable, however, I looked over to where Dick was sitting, and about 50 feet to his right I spotted one huge bull elk. He was standing between two trees just looking around, and I had such a lump in my throat I couldn't speak. Naturally, I couldn't shoot over Dick's head, nor could I make a move or else this trophy would be off and running.

I'm sure we must have had our E.S.P. working, because Dick slowly moved his hand and released his safety. Then he leaned forward so slowly that there was hardly any movement. I was sure that he had seen the bull and was going to get a shot off at it. I only thought to myself, if only I could be in that position! But I was happy for Dick as he swung his rifle to his shoulder.

Then it happened. I heard the loud report of his .308, then another round as he fired from a standing position. I will tell you now that the bull trophy got away. Dick's aim was fine, but he shot an average-sized cow that stood all but obscured from my view! Dick never even saw the bull until he stood up and fired the second round.

What my friend said at that moment I could never begin to put into print! I circled the area and tried everything I knew to track down the bull, but to no avail. I got back just in time to have the pleasure of helping Dick with the final dressing and quartering of the cow. In all the hours it took to get back to camp, Dick was the only one who complained about missing the trophy bull. Over the next few years, I went back to that same area and always brought home a nice bull elk—but nothing like the one that got away!

Hunting Tips/elk

The elk has excellent hearing, smell and eyesight and can travel with an endurance that would be the envy of any marathon runner. • An inveterate climber, uphill traveling presents no problem to the sure-footed elk. So be prepared to ascend to high mountainous areas where the temperature falls to chilling levels. Dress accordingly. • If you get a shot off and don't bring down your elk the first time, don't—and I repeat don't—think that by simply waiting 20 minutes or so you'll be able to walk over and pick up your quarry. The elk will not lie down and lick its wounds as would a deer or moose. An elk will keep moving when injured and has been known to travel a good 10 to 15 miles in this condition. Experience indicates that an elk will head for water when injured. For this reason, a good hunter should always know the terrain and, most important, the location of streams, lakes and other watering holes.

Field Dressing/elk

In dressing out the elk, let's assume you intend to reserve the head and shoulders for a shoulder mount. This means you will want to save as much of the cape as possible. Keep in mind that when an elk is mounted on the wall, you will need a larger space (both width and depth from the wall) for the antlers to clear than you would with a deer.

Before you begin caping the elk, you should open the abdomen to begin the cooling process. Heat builds up rapidly in an animal of this size. Opening the belly will also facilitate bleeding. Do not bleed the animal by sticking a knife in its neck arteries; this will puncture the hide of the cape and ruin it for mounting.

1. Position the animal with its head and upper body elevated. If you are on a steep incline, it is a good idea to tie the elk's head to a tree to prevent it from slipping down the hill. With the animal's rump lower than its head, you will have gravity working to your advantage as you begin to remove the innards.

2. Start by making an incision in the middle of the chest, just in line with the back of the front legs. In the same manner as you would field dress a deer (See "Field Dressing/deer," page 40), use the "V" position and cut through the hide and top layer of muscle down to the genital region, being careful not to pierce any of the underlying digestive organs. Cut through the hide first, then the muscle layer in two steps; one step, depending on your preference, objectives and experience.

3. If the elk is a male, lift up the penis and free it from its base of attachment. Follow the same procedures as you would the deer for tying off the urethral and rectal tubes, male or female.

4. Using your larger knife, cut through the tissue of the inner thighs. You don't want to slice through the thick muscles of the legs, as this will ruin the steaks obtained from these sections; but you want to slice through the area where the legs appear to join the body. This will reveal the aitch, or pelvic, bone which forms an arch over the lower intestinal area between the two rear legs. Cutting this thigh tissue will enable you to spread the legs out to the sides so you can approach the pelvic bone easier (See Figure 2-15).

5. Now cut through the pelvic bone with your knife or a small axe and spread the bone open. Turn the carcass on its side and empty out all the contents of the lower abdomen.

If you have made a gut shot, that is, if the bullet has entered the belly and perforated the digestive organs, you may use a little water to remove the splattered fluids and then wipe the area dry. I prefer to use water sparingly or not at all; it contributes to the growth of bacteria which, in turn, causes breakdown and decay of the meat. The use of water is particularly detrimental when the temperature exceeds 40° F. (4° C.). Wipe the empty cavity with a clean dry cloth. The carcass can remain on its side.

2-15. To facilitate splitting the pelvic bone (which is more difficult than on a deer, for example), make light incisions in the inner thighs first. This will give you more room to get at the bone.

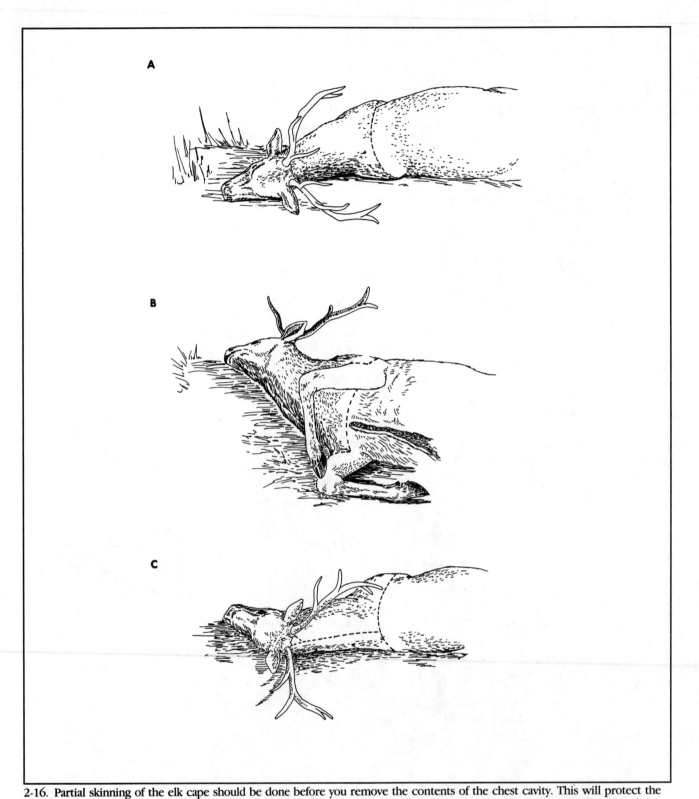

A

B

C

2-16. Partial skinning of the elk cape should be done before you remove the contents of the chest cavity. This will protect the cape from any possible tears or blood stains that might ruin your trophy mount. Starting with a cut behind the front leg, (A) encircle the back of the animal until you reach the other leg. Cut around one leg and (B) continue across the brisket area, ending with a cut around the other leg that joins your initial incision. Following the spinal column, (C) cut from the edge of the cape to the base of the skull, then branch out in a "Y" shape, ending at the base of each antler.

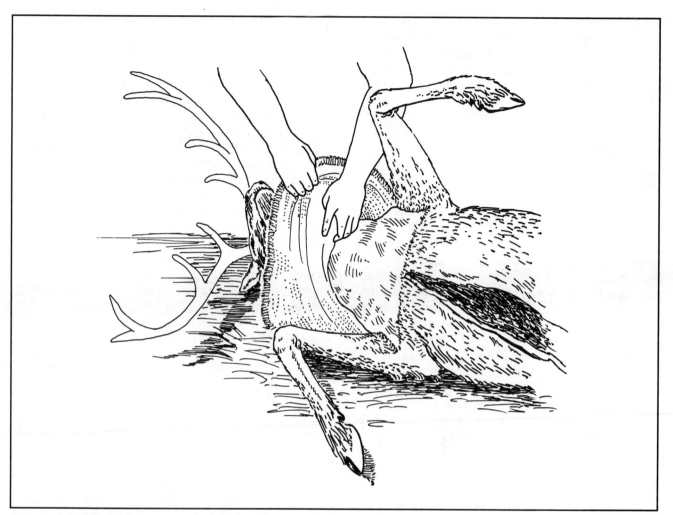

2-17. Peel the hide back to expose the brisket and neck, and your partial caping is complete.

6. *Partial Skinning of the Cape.* At this point, you would ordinarily proceed to enter the chest cavity and remove its contents. Since, however, you intend to mount the head and shoulders, you should first skin out a portion of the cape to protect it from any possible tears or blood stains that may occur during the final steps of field dressing.

With the animal on its side, start cutting through the hide only just behind the front leg and continue around the back of the elk, ending just behind the opposite front leg. Cut around the front leg and across the brisket to the other leg, cutting around this one as you did the other. Join the line of your first incision (*See Figure 2-16*).

Now cut along the middle of the back, following the spine and stop when you reach the base of the skull. Here branch off into two separate incisions, much like the letter "Y," ending at the base of each antler.

Remember to cut only through the hide—the layer of muscle underneath should not be penetrated. Peel the hide only as far back as necessary to expose the brisket and throat, as indicated in *Figure 2-17.*

Now you can finish the field dressing. You will resume skinning the cape when all the contents are emptied from the body and it is propped open for cooling.

7. With the brisket muscles now fully exposed, cut through the underlying bone in a lengthwise direction (*Figure 2-15*).

Spread apart the ribs and reach into the neck to grasp the windpipe and gullet. Follow them up as high as they go and sever them at the highest point; cut away the entire organs, because they spoil rapidly.

Cut around the inside perimeter of the rib cage to free the lungs and heart and to detach the diaphragm, the tough muscle just at the base of the rib cage. Empty out the entire contents of the chest cavity and wipe out the inside of it with a clean dry cloth.

After you have removed the innards, use two or more sticks to prop open the hollowed areas to continue the cooling process.

Skinning/elk

If you intend to use only the hide of the head and shoulders for your mount, you may skip this section on skinning the carcass and proceed to butcher the meat in the manner described in the section on quartering and transporting. Further skinning of the head should be completed after the meat is cared for, or, if you are accompanied by a fellow hunter as is usually the case when hunting big game animals, your friend can begin skinning the cape while you begin quartering or skinning the carcass.

Skinning the Carcass. Begin at the rear of the animal. Reach under the hide and cut the tail away from its attachment to the spinal column, leaving the contents of the tail inside the hide as you skin.

Next, cut a complete circle around the joints of the knees on the rear leags. Then cut straight down the inside of each hind leg. While pulling off the hide, turn the body as necessary. You may have to use a knife in some places, but your muscles and knuckles will get the greater share of the workout in this endeavor.

The hide of the lower body can be removed in one piece, assuming you have already encircled the upper body while doing the skinning of the cape. In hot weather, removal of the hide will also help to cool the meat, since the elk's heavy fur tends to hold in the body heat most effectively.

Salt the hide and process it as discussed in "Skinning and Preliminary Tanning Tips," page 60.

Skinning the Head. Start peeling the hide from the corners of your cut along the backbone. You may want to remove the head at this point, as you would a deer, or you can continue skinning. When you reach the antlers, you will have to use a sharp knife to free the hide that clings to the base of the antlers. When cutting the hide, make the cut so that the hair of the hide projects up around the base of the antlers in order to give the mount a realistic appearance.

To remove the hide from the ears, reach under the hide as you did with the tail and completely cut the ear away from the skull. The inner cartilage will remain inside until further treatment is necessary.

The eyes must be skinned most carefully. Make sure not to cut into or leave any part of the delicate lid

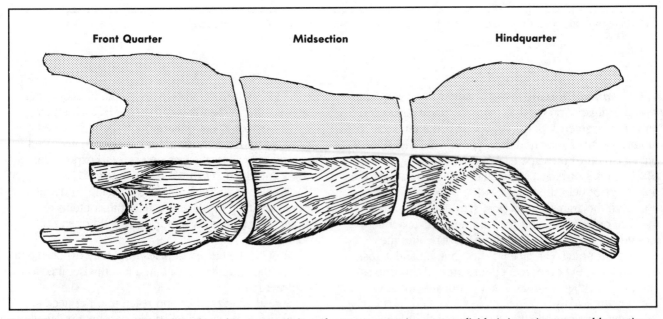

2-18. If you have taken a large elk and need to quarter it in order to transport it, you can divide it into six manageable sections as shown above.

remaining on the skull of the elk. Use your free hand as a guide to gauge the depth of the socket, and carefully peel and cut away the flesh from the skull and socket. Keep your knife as close to the bone as possible. The eyeball itself will remain in the socket of the skull.

When you get to the nose, follow the same procedure as you did in skinning the tail and ear. Leave the cartilage in and cut away from the skull at its base of attachment.

Cut the lips away from the jaw by keeping your knife at all times very close to the bone.

Now you should be able to remove the entire hide from the skull. Treat it with salt the same way you would any piece of hide, using extra care with the ears, nose and lips.

The final step in preparing the mount is removal of the antlers. To do this, you must use some type of saw. A knife or axe will just not do the job. Starting at the back of the skull, saw through the head horizontally at the level of the eye sockets, as shown in *Figure 2-14*. The remaining portion of the head can be severed from the body if you haven't already done so.

Quartering and Transporting/elk

To transport any of the elk meat a long distance on foot, you will undoubtedly have to quarter the carcass and package the meat into manageable sizes. And, if you are only skinning the upper body for a trophy mount, and do not wish to use the rest of the hide, it is acceptable and even advisable to butcher your elk with the hide still on. When cut into smaller pieces, the hide serves as a protective covering for the meat and keeps it free of dirt and insects. The major disadvantage to this, however, is that the meat will take longer to cool and therefore increases the risk of spoilage.

Hang the carcass, if possible, by the hocks as you would a deer. Begin the quartering by first cutting through the entire length of the backbone with a bone saw or small hacksaw. You may cut on either side of the rounded vertebrae, or directly through the middle of each one. This will divide the carcass into two halves. Take one side down and make the second cut just behind the front legs. All the meat to the front of this constitutes the forequarter. The next cut is made in front of the rear leg, severing the hindquarter from the middle section. From the front and hind sections, remove the legs at the joints of the shoulders and pelvis respectively (*See Figure 2-18*).

Repeat the quartering steps with the remaining side. The important thing now is to divide the carcass into pieces that can be transported via horseback or backpack. Later you can properly butcher and process this fine meat (refer to "Butchering and Preserving Game.") Be sure to enclose the meat in properly ventilated meat sacks or cheesecloth to continue the cooling process. The green hide and antlers will also contribute heavily to the overall weight of the load so keep this in mind when you are packing. See the following chapter on moose for proper packing using a horse.

Cooking/elk

Roast Elk in a Cooking Bag
(Serves 6 to 8)

1 5-pound elk loin roast	1 large onion, sliced
4 strips uncooked bacon, diced	¼ cup carrots, diced
	2 cups sherry
salt and freshly ground black pepper to taste	1 16-ounce can crushed tomatoes
3 tablespoons butter or margarine, softened	½ cup flour

Make small incisions all over roast and with the tip of a knife, force bacon pieces into cuts. Sprinkle roast with salt and pepper and rub with butter or margarine. Place in plastic cooking bag and add the remaining ingredients. Close bag and tie. Be sure to puncture bag in several places to allow air to escape. Place in roasting pan and cook 2½ to 3 hours.

Remove roast from oven, slice and keep warm on a heated platter. Arrange onions, carrots and tomatoes around meat. Make gravy by adding flour, dissolved in cold water, to sauce in pan. Spoon some gravy over slices of roast elk; pass the remaining gravy.

Elk Swiss Steak
(Serves 2)

2 1-inch-thick elk round steaks	¼ cup vegetable or peanut oil
flour	1 onion, finely chopped
salt and freshly ground black pepper to taste	1 12-ounce can beer

Combine flour, salt and pepper and pound into steaks with a mallet. Pour oil into a heavy skillet, heat, and add round steaks, browning on both sides. Reduce heat to low, add the onion and cook until transparent. Pour beer over steaks, cover tightly and simmer for 1½ to 2 hours until meat is tender.

Boiled Fresh Elk's Tongue
(Serves 2)

1 fresh elk tongue	1 teaspoon peppercorns
4 cups water	10 whole cloves
1 large onion, sliced	2 bay leaves, crushed
2 tablespoons salt	

In a large Dutch oven, bring all ingredients to a boil. Reduce heat to simmer and cook approximately 30 minutes or until meat is fork-tender. Slice tongue and serve with Horseradish Sauce or Mustard-Mayonnaise Sauce.

Horseradish Sauce:

½ cup horseradish, freshly grated	¾ teaspoon salt
	dash Tabasco sauce
½ cup bread crumbs	½ cup whipping cream
½ cup milk	

Combine first 5 ingredients. Beat whipping cream until stiff peaks form and fold into horseradish mixture.

Mustard-Mayonnaise Sauce:

2 tablespoons dry mustard	1 cup mayonnaise

Blend dry mustard into mayonnaise until completely combined.

Elk Pepper Steak
(Serves 4)

2 pounds elk round steak	6 onions, chopped
½ cup peanut oil	2 to 3 dashes hot pepper sauce, or to taste
1 clove garlic, minced	
1 teaspoon ginger, freshly ground	salt and freshly ground black pepper to taste
½ cup soy sauce	1 tablespoon arrowroot, dissolved in 3 tablespoons water
1 cup beef stock	
3 green bell peppers, cut into strips	½ cup dry sherry wine

Slice the round steak into thin strips. Brown meat in oil, adding garlic and ginger about midway through browning. Add soy sauce and beef stock and simmer until the elk strips are tender.

Add green pepper strips, onion, hot pepper sauce, salt and pepper, and cook for an additional 15 minutes until sauce is well flavored. Add arrowroot-water mixture and wine, and stir constantly until sauce thickens.

SKINNING AND PRELIMINARY TANNING TIPS

Now that you're home from the hunt and have some time to look over your efforts, you realize that the deer hide you've skinned is of such good quality you want to send it to a professional tanner. Or perhaps the head on the elk you brought back is so striking that you think, on second thought, that you really should have it mounted. What should you do?

First of all, tanning and taxidermy should be thought about and planned for *before* you venture into the field. Home tanning and taxidermy can be challenging and rewarding, but they require study, patience and lots of practice. My recommendation is to find a professional tanner and/or taxidermist who is trained to do the job and who is experienced, reputable and reliable.

And don't wait until the day before the season opens. Consult with your hunting cohorts and your local sporting goods dealers and choose a tanner/taxidermist whose work you can see before you give him your head or hide. And check his prices, too; he should be able to

quote you general estimates for various types of jobs. More important, he will be able to guide you regarding his requirements and what you need to do to ensure a beautiful hide or mount.

Basically, here are some of the points you should keep in mind when preparing a head for mounting and a hide for tanning.

1. You'll need two sharp knives, one with a 4-inch blade for skinning, another for removing glands; an 8-inch screwdriver; a meat saw; and salt, either soft ground rock salt or regular table salt.

2. It is easier to skin a younger animal than an older one; it's also easier when the animal is still warm. The longer you wait, the more difficult the job will be and the more likely the meat will spoil (because of heat retention). Start skinning, if possible, within one hour after eviscerating.

3. Winter pelts are more desirable because they are thicker and more luxurious. Spring and summer pelts are

usually sparse, while in the fall new fur is just beginning to emerge. (Black bear can be the exception, since its pelt is often sought after in early spring.)

4. To remove a head for a trophy mount, you'll need to "cape out" the animal first. You can opt to do a partial caping before you field dress (as in the case of a bighorn sheep, for example), but more than likely you'll remove the cape after you've dressed out the animal. In that case, hang the animal by its gambrel joints (lower legs) for easy cape and head removal.

5. Before actually skinning the cape (which encompasses the head and all the hide down to the shoulders), cut through the hide around the entire torso, then make an incision along the backbone, from the edge of the cape to the base of the skull. Then branch out in a "Y" to the base of each antler.

Now, pull the hide from the edge of the cape down and away from the neck, over the head as far as the ears and antlers (or horns). Using a screwdriver, loosen the skin around each antler base (with horned animals, you'll need a knife to cut the skin from around each horn base). After you've finished skinning the head, remove the antlers (or horns) by sawing through the top of the skull (See Figure 2-14).

Remember, to facilitate skinning the head and face, sever the head from the torso at the uppermost vertebra at the base of the neck.

6. The ears, eyelids and part of the inner lip must be removed intact with the rest of the head and cape. Cut under the base of the ear so that it remains attached to the skin (the ear cartilage is removed later). The eyelids must be carefully removed with a sharp knife, using your finger as a guide. Continue on down to the mouth, saving as much of the lips as possible. Finish the process by skinning the nose.

7. To skin the ears, start at the base and remove skin from flesh until there is only cartilage and skin left. Using your thumb, separate cartilage from skin and turn the ear inside out. Cut the cartilage where the ear ends, leaving the ear wrong side out for salting.

8. Scrape away any chunks of flesh from the inner side of the hide and coat it with salt. Rub it in thoroughly and generously, especially around the edges, into the ears and around the lips and nose. Roll the cape tightly with the flesh side in and place the skin in a cool, dry location to drain. After two days, unroll the hide, re-apply the salt and roll again for storage. Be sure to place your head and cape in a cooler or freezer until you get it to the taxidermist.

9. When skinning a deer or other large animal whose head will *not* be mounted, hang the animal by its neck and remove the lower portion of all four legs. Make an incision around the neck and begin pulling down on the hide with your hands. When you reach the tail section, sever only the soft inner cartilage (tailbone) and leave the tail intact as part of the hide.

10. When skinning a bear or mountain lion whose hide is to be used for a rug or life-sized mount, place the animal on its back and take its measurements (See appropriate chapters). Then, starting at the outer edge of the front foot pad, make an incision down one leg, across the chest and up the other leg. Repeat this procedure with the rear legs. Extend the upper and lower ends of the field dressing cut to the lips and tail respectively. Then peel off the skin, making sure to remove all fat from the hide as you proceed.

11. Some animals such as the pronghorn have scent glands which must be removed during skinning. The pronghorn's are composed of small yellow nodules located just below the skin of the white patch on the animal's rump. During skinning, they will usually pull away, but if they don't, remove them very carefully with a knife. Puncturing them could contaminate the surrounding meat.

12. Before salting the full hide, remove all unwanted flesh and fat. Never use a blunt knife, and scrape with great care.

13. When salting the hide, spread it out fur side to the ground. Gradually build up a layer of salt about 1/4-inch thick on the surface of the flesh, rubbing it in vigorously and uniformly. Start at the center and work outward toward the edges, adding extra salt where punctures appear. Once salted, roll the hide fur side out and place in a cool area out of direct sunlight. At dusk, open the roll and let the cool air into the flesh side of the hide provided that it is a dry night.

14. When properly salted, there is little danger of decay or rot. A hide that has been salted and treated correctly can remain at camp as long as a week, if necessary, before being delivered to the tanner.

15. When drying a hide, coat it with a good sheepskin dressing to discourage insects and to help in the drying process. To dry skins in the sun, spread them over a set of parallel poles with the flesh side out. Make sure the hide stays free of wrinkles and does not dry out too quickly. Skins can also be dried in the shade, but you must make sure the area is well ventilated.

16. Once a skin has been completely dried, do not fold it. A hide that is cracked from folding could lose all its value.

Moose

MOOSE

Nothing will be more awesome than your first sighting of the majestic moose. The largest game animal of North America and the largest member of the solid-antlered deer family, it ranges in shoulder height from 6 to 8 feet—taller than the average man. Its length—8½ to 10 feet—is longer than most cars. And its weight—which can reach from 1,400 to 1,800 pounds—is certainly well over what one hunter can carry back to camp.

Three species of moose inhabit the North American Continent: the largest is the Alaskan; the mid-size species, the American or Common moose; and the smallest, the Shiras moose. Collectively, their range extends from the Arctic tundra of the Kenai Peninsula of Alaska across Canada to the Hudson Bay area and into the northern United States, specifically the Rocky Mountains of Idaho, Montana, Colorado and Wyoming, and also into Minnesota.

The distinguishing features of the moose are its unusual, broad antlers, which span an average 5½ feet and can weigh up to 100 pounds, the fleshy dewlap of skin and hair that hangs from its throat and its large overhanging snout. The coloration of both bull and cow is a blackish brown in winter, a dark grayish brown in summer. The male alone sprouts antlers, shed annually, and a mane. The cow grows to about three-quarters the size and weight of the bull.

A graceless beast, the moose walks with a shuffling gait but surprisingly can journey long distances with relative speed. Rarely will you see him run; more likely you will spot him in a lake swimming. He is usually shy and unpredictable and can become quite belligerent during the rutting season.

The name "moose" is derived from the Indian word "musee" which means twig eater. The moose eats between 40 to 50 pounds of browse per day, feeding on twigs of willow, aspen, maple, birch and balsam. Also a lover of aquatic plants, one of its favorite foods is the water lily.

While the natural enemies of the moose are bears, cougars, wolves and man, hard winters and lack of browse have also contributed to their declining numbers. They are usually solitary animals but to ward off starvation, they will form a herd and create a ground or yard, often snow covered. The steady traffic of moose moving in and out keeps the yard trampled down to a level that enables the animals to feed on various herbage lying beneath the snow level. A moose's neck is too short and its legs too long to allow him to graze like a horse or cow but, on occasions, a moose will actually get on its knees to acquire food from the ground if nothing else is available at higher levels.

Hunting Tips/moose

Moose are hunted in many ways and the mode of transport you intend to use is an important consideration before butchering your moose. A horse is always helpful in hunting and packing out moose, but many hunters have accomplished the same tasks on foot with the use of backpacks and fellow hunters. In some areas, it is feasible to hunt from a canoe, since moose are often found near or in the water. It can be useful in transporting the butchered animal back to camp, provided you have carefully packed it so the canoe is evenly balanced. • Where you shoot a moose is probably where he'll fall. Never make the mistake of shooting him as he stands in the water; it is impossible to dress out a 1,400-pound animal while it is half-submerged in a lake.

Field Dressing/moose

Regardless of how you plan to transport your quarry, care and speed are essential in dressing out and skinning. For game as large as this, you will need reliable heavy-duty equipment, including good knives and block-and-tackle gear (please review the field dressing tool requirements for big game, page 18).

To field dress your moose, follow the same basic procedure you would use for deer and elk (please refer to these chapters), making sure you tie the moose to a tree or something stationary so it is securely on its back. Then proceed.

One point of field dressing I haven't discussed yet is what to do specifically with the scrotum. In a small deer, the testicles may not be apparent; in an animal as large as a moose, they are considerable, so you would notice them. You can cut them off entirely and throw them away, or leave them beside the penis. There's no real established procedure. In Eastern Canada, interestingly enough, the French Canadians find them quite a delicacy. They slice them very thin and sauté them, making what they call "Moose Fries" or "Animelles." Do with them what you will.

Keep in mind also that the liver makes very savory table fare.

Skinning and Quartering/moose

Once you have eviscerated the animal, wiped out the carcass and propped it open with sticks, the next step is either to skin the animal or cut it up into smaller sections. One or two of your hunting companions

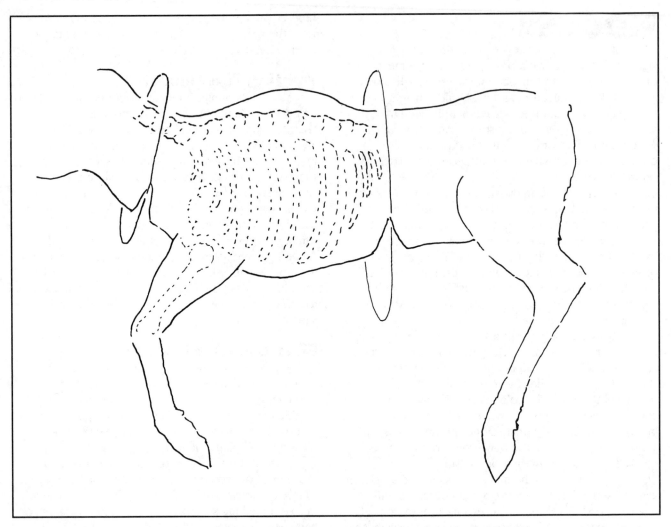

2-19. Since most moose are large, to facilitate transporting, first cut the carcass in two across the midsection at the last rib. Saw through the spinal column of each half, then follow with standard butchering cuts for easy carrying.

could begin the skinning while you are still working on the field dressing. Skinning procedures are the same as for the elk, particularly if you plan to take home a trophy mount.

While you are skinning the skull, remember to remove the tongue by cutting inside each side of the jawbone. Tongue can be boiled or fried in different ways and is considered a tasty dish in some areas. I have included a recipe for moose tongue at the end of this chapter.

If you are a long distance from your freezer facility, or for whatever reason your hunting party is not planning to break camp immediately, here's a tip you can use to preserve your unquartered carcass. Assuming you are in snow country, place the animal on a

snowbank and build a tepee of poles around it. Wrap a tarpaulin around the poles, similar to what an Indian tepee would look like. During the day, fill the moose's opened cavity with snow to keep the animal cold. At night when the temperature is lower, remove the snow. That should preserve the animal until your party is ready to leave.

Now, if you find you have no need for the hide and your group is soon headed for home, quarter the carcass as you would the elk, leaving the skin on. If your moose is unusually large, start first by cutting the carcass in half across the midsection at the last rib (*See Figure 2-19*). Then saw through the backbone of the fore section, followed by the hind section, yielding four large quarters. To facilitate packing and transporting

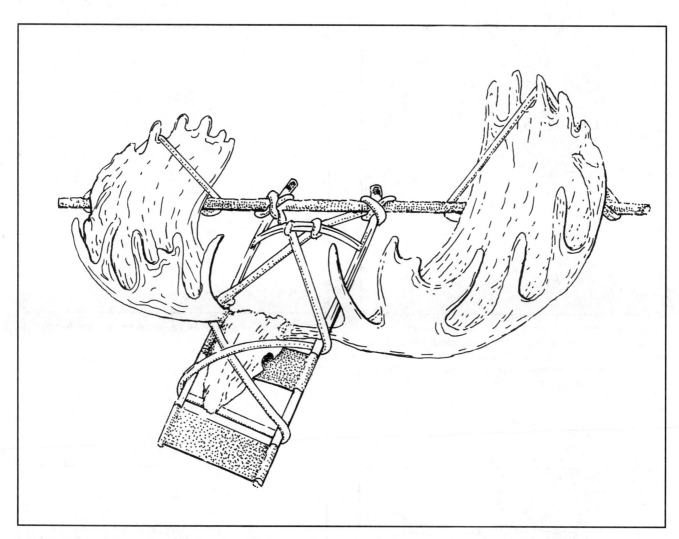

2-20. Packing a moose rack requires great care because of its massive size. Be sure it is securely tied down, balanced, and that strips of bright orange cloth are highly visible from the tines.

and also to dissipate body heat, you can further divide the quarters into smaller, standard butchering cuts. If you want to decrease the weight of your load even more, you can try boning the legs; it helps when pounds start becoming a problem.

Remember that when you're finished quartering, each section of butchered meat should be placed in a proper meat sack or cheesecloth for hanging. This will protect and cool it. Never use plastic bags, as they hold the heat and rapidly cause decomposition of the meat. And, if you find you have no outer covering for the meat, at least keeping the hide on will protect it from dirt, dust and insects, etc.

If, for some reason, you find you are unable to bring the meat back to camp that day, and it is also impossible to hang the meat in sacks, the one precaution you should at least take is to get it off the ground. When meat is flush against the ground, the air doesn't have a chance to circulate around it and provide cooling. Place twigs or brush, etc., underneath the meat, or the whole-dressed animal, if such is the case, so every bit of it is off the ground.

Transporting/moose

Whatever method or mode of transport you use, make sure that the large moose antler rack you are taking home to show off is securely strapped down, balanced, and that strips of bright orange cloth are tied to the tines. This is especially important when you are leaving the field at dusk. *Figure 2-20* demonstrates how

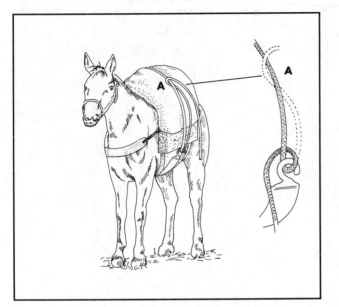

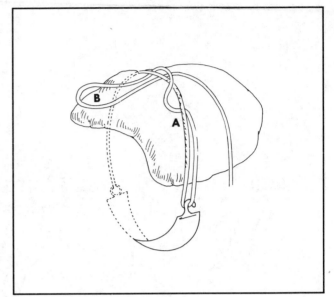

2-21. With panniers and top pack in place, lash rope is thrown over the top of the pack and lash cinch swung under the belly. With point of hook back, cinch is hooked in loop formed in lash rope by twist as shown. Twist is lifted to top of pack after hooking cinch, to point "A".

2-22. Tuck second loop "B" under rope, crossing top pack from rear and enlarged to make large loop for right side of pack.

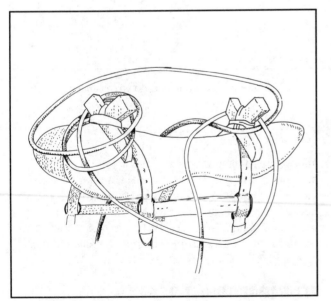

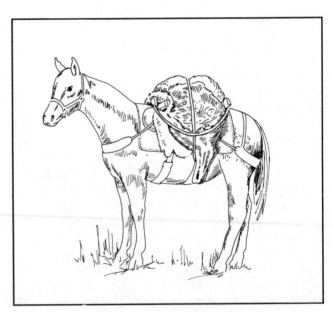

2-25. The sling hitch is used in packing meat without panniers, so sacks of meat should be lashed as high on the saddle as possible. The middle section of sling rope is double-half-hitched on the front fork of the pack saddle. Each end section is loosely looped over the rear fork with the ends down, under the loops, between the front and rear forks.

2-26. The loads are set within the loops on each side; loops are tightened around the loads by pulling down on the rope ends, which are then brought up under the side packs to tie together on top of the load.

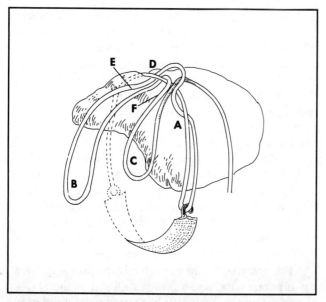

2-23. Leaving loop "B" hanging on right side of pack, pull third loop "C" from between points "A" and "D". This loop "C" is for left side of pack. Now pull up on rope at "A" and across at section "E" of loop "B", tightening cinch as much as possible. Section "E" of loop "B" is then taken back, down and under the rear of the right-side pack and continues up the front of the right-side pack to the center of the top pack, where slack is pulled from "B" at point "F" of loop "C". Loop "C" then encircles the left side of the pack from the front to the rear.

2-24. Final shaping of the diamond and tightening of the hitch is accomplished by pulling back hard on the end of the lash rope, which is then tied under the left pack above the cinch hook.

SQUAW HITCH

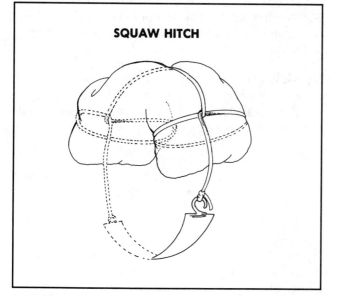

2-27. This is a simple half-hitch in the lash rope around each side pack.

PACK SADDLE

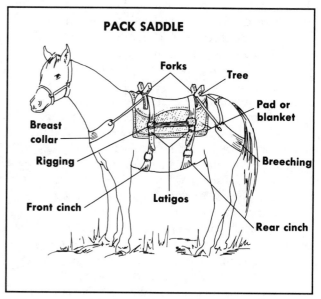

Forks

Tree

Pad or blanket

Breast collar

Rigging

Breeching

Front cinch

Latigos

Rear cinch

2-28. Proper positioning and parts of the pack saddle.

you can bind the rack to a frame pack.

Here is a story—a true one—to think about and hopefully uplift your spirits with the next time you are carrying a quarter and feel that your back is about to break, or the shoulder straps on your backpack have rubbed blisters on your skin.

I was fishing in Maine near the Canadian border. I thought I would do some trout fishing, or perhaps catch some landlocked salmon and also check the area for big game. Being a law enforcement officer, I always carried my .38 with me; you never know what might happen. On this particular day, I was fishing in this beautiful stream and not having much luck. I kept changing flies and moving down stream.

All of a sudden, I heard a strange sound. As I turned a bend in the river, near the bank where the stream had widened, was a large bull moose about 200 feet away. He was splashing around and going under for food. I'd never been this close to a moose feeding in the water, and it was fascinating to watch him go under. There must have been a deep hole in that area of the stream. After a few minutes, though, it dawned on me that this mammoth fellow might not enjoy my presence. I became a bit nervous and began to back slowly up the stream. I hadn't moved more than 100 feet when the moose blared out—it was a sound the likes of which I had never heard before, at least not that I could remember. I had fought in Korea with the Marines, had been associated with police work for many years, so it really took a lot to unnerve me. All I could think of was that the moose must have gotten sight or scent of me, and I knew I didn't want to get in his way.

At this point, all I could think of was the stories I'd heard about dog sled races in Canada and Alaska, when moose would attack the dogs and riders. Would this moose, if provoked, attack me? I really didn't want to hang around to find out. I took my revolver in my right hand, with the fishing rod in the other, and kept moving backward. Finally, I could see a break in the bushes along the shore and I moved toward it.

Completely unbeknown to me, behind those bushes lay a very lovely woman on a chaise lounge, sunbathing in the nude. As I came out of the water—with a gun in one hand and a fishing rod in the other—she leaped up and screamed, "What are you doing!"

With all the calmness of an experienced hunter, Marine, and police officer, I answered: "I'm fishing moose, ah, shooting fish. Oh, hell, I don't know what I'm doing!"

Actually, I was trying to get out of the water

without looking at her. I finally calmed down after she managed to wrap herself in a large towel. It was about that time that I noticed a jeep parked out of sight. The woman and her husband had traveled from Massachusetts for a week-long camping and fishing trip. They had come in from an old road along an abandoned paper mill. He was fishing farther down stream. I tried to explain, a little more calmly now, why I had a fishing pole *and* a gun.

At that point, her husband returned, smiled and said, "Hi." I immediately said that I was sorry that I had barged into their camp, and proceeded to tell him what happened, that I hadn't intended to startle his wife or intrude on her sunbathing. To my surprise, he never said one word about his wife. He just asked, "How's the fishing upstream? It's been lousy down here!"

I'm sure that if anyone walked into my camp with a gun in one hand and a fishing rod in the other, I'd have a few questions to ask him—especially if my wife were sunbathing in the altogether!

Well, as things would have it, I wound up spending the evening with the couple, and the next morning they drove me to my car on the far side of the old mill.

Using a horse is also a common way of hunting moose and you will want to use it to best advantage in carrying your cargo camp or homeward bound. The instructions on the preceding pages have been provided through the courtesy of the Colorado Wildlife and Game Department (original drawings and text by Archie Pendergraft).

Cooking/moose

In addition to relating the adventures of your trip, one final thing remains now and that is to enjoy a meal prepared with moose meat.

Moose Liver Cakes
(Serves 4 to 5)

1 pound moose liver	1 tablespoon flour
1½ cups hot water	salt and black pepper to
½ cup onion, chopped	taste
2 eggs, beaten	bacon slices
½ cup fine cracker	2 sticks butter
crumbs	

Simmer liver in water for about 10 minutes and drain. Chop liver finely with knife or put through grinder on medium blade.

Mix liver with onion, eggs, cracker crumbs, flour, salt and pepper. Shape into cakes and wrap each one in a bacon slice. Fry in butter until well done.

Moose-Stuffed Cabbage Rolls
(Serves 4 to 6)

1 pound ground moose	salt and black pepper to
½ pound ground pork	taste
2 eggs, lightly beaten	½ cup rice, uncooked
	6 to 8 large cabbage
	leaves

Thoroughly mix together moose, pork, eggs, salt and pepper. Add rice to meat mixture and stir.

Cook cabbage leaves in boiling water for a few minutes until tender; drain. Place several generous tablespoons of the meat mixture on each leaf and roll, securing with a toothpick. Place stuffed cabbage rolls, seam side down, in greased baking dish. Pour Sauce over. Cover with lid or foil and bake for 2 hours in a 300 to 325° F oven.

Sauce:

3 tablespoons butter	1 10 ¾-ounce can cream
1 cup onion, diced	of celery soup
1 10 ¾-ounce can tomato	1 cup water
soup	3 tablespoons lemon juice
	1 teaspoon sugar

Melt butter in saucepan; add onion and cook over low heat until tender. Blend in remaining ingredients and simmer about 10 minutes.

Pan-Cooked Moose Steaks
(Serves 2)

2 moose steaks, ¾- to 1-	1 large onion, sliced
inch thick	¼ cup water
salt and black pepper to	2 tablespoons sherry
taste	2 tablespoons
flour	Worcestershire sauce
¼ cup vegetable or	
peanut oil	

Tenderize both sides of each steak by pounding with a meat mallet. Salt and pepper them and dredge in flour. Heat oil in a heavy skillet and brown steaks. Place onion slices on top of each and cook until the steaks

are well browned and the onion is transparent and soft. Pour water, sherry and Worcestershire sauce over steaks. Reduce heat to low, cover skillet and simmer about 1 hour, or until meat is tender.

If desired, make a gravy by adding 2 to 3 tablespoons cornstarch dissolved in ¾ cup of cold water. Add to pan drippings and stir constantly until thickened. Adjust seasoning. Heat until bubbly and simmer for a few minutes.

Simmered Moose Tongue in Vegetables
(Serves 2)

1 moose tongue	1 cup celery hearts,
1 whole medium onion	chopped
2 scallions, white part	1 bay leaf, crushed
only, chopped	1 teaspoon dried thyme
6 pearl onions	1 teaspoon dried
2 rutabaga (turnips),	rosemary
chopped	1½ tablespoons salt
2 cloves garlic, minced	½ teaspoon red pepper
4 carrots, sliced	

Place tongue and vegetables in a large Dutch oven and fill with enough water to cover. Bring water to a boil, then reduce to simmer, cooking 45 minutes to an hour per pound.

Approximately 1 hour before the end of cooking time, add seasonings. When tongue is tender, remove from pot. Return tongue to broth and reheat. Place on hot platter surrounded by the vegetables and serve with fresh Horseradish Sauce (see page 60).

Moose Tongue Hash
(Serves 2)

2 cups moose tongue,	1 medium onion, minced
precooked, cold and	salt and freshly ground
minced	black pepper to taste
1 cup potatoes,	5 tablespoons butter or
precooked, cold and	margarine, or more
chopped	

Combine tongue, potatoes, onion, salt and pepper, and mix well. Shape into 2 large patties. Melt butter in large skillet. Fry patties, turning several times, until golden brown. May be served with a poached egg, topped with a prepared hot mustard sauce or Mustard-Mayonnaise Sauce (see page 60).

Roast Moose with Homemade Barbecue Sauce
(Serves 6 to 8)

1 5- to 6-pound moose
  roast
salt and black pepper to
  taste

1 medium onion, sliced
½ cup Barbecue Sauce
water

Lightly salt and pepper the roast. Place onion slices in bottom of roasting pan and place the roast on top. Cover meat with Barbecue Sauce. Add just enough water to the pan to keep the roast from sticking.

    Place pan in a 350° oven and roast for 1 hour. Reduce heat to 275° F., tent with aluminum foil and roast for 3 more hours, basting occasionally.

Barbecue Sauce:

¼ cup dry mustard
¼ cup sugar
1 tablespoon salt
1 tablespoon black
  pepper, coarsely ground

1 cup cider vinegar
½ cup water
½ cup butter or
  margarine, softened

Mix together first 4 ingredients, then, while stirring, slowly add vinegar and water. Bring to a boil over medium-high heat. Lower heat and add butter. Simmer for 15 minutes, stirring occasionally. Makes approximately 2 cups.

CARIBOU

The last of the cervid game I want to cover is the caribou. Like its other solid-antlered relatives, the caribou sheds its rack yearly, possesses similar physical traits and digests its herbivorous diet with a four-chambered stomach characteristic of all cud-chewing ruminants. The caribou differs noticeably, however, in that both sexes bear antlers with brow tines pointing toward the snout and, as a group, the species is the most gregarious of deer, traveling and migrating in multitudinous herds in search of food.

Sometimes called reindeer because of their large furry hoofs, caribou are derived from a strain of deer originally domesticated from Old World reindeer. The hoofs have a band of white shaggy fur around the upper part and give off a clicking sound when the animal is in motion. To give you some perspective on the size of the hoofs, the feet of an average 400-pound caribou might compare with those of a 1,000-pound moose. This leads to the impression that caribou are larger than they really are. And as all living things must adapt to their environment or perish, the unique pad and size of the hoofs have enabled the caribou, particularly the barren ground variety, to range over vast areas of snow and marshy tundra in the northernmost wilderness of Canada and Alaska.

Barren ground caribou, especially the Porcupine herd, are probably the most famous of the species. Numbering more than 100,000, they migrate each spring from northwestern Canada near the Crow Reservation to the Arctic tundra where they join together with other herds. It is left only to the imagination of man as to why the migrations occur, but most naturalists believe it is their peculiar feeding habits that lead them northward.

The Porcupine herd alone treks over 500 miles to reach its destination, crossing treacherous terrain, fighting storms, sickness and the dangers of wolves, grizzlies and man. Year after year the herd travels the same route, and year after year the Eskimos wait in the same vicinity to bag the 20 caribou each family needs to survive until the next hunting season.

The vernal equinox signals the earth's awakening, and with it come flies and mosquitos that disturb and distress the herds. This often results in violent stampedes or emotional frenzy and eventual death of some of the herd. But as the days expand with the warmth of summer sunlight, it is an awesome sight to see thousands of caribou clustered at the Arctic Circle feeding peacefully on flowers and plants.

Not all caribou, however, are the typical light-colored reindeer-type. There are also the woodland, the mountain and the Quebec-Labrador varieties, so named after the areas they inhabit. These strains tend to be darker in color with a white cape and rump and are slightly larger in size. They might reach to a length of 8 feet, a shoulder height of 4 feet and a weight of 600 pounds. They probably carry the most magnificent set of trophy antlers of any member of the deer family. The spread is as wide or wider, and with more points, than the bull elk. An added conversation piece is what some call the shovel—a flattened thrusted-out, shovel-like rack found on the lower story. This can be a single shovel or a double, all of which make this animal a much-sought-after trophy.

Hunting Tips/caribou

How you hunt caribou depends on which type of caribou you want to hunt. • The barren ground variety of the tundra areas, for example, requires that the hunter come prepared for especially cold conditions with proper clothing and foot gear. Be prepared, also, for the unpredictable. Even though the migration herds reputedly follow the same routes annually, it might just be the year you hunt them that they decide, for one reason or another, to change their past habits. • With any kind of caribou you will need a seasoned guide. He will know the territory and will provide horses or other transportation to the hunting site. Also, he will be keen at finding tracks along the riverbed crossings or recognizing fresh droppings and will be able to follow the trail that will provide you with a shot. • Always keep in mind that caribou are not the docile creatures you may have imagined. They are inquisitive and can bolt faster than a deer when spooked and, believe me, hunting them is work. You will need all your hunting skills to be successful. But it will be worth it.

Field Dressing/caribou

There are many schools of thought on how big game should be dressed out and whether to skin in the field or after you get back to camp. Since you will no doubt have a guide with you, he should be able to assist you with this large animal whatever you decide. We will assume you want the rack and cape for a trophy and will dress out the caribou accordingly. This means you will do a partial skinning of the cape area before you complete the entire field dressing procedure.

Follow the same instructions you would use if you had bagged an elk. Read both the chapters on deer and elk, paying particular attention to Step 6 under elk: "Partial Skinning of the Cape." Because the white cape

Caribou

of the caribou can be soiled easily with blood and dirt, it is very important to keep the animal's head up and away from the ground. Make sure also that your hands are clean when you pull the skin back toward the head. If you must, use your knife to cut away any stubborn tissue. But since the animal will still be warm, you should have little difficulty peeling the hide back.

You should be able to field dress the caribou or any other big game animal in less than 30 minutes. Once you are finished, keep the cavity open with two or more sticks to continue the cooling process.

Skinning/Quartering/ Transporting/caribou

Because of the anatomical similarities among the species of the deer family, you can skin and quarter the caribou just the way you would an elk. And you can transport it using the tips and techniques you'd employ for a moose. So refer to these chapters for the best methods to preserve your trophy mount and/or meat for later use.

Cooking/caribou

If you enjoy beef, you'll certainly love caribou, as I'm sure the following recipes will bear me out.

Caribou Meat Loaf
(Serves 4)

To be really authentic in eating wild game meat loaf, try adding ground entrails to the mixture or surrounding the loaf in a casing as the American Indians did.

2 pounds ground caribou	3 slices American cheese, cut into strips
1 cup bread crumbs	
2 eggs	sausage, parboiled 10 to 20 minutes
4 strips bacon, cooked and diced	
salt and freshly ground black pepper to taste	3 ounces soy sauce

Mix together ground meat, bread crumbs, eggs, bacon, salt and pepper. Shape into loaf and place in a greased baking pan.

Split loaf lengthwise down the center, but do not cut through. Insert half the cheese strips then the sausage and top sausage with remaining cheese strips. Close meat loaf. Make V-shaped notches across the top of loaf and bake at 350° F. for about 1½ hours. Approximately 15 minutes before meat loaf is cooked, fill notches with soy sauce. Return to oven and continue cooking for an additional 15 minutes.

Corned Brisket of Caribou
(Serves 6)

Many people who do not like the taste of any venison meat will rave about it when the meat is corned. The ideal temperature for corning meat is 35° to 40° F. Although pickling is not recommended in temperatures *above* 40° F., if you still wish to try it, be sure to add three pounds of salt to your pickling mixture for every additional 15 degrees of temperature.

1 2- to 3-pound brisket of caribou plus other pieces of same size

Corning Liquid:

6 gallons water, depending on size of container	3 pounds table salt
	3 teaspoons black pepper, freshly ground
10 ounces sugar	1 teaspoon ground cloves
2 ounces sodium nitrate (available at a pharmacy)	4 bay leaves, crushed
	4 tablespoons, pickling spices
½ ounce sodium nitrite (available at a pharmacy)	1 large onion, diced
	3 to 4 garlic cloves, minced

Place caribou and corning ingredients in a large glass container, a ceramic crock or a barrel. Place a weight on the meat so it is completely submerged.

On the 5th and 10th days, remove the meat from the liquid, skim off any scum, stir thoroughly and return the meat to the liquid, opposite side up. At the end of the 15th day, remove the meat, place in a Dutch oven, cover with water and bring to a boil. Skim the foam as it forms on the surface. Simmer over low flame for 5 to 6 hours or until meat is tender. Serve with boiled cabbage.

Over-the-Coals Caribou

caribou steaks, about 1-inch thick, fat removed (1 per person)	seasoned salt
	black pepper, freshly ground
flour	oregano
oil or butter	1 large onion, sliced

Dredge meat in flour. Heat oil or butter in a large skillet; add meat, seasonings and onion, and sauté over hot coals. Fry each side about 7 to 8 minutes. Do not overcook.

Baked Loin Caribou Chops
(Serves 2)

½ teaspoon dried rosemary
½ teaspoon dried thyme
½ teaspoon dried sage

4 loin caribou chops, about 1¼- to 1½-inches thick
1 cup sherry wine

Mix the herbs together and sprinkle over the chops. Place in a glass baking dish and cover with sherry. Cook in a 325° F. oven for 1 hour or until chops are tender. Place on heated plate and cover with liquid remaining in dish. Serve with parsley-buttered new potatoes.

Caribou Meat Loaves with Rice
(Serves 4)

1 pound ground caribou
½ pound ground pork
3 eggs, beaten
1 cup Minute® Rice, uncooked
1 cup tomato paste

1 small onion, diced
1 tablespoon Worcestershire sauce
salt and pepper
1 10 ¾-ounce can tomato soup

Thoroughly mix together ground meats, eggs, rice, tomato paste, onion, Worcestershire sauce, salt and pepper to taste. Shape into 4 individual loaves. Place in a baking dish and pour tomato soup over loaves. Place in 350° F. oven and bake for 1 hour.

PRONGHORN

The pronghorn is the only plains species native to North America, with a history that goes back millions of years. It is often referred to as an antelope, which it is not (true antelope are found only in Africa and Asia), and often thought of as a member of the goat family (the deer family, too) because of its size, habits and horn structure. In truth, the pronghorn is a species unto itself with its own biological family, *Antilocapridae*.

The pronghorn travels in herds, the largest numbers roaming in prairies and desert areas of Wyoming, South Dakota, Montana, Colorado and New Mexico. A cud-chewer with a complex stomach, it feeds on sagebrush, browse, weeds and other plants.

Physically, the buck weighs 80 to 140 pounds, while the doe averages 20 pounds less. At the shoulder, it stands about 3½ feet and measures 4½ feet in length. Its distinguishing features are the two white bands that encircle its neck, the white rump that seems to expand in size when the animal is in flight from danger and, of course, its horns from which its name is derived.

The horns are two-pronged, with the smaller tines pointing toward the nose. The horns of the pronghorn consist of a bony core covered by a horny sheath and it is this sheath only, unlike the deer which grows an entirely new set of antlers each year, that is shed annually. Like the caribou, however, male and female bear horns, the buck's measuring up to 16 inches and the doe's rarely exceeding the length of her ears (*See Figure 2-29*).

The pronghorn has the perseverance and endurance of no other American horned mammal. Its magnificent set of lungs, overdeveloped windpipe and enlarged heart enable it to accelerate in seconds to a bounding speed of 60 miles per hour. Running with its mouth open and tongue partially out, it receives the maximum amount of oxygen necessary for rapid, long-distance travel. Although its legs are thin, they are almost 10 times stronger than those of range cattle.

Other than man, the pronghorn's natural enemies are wolves and coyotes. For defense, nature has equipped the pronghorn with eyesight that is eight times as acute as a human's. Its eyes are set high in its head and it can spot movement and distinguish friend from foe at a distance of three-miles.

Hunting Tips/pronghorn

The pronghorn is a most inquisitive animal and, while it may shy away from hunters, it will often be curious about a vehicle that is driven within 100 yards of it. Some hunters have used this to advantage by parking a jeep, let's say, and stalking the animal from behind as it eventually approaches the vehicle for a closer sniff or peek. ● The guardian pronghorn can give off a musk scent while leading the hunter, or prey, away from the herd. Later, the herd will gather at the same point using the scent that was left behind. ● For the hunter who has never hunted this small but clever animal, don't wait by a fence expecting the pronghorn to jump over it. It will go through it or underneath it without losing speed. Even a five- or six-wire fence will not prove too difficult a maneuver. ● It has been my experience that the horse, especially a stallion, exhibits an aggressive, almost nasty, attitude during a pronghorn hunt. You may be riding and not see anything. Suddenly your horse will become excited, shake its head wildly and whinny loudly when it is within about a one-half mile range of the game. No explanation has been able to account for this phenomenon except that possibly the horse is able to smell the musk odor. Frequently, friends and I have "muscled up" our horses by circling the area and riding into a pronghorn herd for short distances. It is quite an experience for both the horse and the rider and one you will not soon forget.

I used to own a ranch just east of Colorado Springs and quite a few pronghorn would always mix with the cattle. They stayed mostly in small herds, and hardly a day went by that you wouldn't see pronghorn in some area of the ranch. The exception, of course, was during hunting season.

Pronghorn have "outrider guards," and from one to three of the herd will assume this job. These are the ones you'll see first, and these are the ones that leave behind the musk scent, released from their rump glands, when danger is spotted to alert the rest of the herd. Then they take off in different directions.

It's important that if you are in a fixed location and using binoculars to cover an area near a waterhole that you exercise extreme patience before unloosing a shot at a trophy mount. Let the outriders move in and soon you will lay your sights on a real trophy specimen. Keep in mind, also, that even though most of your hunting will be done on the plains, pronghorn can blend into a hillside with rocks. So don't overlook the outcroppings. I've done this on occasion and had several good chances slip away. I feel that since you are allowed only one animal, you should pass up the smaller bucks until you find the one that really counts.

I want to emphasize that stud horses (stallions) do *not* like pronghorn, nor do the pronghorn like them. At our ranch, we used to muscle up our horses, especially

Pronghorn

2-29. Both male and female pronghorn sprout horns. The buck's (left) are beautifully formed and reach to a length of 16 inches, while the doe's are slight and rarely exceed the height of her ears. Another characteristic of both is the large, white bands that encircle the neck.

the younger ones, by circling around them with about six to eight riders. We'd always make sure that we had at least one stallion in the group. We'd be riding in a loose pattern and not see a thing when the stud would start, and get almost tempestuous—like something was brewing. This is the point at which one of us would wave his hat and everyone would form a wide circle at a given sign. We'd ride clear into the middle of the pronghorn herd. The horses were on their own then. They actually acted as if they wanted to "eat up" the pronghorn. We'd have one hell of a ride, with horses and pronghorn going every which way! Of course, this lasts only a few hundred yards and the pronghorn would gallop away, leaving a trail of dust behind them. Needless to say, hard "frolicking" of this kind either makes or breaks you.

Another tricky part was when the pronghorn would go into a draw. In some cases, a draw would be about 30 feet deep. We'd just drop our roping reins and let the horses on their own. You have to make sure that you drop your reins and hang onto the horse or you'll slide down the embankment. If you hold the reins,

your horse will feel the pull and could fall down the draw with you. This is an important point to remember when you are riding on a high trail: if you start to go over, let the horse do the sliding; he can handle it and will keep his balance. This is why you should always do this kind of riding with roping reins. These are reins that are one rein from one side of the bit to the other and not separated like normal reins. If you have to drop them, you won't lose one or the other; they'll be in one piece in front of you right on the horse's neck. If you don't have regular roping reins, just tie your two reins together and it will help prevent an accident or injury.

Chasing pronghorn really starts the adrenalin flowing. And it not only muscles up the horses, more important, it gives you a good idea of where to look for the herds when the hunting season comes.

Field Dressing/pronghorn

Since temperatures can climb quickly on the plains during September and October, the usual hunting months for pronghorn, your main concern after killing

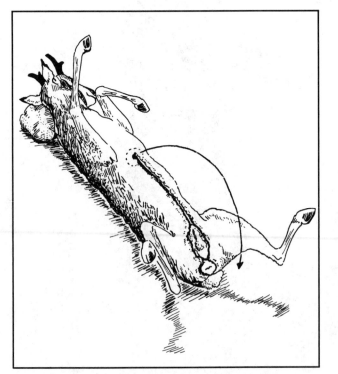

2-30. The first incision in field dressing the pronghorn begins at the sternum and continues through both hide and muscle until you reach the genital region.

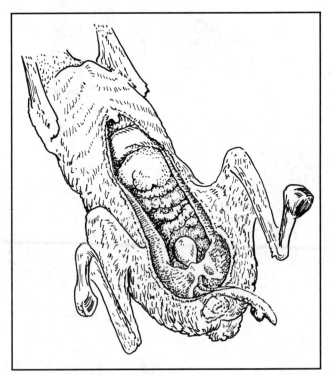

2-31. With a buck, cut the penis down to its base of attachment, then encircle the anus. Gently pull out both until you see the rectum.

one is dressing it out as fast as possible. Once the temperature rises above 46 to 47° F. (8° C.), your chances of losing the meat because of spoilage increase rapidly. Carry a thermometer with you to check before field dressing. This will save you a lot of good meat. Since the pronghorn is fairly small, you should be able to field dress it in about 10 to 15 minutes.

1. After making sure your kill is dead (check the eyes—they should be open and have a glassy film over them), the first step is to place the animal with its head higher than its body. Use a rock or stick to keep the head off the ground. This will ensure that no blood will collect under the neck to ruin or discolor the hair for the trophy mount.

2. Using the "V" formation shown in *Figure 2-3,* insert your knife just below the sternum and carefully cut through the layers of hide and muscle with your blade up. Stop at the genitals (*See Figure 2-30*).

3. If you have caught a buck, cut the penis and scrotum down to the base of attachment (do not remove them). Then cut a deep circle around the anus and pull it out gently until you can see the rectum (*See*

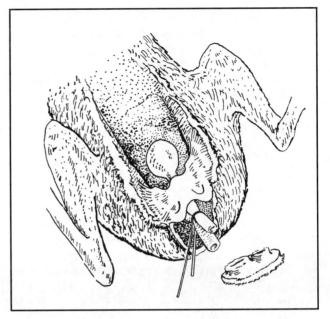

2-33. If you have bagged a doe, simply cut a deep circle around the vagina and anus, which lie close together. Carefully pull out these organs until you see the inner tubes and tie them together.

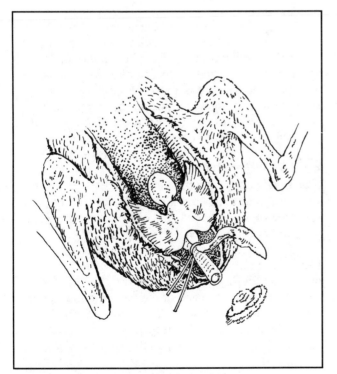

2-32. Tie off the two tubes that lead to the bladder and rectum to prevent the contents from contaminating the surrounding meat when you remove all the innards.

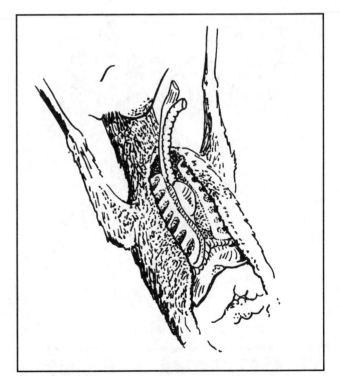

2-34. Open up the chest cavity by cutting through the sternum with a small axe or bone saw. Reach up into the neck area as far as possible and cut out the windpipe and esophagus.

Figure 2-31). Tie off the two tubes that lead to the bladder and rectum, as shown in *Figure 2-32*.

If you have caught a doe, it is a simple procedure to encircle the vagina and anus which lie close together. Gently pull out the organs until you see the inner tubes, then tie them together (*Figure 2-33*).

The purpose for tying off the bladder and rectum, of course, is to prevent the contents from contaminating the meat.

4. Finish work on the lower cavity by cutting through the pelvic bone with a sharp sturdy knife or small axe, being careful not to rupture any of the viscera lying below. Spread open the split bones.

5. Now open the chest cavity by cutting through the sternum, or breastbone (*Figure 2-34*). Reach up into the throat as far as possible and cut out the windpipe and esophagus. With a few quick movements of your knife, you can separate any membrane or muscle that is holding onto the body. If you wish to save the kidneys, heart and liver, cut them loose and place them in a plastic bag. Later they can be transported in the cleaned-out cavity.

6. To remove all the entrails, straddle the pronghorn, grab hold of its legs and turn it on its side. This will facilitate greater control and handling of the animal, and all the contents should easily spill out.

7. At this point, it is very important to wipe the cavity with a clean dry cloth you have brought with you for this purpose. Do not use water, as it can cause an immediate breakdown of the meat, resulting in spoilage. If you have the misfortune of a gut shot and you are near camp, you can wipe out the cavity and organ fluids with a little water, but this is not recommended. Place a stick in the cavity to keep it open for cooling.

Transporting/pronghorn

Your pronghorn should be cooled at least three hours in a shady area before you transport it to your destination. To cool it, cover it properly with a game bag and hang it on the dark side of a truck or rock formation, although this may be difficult to find in pronghorn country.

In any event, if it is colder than 40° F. (4° C.), you can place it on the bed of a truck or on a horse. Never, under any conditions, place it in the trunk of a car, near the fenders or the engine, or directly in the hot sun. If the temperature is above 47° F. (8° C.), you would be wise to skin and quarter the animal right there, depending on the game laws of the state, or at least wait until dark to transport your carcass.

Skinning and Quartering/pronghorn

A warm animal skins like a glove, so you don't want to wait too long before you skin yours. If you are going to keep the head for a trophy, hang the pronghorn by its hind legs at the knee joints. (If not, then hang it from the head.) Cut around the lower joints of all four legs, then up the insides of the legs. Make a cut along the nape of the neck, around the back down to the shoulders. This forms the rim of the cape. Taking a strong grip on the hide (you may use the knuckle method by gripping firmly and pulling away and down) take care to separate the membranes that cling to the hide. Work down the animal, using your skinning knife, if necessary, and the hide should pull away very easily (*See Figure 2-35*).

The scent gland is composed of small yellow

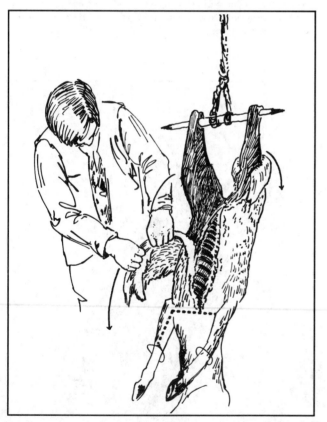

2-35. Skinning a pronghorn is relatively easy, partly because of its small size. Hang it head down if you are planning for a trophy mount. Cut around the lower joints of each leg, up the insides of each, across the brisket area and around the shoulders and back. Then simply pull down with your hands, using your knuckles, until you reach the cape.

nodules embedded just below the skin of the white patch at the pronghorn's rump. During the skinning, they usually pull away with the hide. If you see that some of the nodules have remained on the meat, carefully remove them with your knife without puncturing their outer membrane. You don't want to contaminate any of the surrounding meat. Should you pierce the gland, however, immediately cut away the meat that has been tainted by the secretion.

Now for the trophy head. The same way you would cape out a deer or elk, cut through the hide along the spinal cord down to the base of the skull, then branch out in a "Y" to the base of the horns. Pull the hide with your hands, starting at the edge of the cape and when you get to the skull area use a sharp knife to cut around the delicate areas of the horns, eyes, nose and mouth. As shown in *Figure 2-14,* remove the horns with a bone saw by cutting through at eye-socket level.

Because the pronghorn's head is so small, some hunters will not bother to remove the horns, but will take the entire skinned head along with the salted cape hide to the taxidermist. In any event, remove the head with a saw and a twisting motion, which should free it from the body (*Figure 2-14*).

Once you remove the complete hide, go over the carcass with a strong bristled brush to wipe away any hair that may be left on the body. Now is the time to decide if you want to keep the hide. If you do, start at the edges and begin to scrape away the skin and blood patches or any membrane left on it. Make sure you have about 5 to 8 pounds of plain table salt available. Rub the salt into the skin, working from the center out to the edges. Do not cheat on the edges. And, of course, generously salt the hide from the head, which you are preserving for your trophy mount. You will find that the salt will absorb most of the moisture in the hide. If this in not done, the hide can sour or turn green and you will lose a good portion of it. Roll the hide with the hair on the outside and place it in a cool dry place until you take it or send it to a tanner. (Review also "Skinning and Preliminary Tanning Tips," page 60.)

To quarter a pronghorn, follow the same procedures you'd use for a small deer. And to butcher and process the meat, please refer to "Butchering and Preserving Game."

Cooking/pronghorn

Pronghorn, in particular, has a very delicate flavor and, once you have eaten it, you will know it is worth every minute you spend making your own butchering cuts. For complete instructions, digest the step-by-step procedures that start on page 142 in "Butchering and Preserving Game." Then read on to my special pronghorn recipes and see if they don't set your mouth watering.

Broiled Pronghorn Steaks
(Serves 3 to 4)

Bake 2 steaks in a 375° F. oven until lightly browned. Rub ½ fresh lemon per steak into the meat and sprinkle with any desired spices or herbs, then place a strip or two of bacon on each steak. Broil about 90 seconds on each side.

Fresh Pronghorn Stew
(Serves 4)

¼ cup vegetable oil	2 cups beef broth or
1½ pounds pronghorn,	bouillon
cubed	1 cup fresh tomatoes,
½ medium onion, diced	chopped
½ cup flour	2 to 3 medium potatoes,
1 teaspoon seasoned salt	diced
pepper to taste	1 cup peas
1 tablespoon	1 cup carrots, sliced
Worcestershire sauce	

Heat oil in skillet; add cubed pronghorn and onion. Sprinkle flour over meat and onions and stir until well coated; cook over medium high heat until meat is browned. Add the salt, pepper, Worcestershire sauce, broth or bouillon and tomatoes, stirring well. Reduce heat to medium and simmer for approximately 15 minutes. Add potatoes, peas and carrots, and cover, cooking over low heat until tender, approximately 45 minutes. This is especially good for older pronghorn meat. Serve with warm French bread and a dry red wine.

Sautéed Pronghorn Steaks or Chops

Never overcook a chop or steak because it will become tough; treat it just like the best cut of filet mignon. Melt a half-and-half mixture of butter and oil in a skillet. Sauté the meat, turn every 20 seconds and test with a fork, keeping the meat pink and juicy. Add salt and pepper to taste. For a real treat, pour over a pan of freshly sautéed mushrooms and onions just before serving.

Pronghorn Fondue
(Serves 4 to 6)

Cut 2 pounds pronghorn sirloin steak into 1-inch cubes.

Set up a fondue pot and have your favorite sauces available. (A sauce containing chutney is especially good with pronghorn.) Fill fondue pot ⅓ to ½ full with vegetable or peanut oil. When oil is hot, dip a piece of pronghorn into the pot and cook 1 to 2 minutes, or until desired doneness. Dip into a sauce, and eat. You will not believe the great taste.

Pronghorn Chili
(Serves 8)

1 pound pronghorn, ground or cubed	2 to 3 teaspoons chili powder, or to taste
1 pound beef, ground or cubed	1 12-ounce can tomato paste
1 large onion, diced	1 16-ounce can tomato juice
1 clove garlic, minced	1 to 2 teaspoons salt, or to taste
1 green bell pepper, diced	
½ teaspoon cayenne pepper	

In a large skillet over high heat, brown together the pronghorn, beef and onion and cook until meat is tender. Add the garlic and green pepper; reduce heat and simmer for a few minutes. Add the cayenne pepper, chili powder and tomato paste; stir well. Blend in the tomato juice and salt, and simmer for approximately 1 hour.

Pronghorn Meat Loaf
(Serves 4 to 6)

2 pounds ground pronghorn	5 slices fresh bread, broken into small pieces
½ pound ground beef	1 cup milk
1½ teaspoons seasoned salt	2 eggs, slightly beaten
⅛ teaspoon black pepper	½ cup onion, chopped
1 tablespoon Worcestershire sauce	1 10¾-ounce can tomato soup

Combine all ingredients except tomato soup and shape into a loaf. Place in a lightly greased pan. Pour tomato soup over top of loaf. Bake in a 325° F. oven for 1½ to 2 hours, until desired tenderness.

BIGHORN SHEEP

The dream of almost every big game hunter is the taking of a bighorn sheep. Not only is the hunt exciting, but the meat is among the finest eating of all the big game animals in North America.

A descendant of the Asian sheep, the bighorn came to North America close to a half-million years ago. It was originally a plains animal, but with the advent of civilization, man and predators, it was forced to the far extremities of North America. Today the most common type is the Rocky Mountain variety which derives its name from the mountainous areas it inhabits. The desert bighorn makes its home in the arid regions of the Southwest and Mexico, while its cousins, the Dall's, or white, sheep and the Stone's, or black, sheep are found in the northern reaches of Alaska and Canada.

The perfect description of the bighorn was once given to me by a rancher, who was also a big game hunter: "The bighorn has the characteristics of a fine quarter horse, built close to the ground; it is well muscled, has a chunky body, its feet are proportioned right, it can turn on a dime and has a heart that you don't often find in other animals."

The Rocky Mountain ram stands anywhere from 36 to 42 inches high at the shoulder and measures 60 inches or longer. The weight ranges from 185 to 285 pounds, with a few examples exceeding that. The ewe is about three-quarters the size of the ram. The desert bighorn is a finer boned animal than its northern relatives, with its horns weighing somewhat less than those of the others.

If you look at the bighorn directly from the front, you will see that it stands square and close to the ground, with the brisket area also appearing square. The bighorn has a white muzzle and is white around the eyes. The rump is also white and a white stripe runs down the back portion of each leg. Its tail is short and black. Unlike the thick, seemingly curly wool found on domestic sheep, the coat of the bighorn is smooth, fine-haired and provides excellent insulation and warmth to this mountain dweller.

Sheep do not shed their horns as cervid game do their antlers. Therefore, you can accurately determine a sheep's age by counting the growth rings on its horns. Trophy size is about eight rings, which means an 8-year-old animal. The numerous growth rings of the Rocky Mountain sheep's horns will sometimes form a complete circle. If the horns block off the animal's peripheral vision, which they sometimes do because of their closeness to the face, the sheep will put the tips of the horns into a crevice and work at breaking them off. As a result, you will rarely see a perfect set of horns on a Rocky Mountain ram. However, since the horns of the desert bighorn grow differently, its vision is unaffected and perfect horns are not unusual. Although the ewe also has horns, they are straight and short and unfortunately don't possess the allure of the ram's.

The eyesight of the bighorn is phenomenal. It is said that its vision is equal to using a pair of binoculars, which multiplies vision eight to ten times that of a human being. There are stories, although unconfirmed, that you can stand on a ridge five miles from a bighorn, bend your elbow and the animal will respond by immediately altering its position, as if in fear. However, being a peculiar animal, it may just hold its ground and stare back at you.

The bighorn climbs up and down mountainsides effortlessly. Its great agility is attributable to the confirmation of its feet. Each foot has four toes with two outside hoofs that are used for gripping, as well as two additional dew claws. The interior part of the hoofs has a special adhesive-type tissue, almost like a suction cup, that gives the animal exceptional traction. The cannon bones are the same as those of a horse, and the hoofs, shoulder muscles and spinal column are structured so that when the sheep jumps 20 to 30 feet, or even longer, it is able to withstand the shock from the leap without breaking any bones, which would happen with many other animals. In addition, the bighorn happens to be an excellent swimmer.

As cud-chewing bovids, all bighorn feed on plants. The Rocky Mountain variety eats assorted grasses, including buckgrass, sage brush, bitter brush, small willows and other related foliage. The desert bighorn feed on any type of brush that is available, including cactus—if they are hungry enough—and usually know the location of every water hole or stream in the vicinity.

Mating season usually occurs during November and December for Dalls and Stones, earlier for Rocky Mountain and desert sheep. In October when the rams begin to show interest in the ewes, they often stage feigned battles among themselves. Not so in November, however, when the large rams fight for real—lunging again and again until one of the males finally withdraws. Although they do not fight to the death, if a horn is torn loose, it can prove fatal. The larger, older and stronger rams usually predominate—in the bedroom, as it were, as well as in battle. In fact, after observing their mating habits, one might consider them (the females, too) a lusty lot. And as nature would have

Bighorn sheep

it, once the breeding is done, the males resume their bachelor status, congregating with other males and paying no heed whatsoever to the females.

Hunting Tips/bighorn sheep

Bighorn sheep are found in inaccessible regions, seldom below the treeline, but on occasion in high alpine meadows. As a hunter, you will almost always encounter snow and freezing temperatures. Therefore, you should be: • in excellent physical condition; • equipped with warm clothes and heavy-duty climbing gear; • familiar with the terrain in which the sheep are hunted; and • preferably in the company of a professional guide(s).

Field Dressing/bighorn sheep

If you have taken your sheep in a snow-covered area, you can let it work to your advantage. After making certain the animal is dead (check the eyes—

they should be open and appear glassy), dig out a section of snow to create a hollow area or support in which to imbed the sheep while you field dress it. This will keep the animal stationary.

Before we proceed, let's assume you want to take the head and cape back to your taxidermist for mounting. The remaining carcass you will roughly butcher into large pieces with the hide still left on; it is faster this way, in part preserves the meat and you are not concerned with the rest of the hide because you've got what you want. So, the first thing you will do is to remove the cape and head as quickly as possible. Also, by not gutting the animal first, you will give yourself a better chance of coming home with a nice, clean trophy, and its plenty cold out there, so spoilage is not anticipated.

1. After you have secured the body, cut through the hide only, starting just behind the front legs, and completely encircle the upper torso. Then circle the

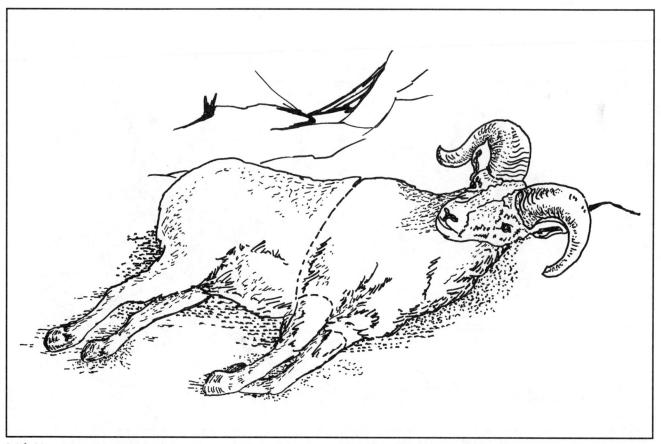

2-36. To remove the cape and head for your trophy mount, begin by cutting—through the hide only—around the entire upper torso and then the front legs as indicated by the broken lines.

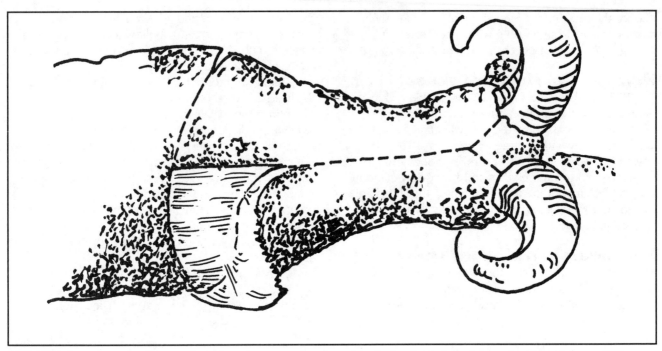

2-37. With the ram on its side, cut along the spine to a point about four inches behind the horns, then branch into a "Y," stopping at the base of each horn.

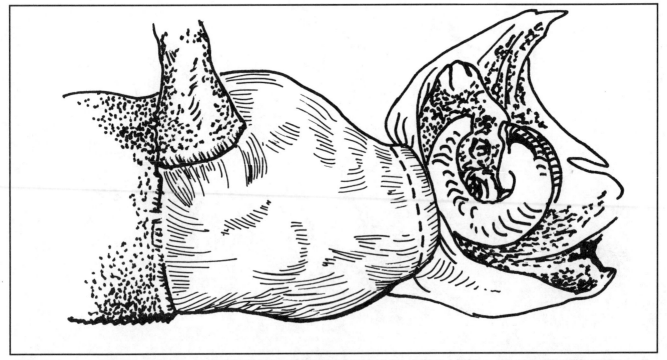

2-38. Starting at the lower edges, peel back the hide toward the head until the neck is completely exposed. Cut through the neck at the base of the skull, and take the horns and twist until the head breaks free. Holding the hide back, drain the head and pat the neck dry with towels. You want a nice, clean, enviable cape, so keep the white fur away from the blood.

INTERNAL ANATOMY OF THE SHEEP

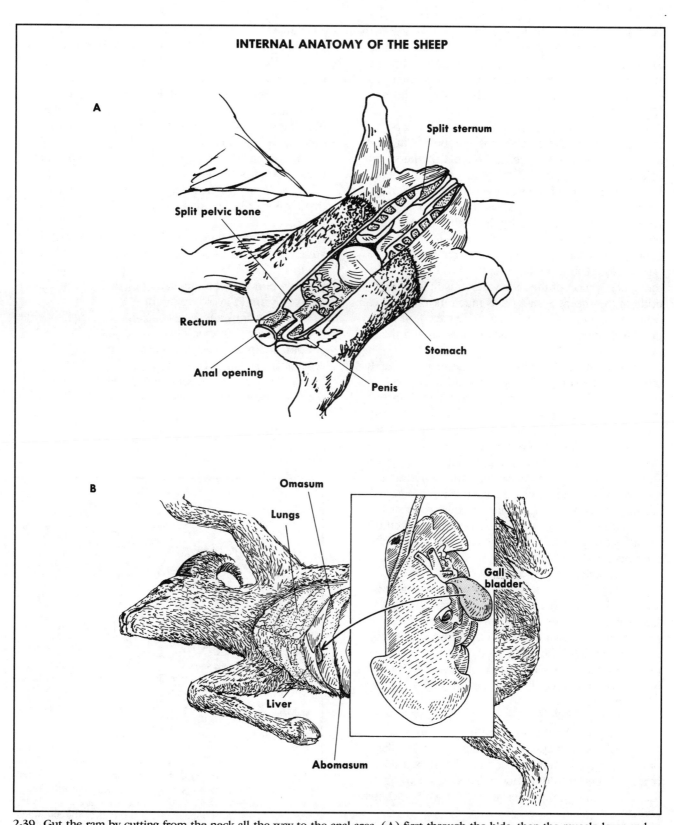

A

Split sternum

Split pelvic bone

Rectum

Anal opening

Penis

Stomach

B

Omasum

Lungs

Gall bladder

Liver

Abomasum

2-39. Gut the ram by cutting from the neck all the way to the anal area, (A) first through the hide, then the muscle layer and last through the pelvic bone and sternum. Be particularly careful with your knife because, unlike cervid game, the sheep has a bile-filled gall bladder (B) which, if punctured, could ruin all the surrounding meat.

front legs just above the knee joints (*See Figure 2-36*).

2. On the back of the neck, cut through the hide along the spine toward the top of the head to a point about four inches behind the horns. Then branch this cut into a "Y," terminating at the base of each horn (*Figure 2-37*).

3. Pull the hide up from the edge of the cape toward the face, enough to expose the neck. Cut through the neck at the highest vertebra on the spinal column, just at the base of the skull, being careful to keep the hide out of the way (*See Figure 2-38*). You do not want to puncture the hide accidentally or stain it with blood. Take the head by the horns and twist until the head snaps free. If it does not, do a little more cutting with your knife until you can remove it.

4. Now you have the complete head along with the upper section of the hide you've taken from the body of the sheep. Scrape off as much meat as you can from the inner areas and salt the hide well. Roll it up flesh against flesh, keeping the fur side out and the salt in contact with only the skin.

Now that you have the area to be mounted safely removed, salted and rolled, you should hasten to eviscerate the animal and butcher the carcass. Since we will not be skinning the lower hide, but allowing it to remain on the carcass as we gut and quarter, it means less work and time involved in getting the sheep down the mountain and back to camp. In addition, it actually serves to protect the surface of the meat at freezing temperatures. Even though the meat is hung outdoors at camp, when the temperatures are below freezing, that mutton can suffer the same type of freezer burn it would get in your freezer at home. Keeping the hide on prevents this.

5. To eviscerate the animal, you will split the carcass open from neck to anus. A knife, a bone saw and possibly a small axe will be your standard tools. Begin at the neck area as shown in *Figure 2-39*. As you proceed to cut down the length of the body, it is not necessary to cut through the hide, muscle and membranes all in one fell swoop. And you certainly will not be able to cut through the sternum and pelvis all in one slice.

So, cut carefully first through the layer of hide and muscle as you near the region of the genitals, cut around the penis if you have a male; do not cut the organ itself, as the urethra, the tube that runs inside it, connects directly to the bladder. Then when you get to the anal opening, completely encircle it with your knife and stop.

6. Go back to the genitals and lightly cut under the shaft of the penis until you reach its base of attachment. Pull it up and lay it to the side of the opening. Carefully pull out the encircled anal area until you can locate the rectum (a larger tube than the urethra, which you will not be able to see). Take the anus and penis and tie a string securely around the tubes that pass under the pelvic arch. This will prevent the contents of the bladder and rectum from spilling onto the rest of the meat.

If you have caught a ewe, cut a large, fairly deep circle around both the anus and vagina, pull on them gently to loosen the rectal and urethra tubes; then tie them together before you proceed to split the pelvic bone.

7. Following the natural "seam" atop the pelvic arch, use your small saw or axe to separate that bone. Do this carefully because too much pressure will possibly puncture the underlying bladder or intestines and you want to avoid doing this.

Pull the anus and penis back into the cavity via the pelvic canal and further loosen the contents of the abdomen. Tip the sheep to one side and allow the contents to slide out onto the ground.

8. Now using your bone saw, split the sternum, the midbone of the rib cage to which all the ribs attach.

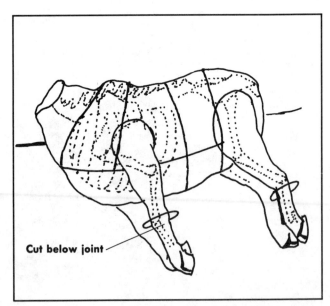

Cut below joint

2-40. To prepare your ram for easy transport, simply quarter the carcass in large sections as shown, leaving the hide on. Divide it in half crosswise in the midsection; then subdivide it again along the backbone; remove the legs at the shoulder joints, further subdivide as necessary. Place in meat bags or wrap in cheesecloth.

Separate it allowing entry into the organs of the chest cavity. Pull down and out on the trachea and esophagus, which are located in the neck. This will aid in loosening the heart, lungs, and liver. As with the other big game animals, you must also cut away the diaphragm muscle by completely encircling the inner perimeter of the rib cage just below the lungs and heart. Be aware, too, that as a bovine animal, the sheep has a gall bladder (unlike a deer), which you should take pains not to puncture. It contains a bitter fluid called bile, which is used in digestion; it can ruin any meat you wish to prepare for the table (*See Figure 2-39*).

If you plan to save the heart, liver or kidneys, be sure to trim off the arteries, veins and fat. Slit the heart open and remove any blood from its chambers. The kidneys are found at about the middle of the back wall of the carcass. If you so desire, just leave them attached while transporting the meat. If not, place all the sweetbreads in a plastic bag. Then remove all the innards from the chest cavity.

9. Use cloths to wipe out the inside of the empty cavity. If a lot of blood has pooled, turn the body over onto its belly and allow it to drain for a minute or so.

Quartering and Transporting/bighorn sheep

Begin quartering with the animal on its back. Locate the last rib in the midsection of the body and follow it to the spinal column where it is attached. This is the location of your first crosswise cut that will divide the body into two sections, fore and hind (*See Figure 2-40*).

On the second cut remove the remaining section of the neck, just above the shoulder bone. This piece should not contain ribs, but don't be upset if a few bone segments get caught.

Now split the fore section of the sheep in two by cutting down the length of the backbone on either side of the round column of vertebrae. You can pack these as is or further divide them by cutting across the ribs at right angles to the direction in which they run. In addition, you can remove the legs for easier and separate transport. Simply cut through the flesh and muscle at the shoulder joint; then twist the leg free.

Split the hind section into two sides as you did the front, by cutting along the inside of the back. Remove the rounds, or thighs, from their attachment to the pelvis the way you separated the fore legs at their shoulder joints. If you cut off the lower parts of the limbs, however, do so just *below* the knee joints. Cut

through the bone here, not through the joint, because you may want to hang the piece later for further smoking, aging, etc., and you would need the joint intact for proper support.

Wrap the sections of meat in cheesecloth or meat bags to protect them from dirt, and to make transport easier. For further butchering cuts, refer to the chapter on "Butchering and Preserving Game."

A single man using a pack frame can transport a whole sheep by making several trips. In some instances, the head and horns alone can weigh more than 50 pounds. For this reason, it is good to have help in carrying your meat back to camp. Sometimes a pack frame is the only method that works in the high, craggy precipes where bighorn sheep are found. When the terrain allows, use an H-frame (*See Figure 1-3*).

When transporting the head of the sheep, make sure the horns do not extend higher than two inches above your head. Pack it fairly low on the form so you will not be mistaken for a sheep. And always remember to tie strips of bright orange to the animal so that it can be easily distinguished at a distance.

Cooking/bighorn sheep

Marinated Leg of Sheep
(Serves 8)

1 5- to 6-pound leg of sheep salt and coarsely ground black pepper to taste	2 cloves garlic, thinly sliced

Marinade:

4 tablespoons vinegar	2 bay leaves
1 cup red wine	½ teaspoon dried thyme
½ cup olive oil	seasoned salt to taste

Trim meat of all skin and fat. Salt and heavily pepper meat and sprinkle with garlic slices. Place in a glass or ceramic dish with a cover.

Combine ingredients for marinade and pour mixture over leg. Cover and marinate for about 24 hours, turning the leg after 12 hours. Keep refrigerated, basting occasionally.

Cook the leg on a spit, if possible, over hot coals for approximately 3 hours or until the meat is tender. The leg may also be cooked in the oven at 325° F. for about 3 hours.

Sheep Stew
(Serves 6)

2 pounds sheep roast, cut into pieces and fat removed
flour
1 large onion, diced
2 tablespoons butter or margarine
1 cup water
2 cups carrots, diced

1 16-ounce can stewed tomatoes or 1 12-ounce can tomato puree
1 10-ounce package frozen peas
½ teaspoon dried thyme
½ teaspoon dried marjoram
salt and black pepper to taste

Dredge meat in flour. In a large saucepan sauté meat and onion in butter or margarine until well browned. Add water, cover pan and lower heat. Simmer, stirring occasionally about 1½ hours until meat is tender. Add the remaining ingredients, and stir well. Cover saucepan and continue cooking over low heat for about another hour.

Roast Sheep
(Serves 5)

1 4- to 5-pound roast (saddle cut)
salt and black pepper to taste
2 medium onions, sliced thin

2 cloves garlic, sliced
4 to 6 stalks celery, diced
½ cup vinegar

Cut off fat from meat and rub with cut sides of garlic clove, if desired; place in roasting pan. Salt and pepper to taste. Arrange slices of onion, garlic and celery atop roast. Pour vinegar over. Place meat in a 425° F. oven for 15 to 20 minutes, then reduce heat to 325° F. Continue to roast, covered with aluminum foil 20 to 30 minutes per pound, depending on age of sheep (20 minutes for young sheep; 30 for older sheep). Serve with mint jelly.

Easy Mutton Meat Loaf
(Serves 6)

2 pounds ground sheep
1 pound ground pork
3 eggs, beaten
1 cup cracker crumbs
1 medium onion, diced
2 tablespoons Worcestershire sauce

1 tablespoon vinegar
salt and black pepper to taste
1 package onion soup mix
⅔ cup water

Mix together meat, eggs, cracker crumbs, onion, Worcestershire sauce, vinegar, salt and pepper. Mix well and shape into a loaf; place into greased baking dish. Mix onion soup and water together and pour over loaf. Bake in 325° F. oven 2 hours. This is especially good for cold meat sandwiches to be eaten the day after cooking.

ROCKY MOUNTAIN GOAT

The mountain, or specifically Rocky Mountain, goat is a magnificent animal. Although a member of the bovid family as the bighorn sheep, the mountain goat taxonomically is also related to the American antelope. Both the male and female bear two slender, black hollow horns that curve slightly backward, the billy's reaching a length of 12 inches and the nanny's around 8 inches or under.

Most mountain goats can be found in the higher, colder slopes of Washington, Idaho, British Columbia and Alaska. And, as inveterate climbers, they possess cushioned, convex-shaped hoofs that provide them with excellent traction and almost adhesive-like footing. The feet appear to be square, with the fore hoofs slightly larger than the hind ones.

A typical goat stands about 42 inches at the shoulder and measures about 5½ to 6 feet in length. Stocky and muscular, it can weigh as much as 300 pounds. Its distinguishing physical characteristics are its white beard and the thick white (slightly weathered yellow) hair that covers most of its body—which contrasts sharply with its black horns, eyes, nose and hoofs.

A ruminant like its cud-chewing cousins, the mountain goat feeds on all sorts of browse, grasses, lichens, mosses and brush and will often make a meal from the bark of juniper and willow trees. Natural salt and mineral springs are also favorites.

Among its other traits are its eyesight, far superior to that of most other animals (as much as three to five miles in range), and the fact that it likes neither stormy weather nor blustery snow falls and will often seek shelter in the nearest protective crags it can find.

Mountain goats are not gregarious by nature, but do tend to live in small herds. And of course the mating season brings them all closer together. The mating season for the goat is the same as that for some sheep—November and December. Unlike the sheep, however, there is virtually no combat among the males for the females. They will charge as if to attack, emit grunts and bleeps, but all this is done for show. The billy goats do not crash head-on to prove their superiority and take charge of the breeding. The male goat does not seem to care—win or lose—but eventually he will mate with a female.

Hunting Tips/ rocky mountain goat

When you hunt mountain goat, you will find yourself in some treacherous territory, in high altitudes where the oxygen level may be low. Therefore, you should: • be in top physical condition; • dress appropriately; • hunt with an experienced guide; and • remember to bring along a pair of binoculars. The goat is so well camouflaged in the snow, where he will often be, that he is difficult to spot. You can search with the naked eye and not see a mountain goat when suddenly you will notice a blur of white movement, and the animal will be gone. Don't miss the shot you've been waiting for by not being prepared.

Field Dressing/ rocky mountain goat

Lay the animal on its back with the head higher than the body, if possible positioning a log under the neck and another under the head. If no logs are available, try to use rocks or build a snow bank to keep the neck and shoulders off the ground (so as not to dirty the white hair for your trophy mount).

Check the temperature. Since most goats are taken in the early or mid-afternoon hours when the sun is at its highest, your meat can spoil rapidly. So rather than remove the cape first, as I suggested with the bighorn sheep, you will dress out your goat before you do anything else. Field dressing procedures are the same.

1. Make the first incision with your knife blade directly between the two front legs at the center of the brisket region below the breastbone. Using the "V" cutting technique illustrated in *Figure 2-3*, take the knife between your index and middle fingers and cut down to the genitals. Be extra careful that the blood or fluids do not come in contact with the cape area, which of course is everything from roughly the brisket up.

2. If you have a billy goat, cut back the penis to its base of attachment. You may detach the testicles completely, but do not rupture the penis, since it contains the urethra, which connects to the bladder. Then with your knife encircle the anus. Gently pull on the anus until you see the rectum, which is directly joined to it. Tie off both rectal and urethral tubes with cord or twine.

If you have a nanny goat, cut a large, deep circle around the vagina and anus, which lie close together. Pull on that round of hairy flesh until you see the rectum and urethra, then tie them together.

3. Split the pelvic bone with a small saw, being

Rocky Mountain Goat

careful not to puncture the bladder, rectum or any of the large intestines underneath. Pull the pelvic bone apart.

4. Now turn the animal on its side and let the entrails spill out. Remove any attached organs and membranes from the carcass, using your knife with quick decisive movements.

If you have difficulty tying the tubes before the pelvic bone is split, by all means split the bone first *very carefully* before you pull the tubes through the lower canal; tie them, then empty the abdominal cavity.

5. Before you proceed to remove the innards from the chest region, partially skin the cape to protect it from bloodstains and animal fluids that could ruin the hide. With the animal on its back, begin by making an incision across the brisket area from one "armpit" to the other, perpendicular to the first cut you made down

the middle (*See Figure 2-41*). Carry this incision completely around the entire torso. Now cut through the hide on the inside of the forelegs, ending at the knuckles. If you wish, you can remove the hoofs just below the lower joint.

Now you have a type of flap in front that you can lift up to expose the throat area. Skinning the head will be completed after you've finished field dressing the chest cavity.

6. Cut through the muscle layer in the brisket up to the sternum and split open the rib cage by cutting the sternum in a lengthwise direction. Spread the ribs apart, and cut up to the throat and the base of the chin. Cut out the windpipe and esophagus and by pulling sharply on those two tubes, you will loosen the heart and lungs, which should be removed at this time. Completely empty the chest cavity. Wipe out the

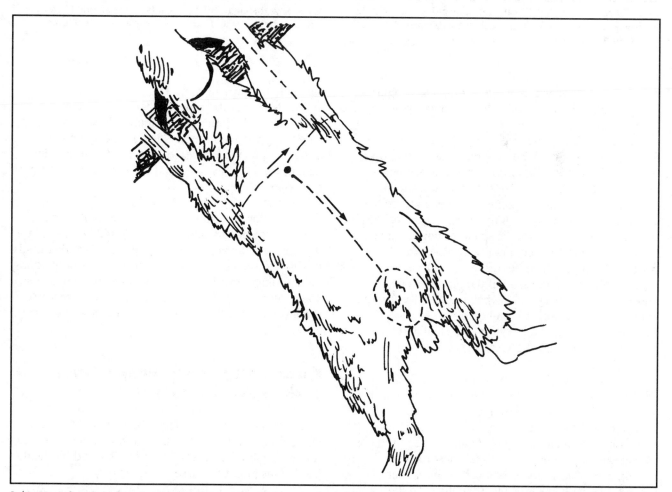

2-41. Your first field dressing incision is the standard cut in the brisket area down to the genitals. Partial skinning of the cape follows by making a cut perpendicular to that first incision and following it completely around the torso and into the forelegs.

2-42. To remove the head easily, carefully pull back the hide to expose the neck, and cut through at the highest vertebra on the spinal column.

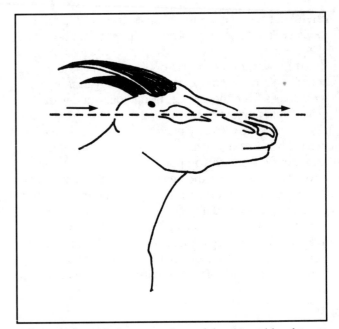

2-43. Saw through the eye sockets of the skinned head to remove the horns and skull cap for your trophy mount.

eviscerated carcass with clean dry cloth, refraining from using water. This liquid will only encourage bacterial growth and meat spoilage.

7. You will now resume caping. Using your fingertips and knuckles, pull the hide toward the top of the skull. Remove the head from the body at the highest vertebra along the backbone to facilitate completion of skinning around the horns and face. Use a strong knife to cut through the neck, just under the skin, and cut back toward the spinal column until you hit that uppermost vertebra just below the skull. Now twist the head until it comes off (*See Figure 2-42*).

Carefully work the skin off the head with your fingers and a very sharp knife, being especially cautious around the lips, nose, eyes and ears.

After removing the hide from the skull and face, saw through the skull at eye socket level to remove the horns (*Figure 2-43*).

Now do a good cleanup job on the skull cap to which the horns are attached, using plenty of salt. Also liberally salt the skin that covered the face of the animal, especially in the lip area. You may want to make some small crosscuts on the inner side of the lips so that salt may be more thoroughly absorbed.

After you have rubbed in a sufficient amount of salt, fold the hide inward so that the fur is on the outside, and place the head in a cool, dry area out of

sunlight and away from heat.

8. Now that the cape has been removed and salted, finish the job by removing the lower portion of hide. Simply extend the first field dressing incision down the inner side of each hind leg. Cut to a point a little beyond the first joint and remove the legs just past this point.

Starting at the upper torso, peel the hide back, working your way down to the hind legs. Roll the carcass from side to side to allow for hide removal in the back. At the tail, cut through the cartilage that holds the hide to the body. If you are concerned about your hide turning green because of warm temperatures, you could flesh it out and salt it there and then; otherwise roll it up, quarter the carcass and head back as swiftly as possible.

Quartering and Transporting/ rocky mountain goat

First, cut off the remaining stump of neck at the base just above the shoulders. Then cut and twist the legs out of their joints. Cut the carcass crosswise in half, so that the fore half contains all the ribs, and the hind half begins just at the base of the rib cage.

If your goat is not too big, you can place these halves directly into game bags or wrap in cheesecloth.

If they are too bulky to carry, however, cut them again lengthwise down the backbone, right down the middle of the vertebrae, if possible. If you so desire, you can also sprinkle pepper on the meat to deter flies and other insects. For finer butchering cuts, see "Butchering and Preserving Game."

Transport as you would other big game, on backpacks, H-frames, etc.

Cooking/rocky mountain goat

Some people believe that goat is not good-tasting meat. They reason that since it takes the goat a long time to get its full growth of horns, it will be older and the meat tough. I think if you try goat meat in some of the recipes we have included here, you will find a contradiction to this belief. Although goat meat tends to be dry, if handled properly, it is as tasty and tender as any meat you will ever prepare.

Curried Goat
(Serves 6)

2½ pounds goat meat, cut into 1½-inch cubes
salt and black pepper to taste
3 to 4 cloves garlic, crushed
4 scallions, diced
2 medium onions, diced
2 tablespoons curry powder
vegetable or peanut oil
2 cups hot water
8 whole allspice
sprig of fresh thyme or ¼ teaspoon dried thyme
⅓ small hot red pepper, sliced
1 tablespoon butter

Season cubed meat with salt and black pepper. Combine crushed garlic, scallions, onions and 1 tablespoon curry powder. Mix together with meat. Let stand at least 2 hours in refrigerator.

Scrape off garlic, scallions and onion and reserve. Lightly brown meat on all sides in hot oil in large saucepan. Add water, allspice, thyme and hot red pepper. Cover and cook over medium heat until fork-tender, about 40 minutes.

Add the second tablespoon of curry powder, butter and the garlic-onion mixture and cook for an additional 10 minutes, until onions are just tender. Serve with boiled rice and chutney.

Goat Stew
(Serves 4 to 6)

2 pounds young kid, cut into ¾-inch cubes
flour
1 teaspoon salt
½ teaspoon black pepper, freshly ground
¼ cup vegetable or peanut oil
2 medium onions, diced
4 potatoes, thinly sliced
1 cup carrots, chopped
1 8-ounce can crushed tomatoes
3 tablespoons Worcestershire sauce
1 teaspoon ginger, chopped
½ cup water

Dredge goat cubes in flour, salt and pepper. Brown quickly in hot oil. Add onions, potatoes, carrots, crushed tomatoes, Worcestershire sauce, ginger and water. Stir while bringing to boil. Reduce heat and simmer for 2½ to 3 hours until meat is tender.

Braised Young Goat
in Wine and Orange Sauce
(Serves 6 to 8)

3 pounds young goat, cubed
1 teaspoon salt
black pepper, freshly ground
¼ cup peanut oil
1 cup dry vermouth
¾ cup orange juice
¼ cup lemon juice
1 tablespoon capers
6 large green olives, chopped
¼ cup pimento, chopped
2 cloves garlic, minced
1 teaspoon Jalapeño peppers, finely chopped
2 whole allspice, crushed
1 bay leaf

Season goat meat with salt and pepper. In a large, deep saucepan, brown meat on all sides in hot peanut oil. Remove meat from pan and set aside.

Pour most of oil out of pan, leaving only enough to glaze bottom. Add vermouth and bring to boil, scraping all brown bits clinging to bottom of pan. Add orange juice, lemon juice, capers, olives, pimento, garlic, peppers, allspice and bay leaf. Return meat to pan and simmer the mixture, tightly covered, for about 2 to 2½ hours, or until meat is tender.

Serve over a bed of hot rice, accompanied by mango chutney.

Black bear

BLACK BEAR

Of all the big game in North America, the bear is the most ferocious and most formidable to hunt. The Kodiak and grizzly bears, both types of large brown bear, possess characteristic humped shoulders and are found in Alaska, western Canada and the American Rockies. Polar bears, the next largest ursine species are noted for their thick white fur, which blends into the snow and ice they inhabit around the Arctic Circle. Black bears, the smallest of the North American bears, are the most numerous and cover a vast area throughout the continent. These are the species hunters most often encounter and most often bring home.

The western range of the black bear includes the states of Washington, Oregon and California and the entire region of the Rockies from Canada to Mexico. The states of the north central region, Minnesota, Wisconsin and Michigan, are also quite popular for black bear hunting. In the east, these bears are abundant in the mountainous areas of the Appalachians from Maine to Florida, and also in the Gulf States.

The male black bear averages 300 pounds, with an unusually large one weighing as much as 600 pounds. It measures 3 feet high at the shoulders and 6 feet long from nose to tail. (The female is considerably smaller.) The black bear has a short tail, a long muzzle and small rounded ears, which occasionally get buried in its thick fur. Its coloring ranges from brown to black to almost white, but its face is always brown, and on its chest you will see a splash of white fur.

In addition to its smaller size, the black bear differs from the brown bear in that it has shorter hind feet and claws, and possesses a more uniform covering of fur. Many bears, especially larger ones, have areas of hide that are sparsely furred.

The bear is a plantigrade mammal which, like man, walks on the entire soles of its feet. Each foot has one main pad and five smaller pads, with one claw extending per toe. Because of the tenderness of its feet, the bear will often travel along the banks of streams, dusty trails and other relatively soft surfaces. Interesting also is the fact that the claws are nonrectractile, that is, they cannot be drawn back or in, as, let's say, the mountain lion's. This, however, contributes to the bear's reputation as a digger and a climber, and it is not uncommon for a mature bear to be seen clambering up a tree. (Incidentally, bear feet are delicious to eat when cooked over the coals of a campfire; see the recipe I have included later on in this chapter.)

Although you might imagine the bear to move at a slow, ambling pace, it is quite the runner. Usually a solitary wanderer, it is always on the move (swimming in the water as well), but seems to stay within a range of about 10 miles.

Because its teeth are well adapted to eating everything, the black bear enjoys the varied diet of an omnivore. While the polar bear, the most carnivorous of the bears, dines on fish, birds and other game, such as caribou and fox, and the grizzly favors salmon, snakes and frogs, the black bear leans more toward berries, buds, roots, honey and insects, as well as small mammals and fish. If it is ravenous, the male will even eat other bears.

Contrary to common lore, the black bear does not truly hibernate. Sometime in November or December, it will begin its winter sleep, which may end anytime from late March to mid-May, depending on the region, length of season, snow cover and individual habits. The body temperature and metabolism of the bear remain unchanged, however, as is evidenced by it being roused during warm spells when it emerges from its den.

Hunting bear can be as different from state to state as hunting bobwhite. They never act the same way you expect them to and you realize that bears can neither read boundary maps nor are they the slow creatures many hunters believe they are.

I remember being in Vermont in the early 50's when my father and I had a maple sugar operation as a part-time business venture. We converted a few buildings to bunkhouses for hunters who came up for the deer season from New York, New Jersey, Massachusetts, Connecticut and Rhode Island. We'd always check their weapons, especially the personal weapons that they all brought along. Remember, this was during the days when firearms laws were not so tight.

I can remember sitting around one of the three fireplaces in the main house. The night before an actual deer hunt began, we always passed out printed material to everyone, telling them what to do if they downed their game, the proper signals and what to do if they got lost, plus other items of interest. Well, a few men told some wild stories about bear and even mountain lions, which I never saw or heard of in that area. My father was a smart man, and about two hours after everyone had gone to bed down for the night, he and I would take our lanterns and go into the bunkhouses. There were four to five hunters in the two bunkhouses, and we could always tell the new ones or those whom the stories had affected quite a bit. You'd find a pistol next to their pillow or sometimes under their hand.

This one time Dad got everyone up about an hour

and a half before dawn and, after they'd finished their breakfast, we positioned them on still runs. Each hunter was told that since there wasn't any snow and it was very dry, the best luck this day would be still hunting. About 9 A.M., my father and I were "dogging the swamp," i.e., tramping through the woods below the hunters, hoping that our rustling would move deer toward them. It was then that we heard two shots, but no signal from the hunter who had fired. So we assumed he'd missed. As we picked up the hunters, we came to the one who had fired and asked him how large the deer was that he'd missed. His answer was, "Oh, I didn't shoot at a deer; it was a large black bear." It had been about 50 yards above him.

I didn't say anything to him, but I went up to the area and, sure enough, plenty of blood was everywhere. He hadn't even told us that he'd hit the animal. My only thought then was that the side of the mountain still had hunters on it, and a wounded bear was no animal to have stalking around.

We immediately sent a man toward the adjacent area to pass the word about the wounded bear. We were preparing to go up the slope and hunt down— which is usually the best strategy because the wounded bear would have to travel uphill against us—when we heard a loud noise about 100 yards from where I'd just come from. There it stood: one of the biggest black bears I'd ever seen, blood covering the front of him and spilling out of the eye that had been wounded. He was as mad as any animal could be.

Dad had always told me that if a bear's mind is made up, he'll kill you. I turned to get off the trail and shouted at the others to move. We all began firing at it and, as we did, the bear began rolling end over end. I figured that the bear *had* to be dead; we'd put at least nine rounds in it. I had a .30-06 Sporter model with a 150 grain soft tip. The bear landed next to a tree about six feet from us. He had died, but not before taking a swipe at the big pine which, in his confusion, he must have thought was a man. The piece of bark he'd whacked with his claws looked like an axe had hit it. Incidentally, the fellow who had initially fired at the bear was nowhere in sight, and was, I assumed, probably halfway back to camp when the bear had appeared.

We dressed out the animal and, when we got it back to camp, we skinned and hung it from a rafter in the barn door. We counted nine rounds in it, two or three in the sternum. Some had actually turned around in the fat, as bird shot would do in a bird. We didn't weigh the bear; the weather was quite warm so we butchered it right away. Naturally, a lot of the meat was unusable. As for the skin, you guessed it, it was demanded by the hunter who did the original shooting.

My father told this story many times, because in all the years he had hunted, he had never seen a bear roll; never have I. It just goes to prove that no matter what animal you are hunting, no two kills are ever the same.

Hunting Tips/black bear

The bear is a formidable beast that may attack a human if it is hurt or startled; extreme quiet and caution are musts when you hunt bear—also the proper ammunition and mental preparedness. • Look for damage to tree branches and claw marks on trunks; also tracks along river banks and other soft-walking surfaces. These are good indications that black bear are in the area. • If you are looking for a bear hide or a special mount, it is best to plan your hunt for the spring, around the time when the bear awakes from its winter sleep. This is when the fur is in its best condition. Second choice would be late fall, just before the bear beds down again.

Field Dressing/black bear

Once you are completely certain your bear is dead, be quick about dressing it out. Any delay could result in serious damge to the quality and taste of the meat. Field dressing is basically the same as for other big game animals, except that I don't bother to split the pelvic or breastbones, as you would do with a deer, for example. The bear's bones are pretty solid and hefty, which makes splitting them difficult. Also, the bear is large enough that you can maneuver underneath the large bones. So save yourself some time, and just reach under with your hands.

1. First turn the animal on its back. Starting just below the base of the rib cage, insert a sharp knife about one inch deep; cut down just enough to allow the index and middle fingers of your free hand to slip under the hide, and position those fingers with one on either side of the knife blade (*See Figure 2-3*). Using your fingers as a guide, cut down to the genitals, first through the hide, then through the muscle layer. You could try to do it in one step, but remember the fur is pretty thick, so it could lead to mistakes you don't want.

2. As all animals whose meat you are going to eat, you want to tie up the tubes leading to the bladder and rectum so the meat will not become tainted by their contents when you empty the animal of its innards.

If you have a male, loosen the penis with your knife by cutting it down to its base of attachment. Then cut a deep circle around the anus. Gently pull the penis

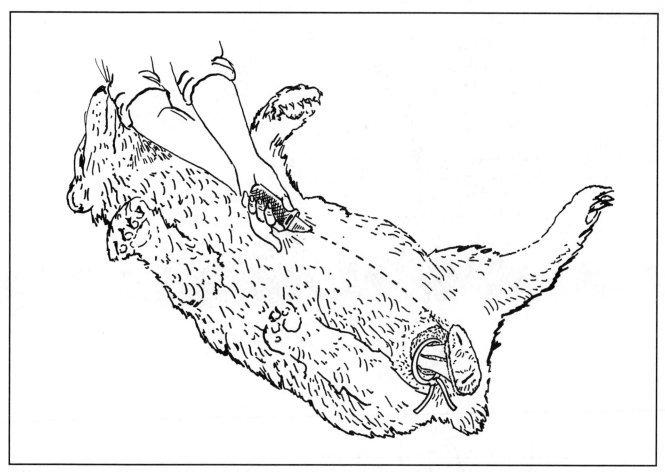

2-44. Field dress the bear as you would other big game. First open up the animal with a straight incision from the breastbone down to the genitals, cutting around them and tying the rectal and the urethral tubes.

and anus out until you can see the rectum, a large tube that contains the bear's fecal matter. Tie the two tubes together.

If you have a female, simply cut a large circle around the vagina and anus, which lie close together; gently pull them out and tie the tubes (*See Figure 2-44*).

3. Now turn the bear on its side and the intestines, bladder and organs of the lower digestive tract should begin to spill out. Guide the tied tubes under the pelvic arch, being careful not to damage the bladder or intestines (*See Figure 2-45*).

4. With the animal still on its side, cut a circle around the inner perimeter of the rib cage as shown in *Figure 2-46* to separate the diaphragm muscle, connecting the upper chest cavity with the lower abdominal cavity. Reach up into the chest cavity and cut loose the lungs; carefully pull them and the other upper organs out of the cavity, severing what might be

difficult to remove, such as the windpipe and esophagus. If you plan to save the heart, liver and kidneys for later eating, detach them, cutting off any arteries, etc., and place them in a plastic bag for transport. According to Indian legend, the liver will impart to whoever eats it the courage and strength of the bear.

5. The body cavity should now be completely empty of all viscera. Turn the bear on its belly and allow the blood to drain about five to 10 minutes. Roll the animal on its back again and wipe out the empty cavity with clean dry cloths. If you are tempted at this point to wash away with water the blood still remaining in the carcass—don't. It is this thin film of blood that actually helps to preserve the meat until actual cooling takes place. Now prop open the empty cavity with one or two sticks, which will aid in cooling the meat.

2-45. Slide the tubes under the uncut pelvic bone and empty the lower cavity of all its contents. (The bear is one animal whose pelvic and breastbones you don't split to remove the innards underneath.)

Skinning/black bear

If you intend to send your bear skin to a taxidermist for treatment, there are a few measurements you must take before and after it is skinned. Measure the length of the bear from its nose to the tip of the tail; the length of the head from the nose to the base of the skull; and the length of the tail. After you have removed the complete hide, stretch it out and again measure the distance from nose to tail, and add to that the distance from one front paw to the other front paw. Divide this sum by two and you will have what is known as the "square of the bear."

Skinning should be accomplished within one hour of the animal being killed and dressed out. The longer you wait, the more difficult the job, and the greater chance of meat spoilage. For one, the heavy fur and thick skin retard heat loss and inhibit cooling of the meat. Second, with bears that are actually black in color, the dark fur tends to absorb heat. Finally, the bear fat underlying the hide is similar to pig fat in that it freezes poorly and spoils quickly. Rancid fat left on the hide will rot the flesh and cause the hairs of the hide to fall out. (Remember also that the best hides are obtained in early spring.)

The following method for skinning a bear is one I use when I am saving the hide for a rug or life-sized mount.

1. First, if possible, place the bear on a clean tarpaulin or other protective surface. With the bear on its back, lengthen the original field dressing incision up to the chin, about four inches below the jaw, as shown in *Figure 2-47*. Be sure you do not extend this cut up to the lips.

2. Next, starting at the outer edge of the front foot pad, cut down and across the chest and continue up the other leg, ending at the opposite foot pad. Repeat this with the hind feet and legs. Extend the lower end

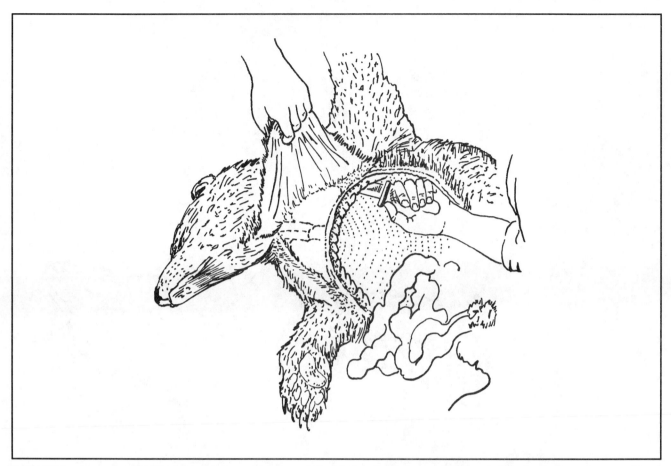

2-46. Without severing the bear's breastbone, reach in and detach the diaphragm muscle by circling the inner perimeter of the rib cage. Then empty the chest cavity, cutting away such organs as the windpipe, lungs, etc.

of the field dressing cut all the way to the end of the tail.

3. Starting at the rear, begin peeling away the skin, as though you were peeling off a snow suit. Since there is usually a lot of fat under the skin, this means two things: (1) time and care are necessary to remove the fat from the hide as it is peeled off; and (2) the blade of your knife will be dulled often as you proceed. I strongly advise skinning correctly and carefully the first time as opposed to doing a clumsy job initially with the intention of cleaning it up later. The longer you wait, the tougher it becomes to scrape away clinging pieces of tissue, and by waiting, you risk a greater chance of losing all or part of the hide through spoilage.

When you skin the feet, remember to skin to the last joint and leave the claws and pads intact.

4. The neck and the head are skinned last. Once you have pulled the entire hide up to the point at which the neck and skull join, you may sever the head from the body. Being careful not to cut into the hide, cut through the joints at the base of the skull and twist until the head is free from the body. At this point, you should have a completely skinned body and a head that is still attached to the skinned hide. Having separated these makes skinning the ears, eyes and lips an easier task.

The hard inner structure of the ear is attached to the skull by tough connective tissue and cartilage. When you have pulled the hide up this far, you must reach under and cut the ear from the skull at the base where it attaches. The cartilage of the ear can remain inside until you have finished skinning the entire head. Then you simply turn the ear inside out and cut it away from the flesh. The eyelids, nose and lips are skinned in the same careful manner. When you are removing such structures from the skull, always keep the knife as close to the bone as possible and use your free hand as a guide to make sure you do not cut into these delicate

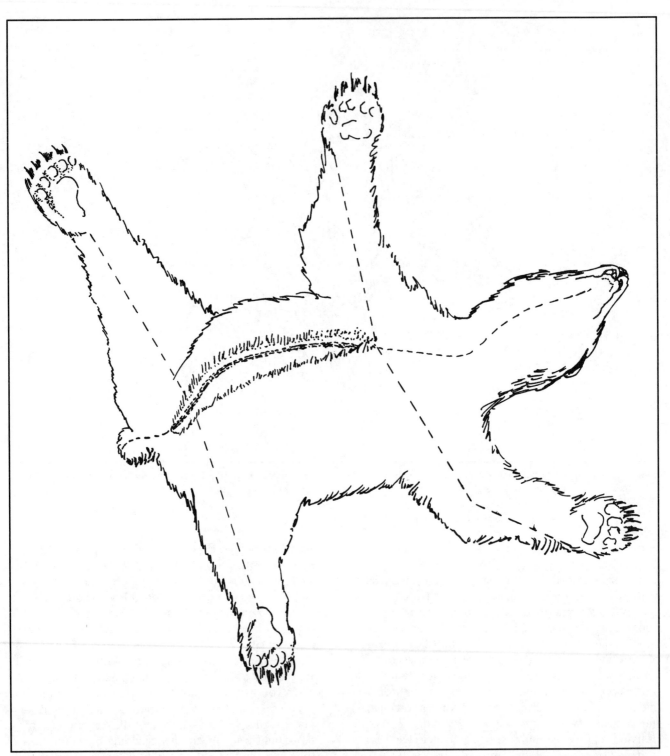

2-47. Before skinning, measure the entire length of the bear from the nose to the tail, then the length of the head and the tail separately. Cut through the hide along the dotted lines indicated and start at the hind end, peeling away the skin from the flesh. Be sure to scrape off the layer of fat as you skin or rancidity will swiftly set in.

parts. After you have skinned the lips of the animal, split them from the inside, and remove any meat around them. Then salt generously.

If your bear has an unusually large skull (which in most cases accompanies an unusually large bear), you may want to save it for the archives of Boone and Crockett, one of the recognized recording organizations and somewhat of a Guinness record group for sportsmen. Another reason to preserve the skull is that it makes an interesting kind of secondary trophy. The proper way to treat the skull is to scrape away all excess tissue, muscle, etc., and boil the skull for several hours in a solution of sal soda to sterilize and remove any remaining flesh and vermin. After boiling, dry and sprinkle the skull with borax. The use of borax is additional insurance against having tiny microscopic organisms living in your trophy. If you desire a whiter appearance to the skull, it can be bleached with straight peroxide or regular chlorine bleach diluted with water.

Now that you've spent so much time and expended so much effort skinning your bear, you will want to ensure that the hide does not spoil. If you are an hour or less from home and the temperature is relatively cool (47° F., 8° C., or below), you can roll up the hide fur side out and later put it in a refrigerator or freezer until you can get it to the taxidermist. If this is not the case, then you must very thoroughly salt the hide to prevent decay and rot.

You will need about 25 pounds of regular table salt and a clean place to spread the hide. The finer texture of table salt makes it superior to more coarse salt in that it spreads more uniformly and penetrates more deeply. And you will get the best results by using dry salt. If salt has been allowed to dampen and clump, break up the lumps and dry the salt in a pan over a fire. Any fat left clinging to the hide will impede penetration of the salt and thus cause degeneration of the hide and fur. It is important to have removed all the fat.

Start at the center and work the salt toward the edges of the hide. Be sure to salt all edges liberally, especially those around puncture wounds from bullets, etc. Rub vigorously. Once you are sure that all areas of hide have been thoroughly and evenly salted (the salt's layer should be about one-quarter-inch thick throughout), fold up the hide, edges in and fur side out, so as not to spill the salty brine that will begin forming on the skin side. Place the folded hide in the shade and allow it to rest for a few days. This will give the salt sufficient time to draw the moisture out of the hide.

Finally, dry the cured hide by hanging it over a

fence or clothesline, not in direct sunlight. If rain seems imminent, cover the hide with a tarpaulin so it won't get wet. When dry, the hide can be brought to the taxidermist for further processing.

Quartering and Transporting/black bear

If you have an unusually large bear, you may want to quarter it to reduce it to manageable pieces before you transport it. In this case, proceed as you would an elk, for example, by hanging it by its hind legs (see page 59). Insert a heavy pole between the bone and the tendon as shown in *Figure 2-48*. Tie a rope onto this pole and hoist the carcass to a level at which you will be comfortable working. Or use a basic block-and-tackle setup. A very strong tree limb or wooden rafter can be used to support the hanging bear.

First, remove the neck by cutting through the spine just in front of the shoulders.

Your second cut will be a long one from the tail to the neck area. To do this, you will need a small hacksaw or bone saw. After locating the vertebral column, begin sawing down one side of the spinal column cutting through the ribs at the top of the vertebrae, and cut through the entire length of the carcass. You will now have two relatively equal sides of meat.

Divide each side into thirds by severing the fore-

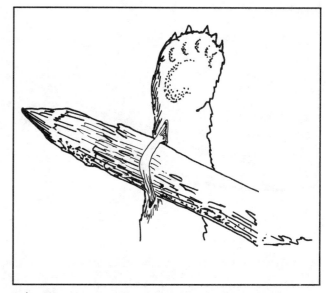

2-48. To quarter your bear for transport, hang it by the hind legs, inserting a sturdy pole between the bone and the tendons, and proceed much as you would an elk.

and hindquarters from the midsection, and you will have six good-sized pieces to carry back to camp or home. Place each piece in a cheesecloth-type game bag, which allows for cooling. Perhaps, too, you may want to pepper the meat to keep insects away until you can properly process it. For further butchering cuts, refer to "Butchering and Preserving Game," page 142.

If you decide you can cart the carcass in one piece, you can construct a rig like the one shown in *Figure 2-49*. You'll need five pieces of wood and rope or nylon cord. Cut two wooden poles of approximately 10 to 12 feet in length from nearby trees. Then cut three cross-poles about 3 to 4 feet long. With about 20 feet of rope or cord, "lace" all the poles together, crisscrossing the rope between the crosspoles and at each juncture. Allow for shoulder straps, which can be padded by placing some folds of cloth beneath them. Now with some additional cord, strap the bear to the pack as securely as you can, trying to distribute the weight as evenly as possible. Also, be sure to tie strips of bright orange cloth onto the bear as a safety precaution. Needless to say, I'd only attempt to transport a bear this way if I were in extremely fit physical condition and the journey back to base camp was not too far.

2-49. If you don't have many hands to help you carry out your quartered bear, you can rig up your own backpack to carry it out whole. "Lace" five poles garnered from nearby trees with about 20 feet of rope or cord, allowing for shoulder straps to assist in the pulling.

Cooking/black bear

Corned Bear
(Serves 6 to 8)

Corning bear has been a culinary tradition in England since the early 1700's. Its popularity through the centuries really isn't surprising—the results are delicious! This recipe for corning not only enhances the flavor of bear meat, but also complements moose, elk, caribou, deer and antelope.

When pickling, use a nonmetal container with about a 5-gallon capacity. Get a good pickling crock or a large barrel with a tight cover and an opening large enough to place through it a heavy ceramic saucer to keep the meat below liquid level. Throughout the corning process, keep the liquid at 36° to 38° F. (2° - 3° C.) to ensure its effectiveness.

several top round bear
   roasts of 2 to 3 pounds,
   trimmed of all fat

Corning Liquid:

3 gallons water, depending on size of container	1 tablespoon black pepper
1¼ ounces saltpeter (available at a pharmacy)	½ pound white granulated sugar
2½ pounds salt	1 large onion, chopped
1 ounce mixed pickling spices	1 clove garlic
	2 to 3 bay leaves
	½ ounce of your favorite spice, such as cloves, thyme, etc.

Put water into pickling container, large crock or barrel, add the saltpeter and 1 pound of salt and stir 3 minutes. Add the pickling spices and black pepper and stir for another 3 minutes. Mix together the remaining salt (1½ pounds) and the sugar and add to the liquid, stirring again. Be sure you add the ingredients in the order indicated. Add the vegetables, herbs and spices and do a final 2-minute stir.

Place the meat in the crock and weight it down so it is completely covered with corning liquid. Let stand for a week; turn the meat over, stir the liquid for about 3 minutes and weight and cover the meat again, leaving it for another week.

To prepare the meat for eating, remove it from the crock and place it in a Dutch oven, completely submerged in cold water. Bring to a boil and boil for about 5 minutes to remove the scum that has accumulated during the corning process. Spoon off the scum or place a few lettuce leaves in the pot to absorb the unwanted impurities, then remove the leaves. Simmer the meat for 4 to 5 hours, at which time it should be tender, bright red in color and fine tasting.

Roast Bear with Wine Sauce
(Serves 6 to 8)

1 5- to 6-pound bear roast	black pepper, freshly ground
seasoned salt	

Wine Sauce:

½ cup melted butter	1 bottle port wine
1 18-ounce jar crabapple or currant jelly	

Place roast in a large roasting pan and add just enough water to cover bottom of pan. Season with salt and pepper to taste. Cover and roast in a moderate 350° F. oven for approximately 30 to 40 minutes per pound, or until tender. Baste with Wine Sauce about every 15 minutes during roasting. Pass any remaining Wine Sauce in a gravy boat.

Wine Sauce: Melt butter in saucepan over low heat. Add jelly and stir occasionally until melted. Turn off heat and add wine, stirring until well blended. Serve over sliced cooked meat. This sauce is good with any type of game meat.

Barbecued Bear Sloppy Joes
(Makes 6 to 8 Sandwiches)

2 pounds ground bear or leftover cooked bear meat, shredded	2 tablespoons Worcestershire sauce
1 large onion, diced	¼ to ½ teaspoon cayenne pepper, or to taste
1 medium green pepper, diced	1 teaspoon dry mustard
1 cup catsup	1½ teaspoons salt
⅓ cup dark brown sugar, firmly packed	½ teaspoon black pepper, or to taste

Brown ground meat in a large skillet; add onion and green pepper and cook until tender. If using shredded meat, brown onions and green pepper first in a small amount of butter, then add meat; simmer for a few minutes. Add remaining ingredients and stir well. Cover pan and simmer for about 20 minutes. Serve in club or hamburger rolls or on your favorite bread.

Bear Stroganoff
(Serves 4 to 6)

2 pounds bear meat,
  cubed
flour
¼ cup vegetable oil
1 large onion, diced
2 cups fresh mushrooms,
  sliced
2 10½-ounce cans beef
  consommé
2 10¾-ounce cans cream
  of mushroom soup

2 tablespoons
  Worcestershire sauce
salt
pepper
1 cup sour cream
1 8-ounce package egg
  noodles, cooked
  according to package
  directions

Dredge meat in flour. In a heavy skillet, brown on all sides in hot oil. Reduce heat; add diced onion and cook until onions are golden brown. Stir occasionally to prevent sticking.

Add mushrooms and consommé; stir until mixture begins to bubble. Add mushroom soup, Worcestershire sauce, salt and pepper to taste. Cover and simmer approximately 2 hours, or until meat is tender. Blend sour cream into gravy and heat but do not boil. Serve over noodles.

Bear Casserole
(Serves 10 to 12)

2 pounds ground bear
½ pound ground pork
1 large onion, diced
1 large green pepper,
  diced
1 16-ounce package egg
  noodles, cooked
1 pound sharp cheddar
  cheese, grated
1 cup salad olives, diced

½ pound fresh
  mushrooms, sliced
¼ cup chili powder
1 12-ounce can corn
  niblets, drained
1 12-ounce can stewed
  tomatoes
seasoned salt and black
  pepper to taste

Mix bear and pork and brown in a large oven-proof skillet or Dutch oven until well done. Add onions and green pepper; simmer until tender. Spoon off fat.

Cook noodles according to package directions, drain and add to skillet. Add half the grated cheese and all remaining ingredients to skillet and stir well.

Bake in a 300° F. oven for 2 hours. Sprinkle on remaining cheese 3 to 5 minutes before end of cooking time or just prior to serving. This dish freezes very well.

Mud-packed bear feet—different and delicious.

Mud-Packed Bear Feet
(Serves 4)

4 bear feet

black, red or cayenne
  pepper to taste

Cut off bear's feet as shown (A). Surround each foot with a wet ball of mud that measures 8 inches or more in diameter. Some hunters wire the feet before packing them with mud to help keep the feet together while cooking.

Place wet mud ball in, not over, hot coals for 3 to 4 hours, turning occasionally. With a small hatchet or hammer and chisel, break the hardened mud ball in half and extract the meat (B). If desired, bear feet may be seasoned with black, red or cayenne pepper and quickly pan-fried over hot coals.

WILD BOAR

"I was scared. The sow was lookin' at me. And growlin'. I could see her tusks. They were about two inches long. Her teeth looked sharp, too. You'd think she would've run off when I yelled at her, but she didn't. She just kept comin'."

She did indeed keep coming at Bobby Zellner until she trapped him and knocked him down in a mud-filled marsh at the Aucilla Wildlife Management Area in northwestern Florida. As reported in the *St. Petersburg Times*, this 200-pound feral hog had been wounded by Zellner's son, Paul, and she was mighty mad. She pinned Zellner to the ground, but luckily he was able to cock the hammer of his Winchester and get off a shot. It hit the sow above the left eye and she dropped dead instantly. For the Zellners it was a successful hunt; but it was also a dangerous one that had caught them both off guard.

That's the chance you take when you hunt feral hogs (or razorbacks and wild boar, as they are also known). The true wild boar is a European species of the *Suidae* family and was introduced to North America by sportsmen for hunting. The wild hogs found here today are believed to be their descendants. Both species, however, still exist in various parts of the country and sometimes they interbreed. Wild boars have been found in New Hampshire, New York, Tennessee, the Carolinas and California; feral hogs are most often found in Hawaii, Florida, the Carolinas and the Gulf States. The domesticated hog is also descended from the European wild boar; it was introduced to the New World by the Spanish in the 1600's for its variety of leather goods, its bristles for use in brushes and its porcine meat products. Feral hogs have apparently evolved through the decades as domestic hogs gone wild.

Despite their fierce nature and the similarities in their physical appearance—cloven hoofs, long snouts, sharp teeth, tusks and coarse, bristly hair—the two species differ in some respects. The average adult boar stands 3 feet high and 5 feet long, and it weighs about

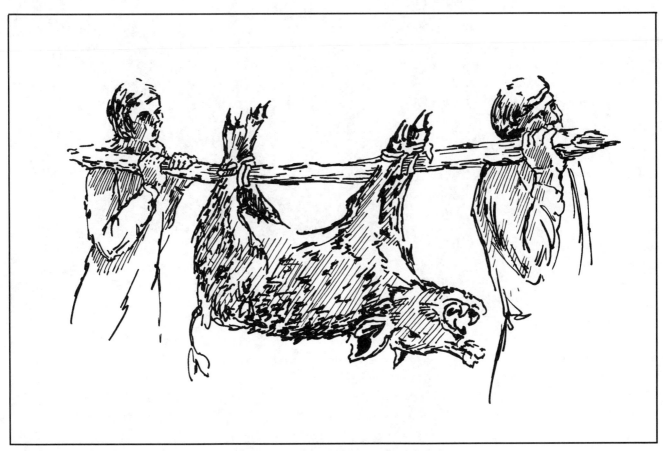

2-50. To carry a wild boar back to camp, tie its front and rear legs to a stout pole as shown.

Wild boar

300 to 400 pounds. The feral hog is usually smaller; in fact, the "pig" (classified as a small hog) weighs under 100 pounds. The ears of the wild boar stand erect, whereas the feral hog's may droop. The boar's tusks have been recorded at as much as 12 inches, considerably longer than those of the average feral hog. The bristly hair of the boar is usually longer and darker than that of the feral hog, although both range in coloration from light gray to almost black. The boar piglets, interestingly enough, have stripes running lengthwise across their bodies.

Hunting Tips/wild boar

As Bobby Zellner will readily attest, wild boars and hogs are fierce fighters. Their pointed tusks make natural weapons for charging and tearing apart their enemies. • Most wild boar hunters prefer to wait in tree stands and fire when the animal gets close. They don't stop firing, either, until they are sure the animal is dead. • Other hunters prefer to stalk their prey, using hounds or bulldogs. These fearless dogs often attack a hog at its ears or legs, then hang on until the hunter can finish the job. • Because wild boars are so unpredictable—some may charge, while others will wait you out—it may be wise not to hunt these animals at all unless your reflexes are exceptional and your aim is extremely accurate. • You should also know the area you're hunting in and hunt with someone who knows what he's doing.

Since there is little fat on a wild pig, some hunters have been known to track, trap, and "fatten" a wild pig, waiting several weeks before the actual slaughter. A younger, medium-sized animal will, of course, produce the best meat in taste and quality.

Debristling/wild boar

When dressing out a wild pig, boar or hog, you must "debristle" (remove the outer bristles) from the hide *before* dressing out the animal. This debristling process can be handled most efficiently at your camp or home; this usually means, however, that the carcass must be carried some distance. *Figure 2-50* illustrates how two people can transport the animal by tying it to a sturdy pole.

The simplest way to debristle a hog is by scalding it in a large, tall drum or barrel. Hang the animal in block-and-tackle fashion by inserting a pointed-edged gambrel stick between the two tough gambrel ligaments located on the lower hind legs (*See Figure 2-51* for details). Tie a rope to the center of the pole and thread it through a pulley that is secured to a supported pole or beam (*See Figure 2-52*). This device

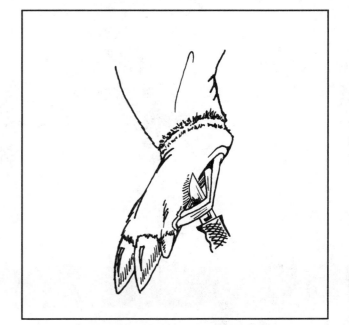

2-51. Detail of gambrel ligament separated at the joint where you would insert pole for hanging carcass.

provides flexibility in dousing, gutting and butchering the hog.

Fill the drum with scalding (not boiling) water so as not to cook the skin or set the hair. Then lower the animal into the water, completely submerging it to ensure uniform scalding. Keep the hog under water two to three minutes at a time. For a 250-pound hog without its heavy winter coat, allow about three to six minutes to loosen the hair. Have enough hot water on hand in case the water in the drum cools too rapidly.

Then, using a muslin cloth or similar coarse material, rub the hide in a circular motion until the bristles are removed. This process may require two or more people, because the bristles must be removed as fast as possible before the skin cools down. Some hunters use scrapers to speed up the debristling process.

If no drum large enough for dunking is available, simply pour scalding water over the carcass where it lies and rub the skin hard with a rough cloth. Repeat this process until the hide is free of bristles (*See Figure 2-53*). When the skin is completely clean, rinse the carcass with cold water; if you intend to use the hide, it must also be shaved.

Field Dressing/wild boar

The next step is to skin and eviscerate the animal. This can be done most effectively with the carcass

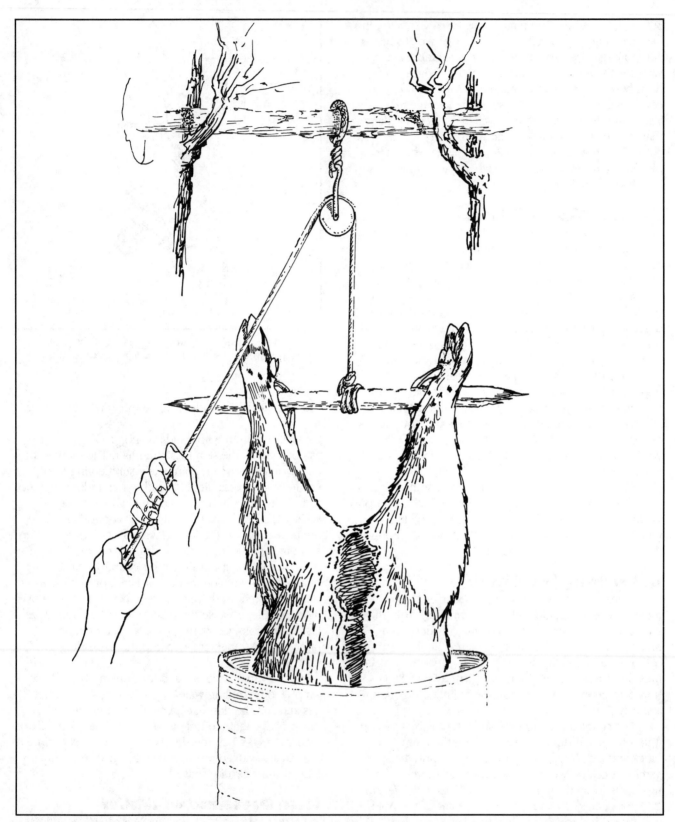

2-52. This simple block-and-tackle device enables the hunter to scald the hog prior to debristling. Keep carcass submerged long enough to loosen hair.

2-53. Rub skin hard with a rough cloth to remove hair. If hide is to be used, remaining hair must be shaved off.

suspended on the gambrel stick *(See Figure 2-54).*
Begin by removing the head. First, cut the neck with a
sharp, clean knife at the back of the skull through the
bone joint that connects the skull to the neck. Continue
cutting around the front of the head to a point just
behind the jawbone, leaving the jowls *(See
Figure 2-55).* This method provides an outlet for
draining the blood as well as severing the windpipe
and gullet. Be sure to place a bucket or some other
container beneath the carcass to catch the blood.

If you intend to make souse (see recipe on page
115), the head should be cleaned. First remove the
tongue with a sharp knife, wash it with clear water and
hang it up to dry. Then cut the muscles on either side
of the jaws and pull the jaws apart. Remove the lower
jaw, trim off any usable meat and discard the remnants.
Next, clean out the inner cartilage on the underside of
the ears. Cut out the eyes and snout and remove the
skin from the face. Finally, saw off the face bones, cut
through the skull lengthwise and remove the brain.
Rinse the remaining head with cold water.

If you intend to make head cheese, pull the skin
over the head of the pig, using your knife the same as
you would on a deer, cutting very carefully around the
entire neck. Remove the head, cut off the ears and cut
out the eyes and tongue. Remove any bristles that may
be present, but leave the skin on the head. Then cut
the head into four pieces and place them in boiling
water. Cook until the meat is tender enough to scrape
or fall off. To this soupy mixture add onions and
spices, according to taste. Chill the mixture in a bowl
until it has the consistency of gelatin. You have now
made a good supply of delicious head hog cheese.

Getting back to the skinning and gutting operation,
it makes little difference which comes first. Most
hunters prefer to gut the body before skinning, so let's
take that step first. Before you begin, though, note that
immediately beneath the outer layer of hide and fatty
deposit lies a layer of muscle; and just below that are
separate membranes which enclose the organs of the
abdomen and chest cavity.

Beginning at the neck end, proceed to cut upward
through the skin and muscle layers to the end of the
breastbone. Split this bone and open it up slightly to
allow for cooling. Do not cut beyond the chest cavity
and into the stomach; that area is best approached from
above.

Next, make an incision lengthwise down the
abdomen and through the muscle layer *(See Figure
2-54).* Do not penetrate the membrane underneath it;
only the layers of hide and muscle should be opened.
Then, cut around the anal region, loosen the opening

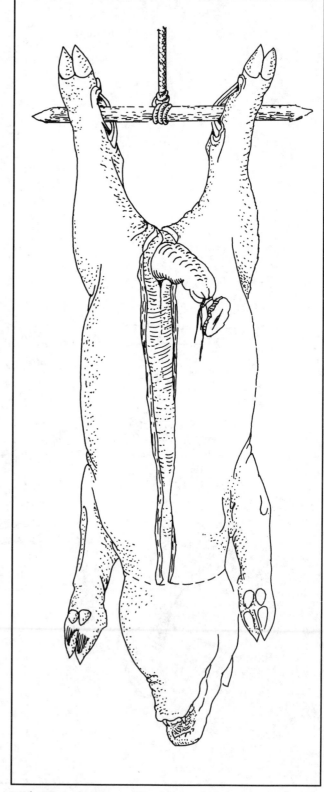

2-54. When skinning and gutting a wild boar, hang it upside
down on a gambrel stick as shown. Remove head and make
incision lengthwise down the abdomen.

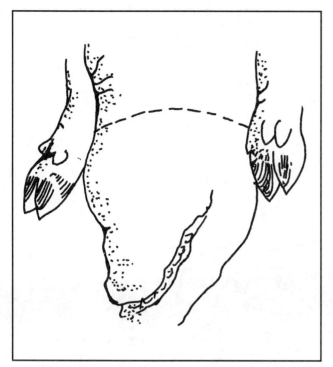

2-55. To remove head, cut neck starting at back of skull and continue around to jawbone, leaving jowls intact. Place bucket beneath head to catch blood.

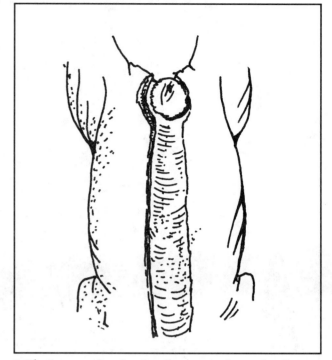

2-56. Cut around anal region, loosen opening, and pull out connecting rectum.

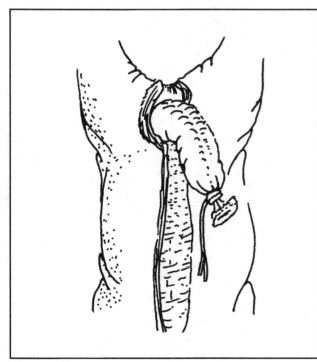

2-57. Tie off rectum as shown to prevent spillage.

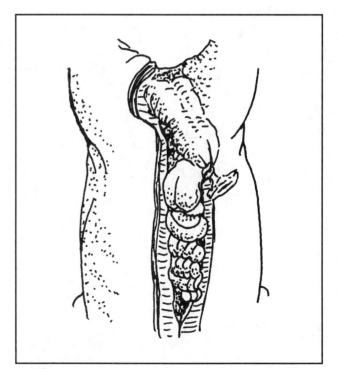

2-58. Split pelvic bone and pull out intestines and other organs. Wipe empty cavity clean with a cloth.

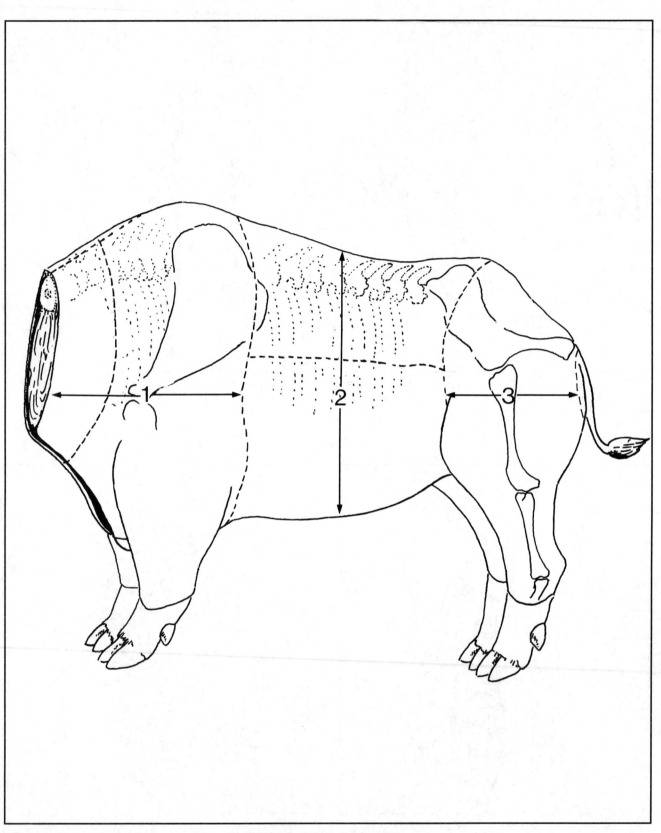

2-59. Quarter your hog into three or five sections, as indicated by the dotted lines.

and pull out the connecting rectum *(See Figure 2-56)*. Tie this organ as shown in *Figure 2-57*.

Now slice carefully through the membrane enclosing the lower abdomen and split the pelvic bone *(See Figure 2-58)*. Begin pulling out the intestines with one hand and work your way down to the chest area, severing the diaphragm and other organs with a knife as you proceed. With the carcass still hanging upside down, wipe the empty cavity with a clean cloth and prepare to quarter the hog.

To quarter the hog, first cut off the tail as close to the base as possible, so that the underlying backbone is visible. Using the center of the backbone as a guide, saw through the middle of the carcass straight down through the neck, making two halves.

Place one half on a table and cut it up into 3 or 5 large sections, according to the diagram *(Figure 2-59)*. The first cut begins just behind the shoulder blade, separating the forequarter from the midsection. You can further divide the forequarter by cutting off the jowel section.

Now remove the hindquarter. Cut the midsection into two pieces (see horizontal line in *Figure 2-59*) to make five good-sized chunks. These should be cooled and thoroughly cleaned before preparing the meat for preserving or cooking.

The cuts described above are rough, preliminary cuts. Instructions for final cuts—steaks, chops, roasts, spare ribs, and the like—are found in the chapter on "Butchering and Preserving Game."

Cooking/wild boar

Sweet and Sour Wild Pig
(Serves 5 to 6)

1½ pounds lean pig, cut into bite-size pieces (shoulder cuts are best)	2 tablespoons soy sauce
	1 tablespoon dry mustard
½ cup shortening	½ teaspoon salt
½ cup water	2 tablespoons cornstarch
1 8-ounce can pineapple chunks (reserve juice)	¼ cup dark brown sugar, firmly packed
¼ cup lemon juice	1 large green pepper, diced
¼ cup cider vinegar	1 medium onion, diced

Melt shortening in a large skillet over high heat and brown pig pieces. Reduce heat to simmer and add water, cooking until meat is tender.

In mixing bowl, combine reserved pineapple juice, lemon juice, vinegar, soy sauce, mustard and salt. In a separate bowl, combine cornstarch and brown sugar and mix into pineapple juice mixture. Slowly pour over pig, stirring until thickened. Add pineapple chunks, pepper and onion and continue cooking over low heat for 5 to 6 minutes. This is delicious served over wild or long grain rice.

Souse
(Serves 4 to 6)

1 pig's head, without tongue, cleaned	1 bay leaf
	salt and freshly ground black pepper to taste
4 pig's feet, cleaned	¾ cup cider vinegar
4 pork hocks, cleaned	2 medium onions, sliced
water	
1 teaspoon mace	

Place meat in large Dutch oven and add enough water to cover. Cook over medium heat until meat is tender. Transfer meat to platter to cool; reserve liquid.

Remove the meat from the bones and cut into bite-size pieces. Add mace, bay leaf, salt, pepper, vinegar and onion to the reserved liquid and boil until liquid is reduced to about one half. Strain the liquid, cool and skim off fat.

Heat the meat in a large crock. Pour into the crock as much of the liquid as it will hold or until the meat is completely covered. The meat may be used for sandwiches, salads or heated as a main dish.

Barbecued Pig
(Serves 4 to 6)

3 to 4 pounds pig, any cut, trimmed of all but a thin layer of fat	1 lemon, halved
	2 medium onions, sliced
	1 16-ounce bottle barbecue sauce

Rub meat with lemon and place in a roasting pan, fat side up. Cover with thin slices of onion and roast in a moderate 350° F. oven for 1 hour.

Remove from oven, pour barbecue sauce over meat and tent with aluminum foil. Reduce oven temperature to 325° F. and roast for an additional 1 to 1½ hours until meat is tender.

Javelina

JAVELINA

The collared peccary, white-lipped peccary, musk hog, desert hog and wild pig all refer to the same mammal found in the southwestern United States: the javelina (pronounced ha-vah-*lee*-nah). In appearance, mannerisms and the taste of its meat, the javelina resembles a pig—but it is not a true pig. Because it is indigenous to the Americas and is anatomically different from the Old World swine, the javelina is classified in the *Tayassuidae* family. Its name comes from the Spanish word for *javelin,* which accurately describes the animal's long shape and the slashing motions of its canine teeth, or tusks.

The javelina is smaller than the wild boar, measuring only about 20 inches at the shoulders and 35 inches in length, and averaging about 50 pounds in weight. Its sharp, downward-curving tusks are used for fighting and rooting for food. It has a large head, long snout, cloven hoofs and musk glands on its rump (which must be removed before skinning). Unlike the wild boar, its skin is smooth and thin, making it especially suitable for gloves, purses and other fine leather products.

The javelina, or collared peccary (so named because of the white band encircling its neck), is most abundant in the arid scrub regions of southern New Mexico, southern Arizona and southwestern Texas. The white-lipped variety, which features a white stripe across its chin, is found in lesser numbers and farther south, mostly in the forests of Mexico and South America.

Javelinas travel in small bands and are often found feasting on their favorite food, the prickly pear. Although the animal has very poor eyesight, its senses of smell and hearing are extremely well developed.

Hunting Tips/javelina

When hunting the javelina, it is wise to approach it from a downwind direction so that it cannot pick up your scent. • Strict silence should be maintained when stalking these animals, for the slightest noise can startle a group of them into running at top speeds of nearly 25 miles per hour.

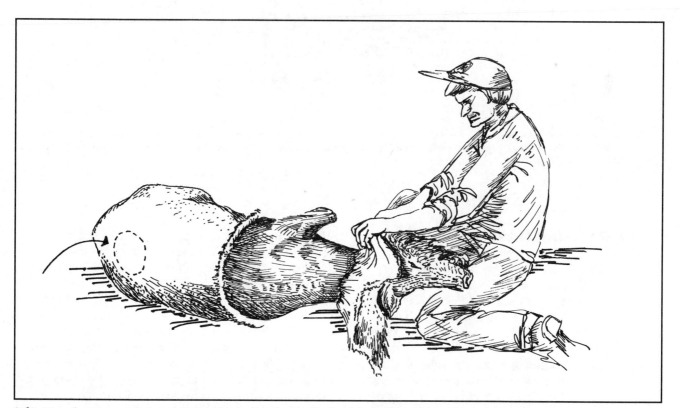

2-60. Many hunters, as the one pictured here, save the javelina's white collar and head for a trophy mount. In skinning this animal, be sure to remove the musk gland (circled area near tail).

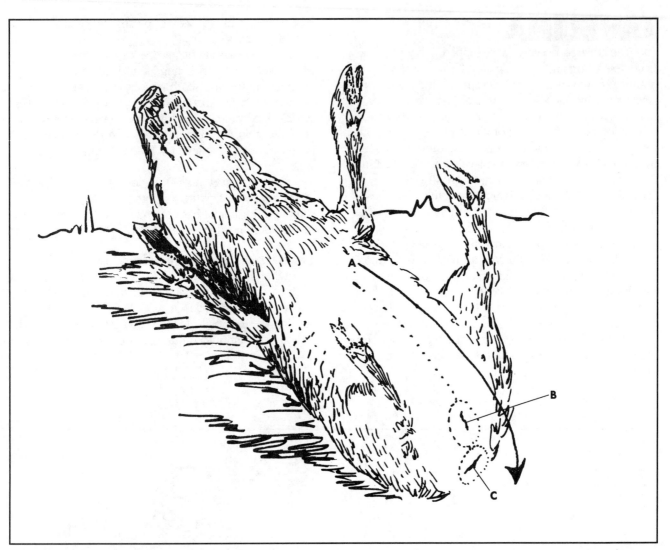

2-61. To dress out the javelina, begin cutting at point "A" and proceed to point "B". Cut around reproductive organs (circled area at "B") and also the vent (circled area at "C").

Field Dressing/javelina

Once a javelina has been killed, it should be dressed out immediately; otherwise, the high temperature of its native habitat will quickly spoil the meat. Because of its small size, the dressing out process takes less time than it does with a wild boar. It requires no bleeding, for example. I recommend that you field dress the javelina much as you would a mountain goat; that is, partially skin the cape area and save the white collar and head for a trophy mount. Before skinning, make sure you cut out the musk gland on the rump *(See Figure 2-60)*. This musk gland is a sac-like bursa located under the hide about seven inches above the

base of the tail. Its contents, should they not be removed, could spoil the taste of javelina meat. Use a separate knife for this operation, circling the area and cutting it away from the underlying muscle and fat. Should any of the whitish secretion touch your hands, wash and wipe them clean before proceeding.

The first steps in dressing out the javelina are shown in *Figure 2-61*. If you plan on saving the head for a trophy mount, start cutting at point A—about four to five inches behind the front legs—and continue on down to point B. Next, make a circle around the reproductive organs, but don't cut too deeply—you might rupture the bladder or intestines. Then, at point

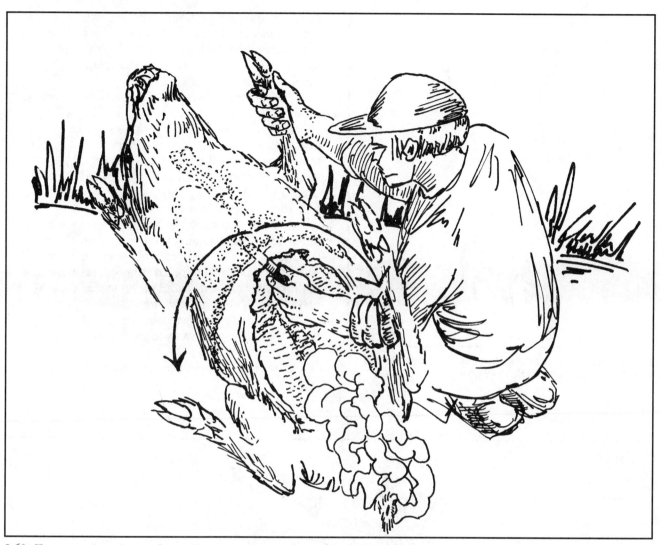

2-62. To remove intestines and reproductive organs, cut through pelvic bone and spread apart. Empty chest cavity and cut along the rib cage toward the throat area.

C, make a deep cut around the vent (anus) and pull the vent area out and away from the surface skin. Do the same with the reproductive organs. Now cut through the pelvic bone and spread it apart *(See Figure 2-62)*. Reach into the abdomen and carefully pull out the contents—including the intestines, bladder and reproductive organs—from between the rear legs.

The next step is to empty the chest cavity. Make a cut along the inner perimeter of the rib cage until you can separate the diaphragm muscle from the abdomen *(See Figure 2-62)*. Then reach up into the throat area, grasp the windpipe and esophagus and cut them out. As an alternative, you can peel back the hide and enter through the throat opening.

Pulling down and out on the trachea and esophagus will now help loosen and remove the heart and lungs; the stomach and liver, which are connected to the esophagus, should also come out at this time. Finally, cut the kidneys away from the back wall, discard them and wipe the cavity clean with dry cloths, cutting away any bad or shot meat.

Skinning/javelina

If skinned and preserved correctly, the hide of the javelina can yield a number of rewarding products, including gloves, jackets and purses. These items are

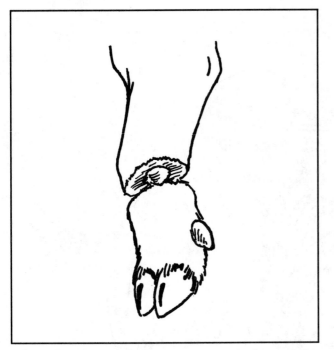

2-63. Before skinning the leg areas, remove the feet at each knee joint with a sharp knife or bone saw.

especially beautiful because of the fine, thin quality of javelina leather. The head of the animal is also very handsome when mounted for display. For these reasons, the hide of the head and lower body are skinned and used separately.

The skinning process itself involves the following steps:

1. If you have not already done so, make a cut that encircles the entire body, starting at a point four to five inches behind the front legs. Get a good grip on the flesh at that point and pull hard toward the tail, using a knife to separate those sections where flesh and hide stick to the carcass.

2. When you reach the rear legs, you must first remove the feet by cutting through the outer layers at the knee joints *(See Figure 2-63)*. Bend the joints back with your hand and cut or saw through the bone. It is not necessary to slit the sides of the legs as the skin will pull off as it is drawn back (step 1 above).

3. When the hide has been stripped from the body, it must be generously salted and rolled up for transport in a meat bag.

4. Now position yourself at the opposite end of

2-64. To skin the head section, pull the hide toward you. Make sure to retain whole ear (see above) by cutting cartilage away from skull.

the animal *(See Figure 2-60)* and begin skinning the head section. The front feet are, of course, removed in the same manner as the rear legs (see above). The hide is then pulled upward and toward you, much as you'd remove a shirt. When you've reached the ear, cut the inner cartilage structure of the ear away from the skull *(See Figure 2-64)*. The whole ear remains part of the hide. The soft bony material inside the ear can be removed simply by turning it inside out and cutting it away.

5. The eyelids, nostrils and lips are treated in the same manner as the ears. These structures are all attached to the skull by connective tissues which must be cut away so that they all remain part of the hide when peeled off. As you proceed, be sure to trim off the excess pieces of tissue still clinging to the hide. This will prevent spoilage and damage to the leather.

6. Salt the inner side of the head section as you did the lower portion of the body and roll it up as well.

Final butchering of the javelina can be done at camp or home, depending on the length of time that has elapsed since the kill. Directions for dividing the carcass into sections suitable for storage are found in the chapter on "Butchering and Preserving Game."

Cooking/javelina

Javelina Chops and Sauerkraut
(Serves 5 to 6)

10 to 12 javelina chops or	black pepper
3 pounds spareribs	1 quart sauerkraut
salt	5 to 6 medium potatoes

Brown meat in a Dutch oven on top of stove. Add salt and pepper to taste. Place sauerkraut over meat and cook in a slow oven (300–325° F.) for 1 hour. Remove from oven.

Peel potatoes and cut in half lengthwise, salting and peppering to taste, and place on top of sauerkraut. Cover and return to oven for an additional hour, or until meat and potatoes are tender. Serve with spiced apples.

Javelina Roast
(Serves 6)

1 3- to 4-pound javelina roast	2 cups beef broth
	seasoned salt
4 tablespoons shortening	black pepper, freshly
4 tablespoons lemon juice	ground
1 clove garlic, minced	

Gravy:
pan drippings
3 heaping tablespoons cornstarch
⅓ cup cold water

Dredge roast in flour. Melt shortening in Dutch oven and brown meat until crisp. Sprinkle top of roast with lemon juice and garlic. Salt and pepper to taste. Add beef broth and cover. Cook in slow oven (300–325° F.) for 2½ to 3 hours.

Remove roast from Dutch oven and prepare gravy. Bring drippings to a simmer on top of stove. While stirring constantly, add cornstarch, diluted in water, a little at a time until gravy thickens to desired consistency. Serve with glazed sweet potatoes or carrots.

Mountain lion

MOUNTAIN LION

The mountain lion (also commonly known as panther, puma or cougar) has probably had more stories written about it and told about it than any other hunted animal. It has been blamed for countless attacks it has taken no part in and has a reputation as an aggressor that is undeserved. I have seen ranchers band together and spread fear among small communities after only one cat appeared in their pastures. I've heard stories of how the mountain lion has attacked and hunted man—how it has jumped from ledges and knocked riders from their horses for the purpose of killing or mutilating them. In point of fact, mountain lions rarely attack humans and will go out of their way to avoid them. And I have yet to meet an individual who could claim that he has actually been assaulted by one.

Mountain lions will raid ranches and kill sheep and lambs in search of food. They also have been known to attack horses. However, if deer are available to them as prey, this is their preferred diet. When they do go on a killing spree destroying ranchers' herds, then preventive action must be and usually is taken.

The mountain lion's greatest enemy probably is man, and along with him his dog. In Colorado, prior to elimination of the $50 bounty paid to mountain lion hunters and the institution of the law allowing a hunter only one mountain lion per year, I knew professionals who trapped and/or shot and killed over 200 of these animals purely to collect the money. With new game laws in effect in such states as Washington, Oregon, Idaho, Arizona and New Mexico, the population of the mountain lion is being better controlled and secondarily is producing stronger strains of the species.

I have, in my time, freed several mountain lions. I have also experienced face-to-face encounters with them in attempts to capture them for transport to local zoos. In fact, one time Bill Reed, who was one of the country's experts in lion hunting, a few buddies and myself went out to the area south of Canyon City, Colorado, to capture one for a zoo. After several hard hours of riding in the rough terrain in what we call the "Purgatory" area, our dogs gave chase to a big cat, which we managed to tree. Bill handed me a two-foot stick and told me to go up the tree and try pushing the cat out. The dogs would then do their job of getting him stretched out once it hit the ground. The rest of the men had ropes to help.

I personally didn't favor the idea, but since I had been "elected," up the tree I went. I was sure that since the cat was more or less "cornered," he would attack me. To my surprise, it screamed at me as I got closer, and it struck out at the stick several times, but it did not try to attack. The stick by this time began to feel like a pencil in my quivering hand. But still the cat did not lunge out at me. Instead, it kept backing up on the limb, till it finally fell from the tree.

The dogs pulled at him and the ropes went around him. Then Bill put what I call a bit block into its mouth from behind and quickly tied it into place. The cat's legs were then tied and secured. Blankets were placed around it to keep it warm and a blindfold was put over its eyes, mainly to keep the animal from going into shock and to keep its body temperature at a normal reading. Unfortunately, in the short amount of time they are in captivity during transport, if the animals are not properly administered to, they will often become hypertensive and experience heart attacks, resulting in death. And, after all, the purpose of retaining them in zoos is not only to study them, but to extend their life spans and allow their magnificence to be appreciated by many.

Well, the cat was brought out alive and happily received by a zoo in Colorado. I might add, too, that unless you have a horse that is broken for this kind of transporting, don't try it.

Can you imagine your delight (or fright) on encountering in its own habitat this large member of the felid, or cat, family? It might stand 6½ feet in length, 2½ feet high at the shoulders, weigh about 175 pounds and wave a 3-foot-long tail. Its short-haired unspotted coat would vary from a russet color to gray, depending on the season. Its yellow eyes and muzzle would be marked with a darker coloration, while its lower flanks, stomach and the front of its mouth, including its whiskers, would be off-white.

The mountain lion is not an extremely fast runner. It can sustain great speed for only about 300 yards, at which time it tires and slows down considerably. This is one of the main reasons it stalks its prey and waits for the animal to come close before launching its attack. Relying heavily on its exceptional eyesight and hearing, the puma will ever so quietly sneak up on its prey and, with great agility and grace, pounce at the most unsuspecting moment. After the kill, the puma will eat its fill, then hide the remainder of the carcass, returning to feed at intervals when it is hungry, or until the meat has been consumed or begins to spoil.

The mountain lion has a characteristically shrill cry that can be heard from as far as a mile away. And like other felines, it yowls, growls, hisses—and even purrs when contented. Incidentally, while its sense of smell plays an important role in its life, it is not nearly so keen as that of members of the canine family.

Although it is not a migratory animal, the mountain lion may travel as far as 20 miles a day in search of food. Its entire range can span as much as 70 miles. The female, about two-thirds the size of the male, does not roam as wide a territory as the male, particularly when she is caring for her young in the den.

The mountain lion is a solitary animal by nature. Usually the only time you will see mountain lions together is when the female is accompanied by her young. These cats seem to enjoy no definite breeding season, although most of the young, it appears, are born in the spring. The males are polygamous and will breed with as many females as are available to them. They will even fight to the death over a female.

The meat of the mountain lion has been compared with veal or lamb. However, due to the fact that little fat is found on the animal, proper cooking would require mositure and additional fat. Most hunters usually prefer not to eat it at all, since they are interested primarily in the hide or a trophy mount. For this reason, I have not included instructions for butchering or any recipes for preparing the meat.

Hunting Tips/mountain lion

Because the mountain lion possesses such great agility and craftiness, it will jump wide crevices and ledges, climb any obstacle and generally choose the most treacherous course to avoid being caught. • Hunt with a professional guide, which most states that allow

2-65. To insure a realistic trophy with accurate dimensions, before you skin the mountain lion, photograph it from different angles and measure its length, shoulder height, head, neck and feet.

hunting of this kind require. The guide will provide dogs and mountain or trail horses that are basic hunting requisites. The dogs will pick up the scent and will eventually tree the cat or hole it up in a cave. The horses have the sure-footedness and temperament to climb narrow mountain paths without being spooked by jack rabbits or pieces of shiny paper which, with other animals, could lead to spills or eventual disaster. • You should be in excellent physical condition to withstand the chase over rugged terrain, oftentimes at altitudes of 4,000 feet or higher and to endure a long, bumpy ride on horseback. • Always be mindful of the feline's keen senses of sight and smell, its ability to burst with speed over short distances and its indomitable spirit of survival.

Field Dressing/mountain lion

Because you will be transporting only the hide back with you, the actual field dressing will take a very short time. You will not need to take any special precautions during the evisceration, but it should be done nonetheless, quickly and before you skin the animal.

Begin by placing your cat with its head in an uphill position if you are on a slope. If not, prop the head with rocks or whatever you can find.

1. With a sharp skinning knife, cut a good-sized circle around the genitals if it is male and completely remove the penis and scrotum. You need not be concerned with tying the bladder and rectum as you ordinarily would with other animals whose meat you might eat. If you have caught a female, cut a deep circle around the vagina and anus, which lie close together in between the back legs.

2. Make a long incision from the genitals, up the stomach to the middle of the chest or, if you prefer, start at the chest and cut downward to the circle. Keep the knife blade just under the layers of skin, using the "V" cutting technique discussed in *Figure 2-3*. Try not to puncture any of the inner organs—only because it makes it messier.

3. Turn the animal on its side and as swiftly as possible clean out the entrails, cutting them away, if necessary. (And don't hesitate to wear plastic skinning gloves that are designed to protect your hands during this procedure.)

Note in field dressing the mountain lion that, unlike other animals such as the deer, for example, whose pelvic and breastbones must be split separately in order to remove the innards (some of which you would also save, like the heart, liver, etc.), you can

eviscerate the mountain lion in virtually three simple steps.

4. The only thing remaining is to reach up into the throat as high as you can and cut out the trachea, esophagus and lungs.

5. Wipe out the cavity with clean dry cloths and try to soak up as much blood as possible to prevent it from soiling the hide you are now going to remove.

Skinning/mountain lion

A camera (a Polaroid will do) and a retractable tape measure, both of which are light and easy to carry, will be great assets to you before you embark on the skinning. To make the taxidermist's task easier, take photos of the animal from different angles before you skin it (perhaps, too, before you even gut it). Measure the cat from head to tail; its head, from the mouth to the back of the skull; its height at the shoulders; the width and circumference of its neck; and the size of its feet or pads *(See Figure 2-65)*. This way the taxidermist can work from actual measurements and do an accurate job of recapturing in a trophy what you have taken in the wilds.

You can skin the body of the cat on the ground while you are still in the field, but you will want to do the "fine" work of skinning the head and salting when you have more time—back at camp or at home. As you skin, be careful not to get blood on the hide, the cape in particular, as this will tend to ruin a good mount. On the underside of the animal, make deft cuts with a sharp knife through the hide only, along the broken lines shown in *Figure 2-66*. Starting in the middle of the body and working toward the limbs, pull back the hide with your hands and it should come off like a glove, since the animal is still warm. Leave the tail on and when you get to the feet, with your knife detach them from the legs at the lowest point possible, leaving the feet and surrounding hide intact. Don't bother to fuss at this point with any of the flesh left in the feet, you or your taxidermist will get to that later.

When you have skinned as far as the head area, stop. As you would do with other trophy mounts, at this point peel the hide back to expose the neck and sever the neck from the body at the highest vertebra on the spine. Once you've done this, you should have a hide—in one piece—with the feet, tail and head still attached. If you need to, drain the neck and pat it dry with towels. Roll the hide skin to skin with the fur side out and get back to camp quickly.

At camp or wherever, proceed first to skin the head, then salt the entire hide. Skinning the head is

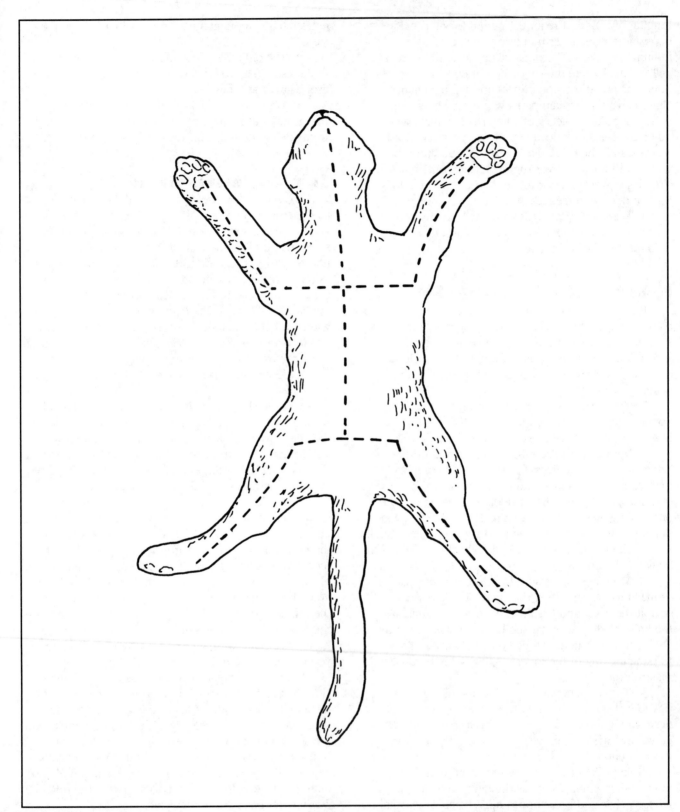

2-66. Following the broken lines above, make incisions through the hide on the underside of the animal to facilitate skinning and eventual mounting.

time consuming and tricky business, so be especially cautious with your knife around the ears, eyes, nose and lips.

Since the hide can sour quickly, depending on the temperature, scrape as much flesh from it as possible; you will have a much better hide if you do. Pay special attention to the area where the bullet entered and/or exited the animal.

Once you are satisfied that you have scraped off all the fleshy matter you can, begin to rub the salt into the skin. You will need about 15 pounds of fine table salt or ground rock salt—and several hours. Place a bunch of salt on the center of the hide and work it out toward the edges. When you are sure your skin is thoroughly salted, roll the skin hair side out. Both the hide and head should be wrapped, and transported to a cool place, keeping them away from heat and out of direct sunlight.

Alligator

ALLIGATOR

For those who seek the ultimate hunting adventure, catching 'gators offers more excitement than a sportsman could ever hope for. A full-grown adult alligator ranges in length from an average of 8 feet to a record-breaking 19 feet, and its weight varies from 100 to 300 pounds.

Looking like an overgrown lizard, the alligator derives its name from the Spanish word *el lagarta,* meaning "the lizard." Indeed, its broad, rounded snout and powerful tail are reminiscent of the formidable dinosaurs of prehistoric days. Its tail can knock a man senseless, and its huge, gaping jaws can crush its prey to death in one moment of violence. It feeds mostly on fish, turtles and small mammals, but large alligators have been known to attack and kill men, especially when threatened.

Why hunt alligator? For profit, to begin with. For centuries, pocketbooks, wallets, shoes, belts and other products made from alligator skins have stood the test of quality, durability and alluring good looks. And as a food source, the alligator offers much to the consumer. Its meat is tasty, and it contains more protein than beef or pork—including a bonus of extremely low fat content.

Prior to the 1960's, this carnivorous reptile of the *Crocodilian* family was freely harvested. Hunters pursued it along the river banks of the southeastern United States, from North Carolina through Florida and west along the Gulf States. But by the 1960's the alligator population had declined alarmingly, causing game departments to respond by placing bans on alligator skins and meat. Today, Louisiana is the only state that permits a limited harvest, made possible by the state's excellent management and preservation program.

Although the alligator is still a protected species in Florida, approximately 2,000 are harvested each year under the aegis of the Nuisance Alligator Program. Florida's Wildlife Research Laboratory, a division of the Game and Fresh Water Commission, has conducted extensive studies on the impact of a hunting season on Florida's alligator population. Experimental harvests were conducted recently in a controlled area of the state. Results of these test harvests are still being carefully evaluated. The National Alligator Association, based in Orlando, is also working hard to promote the controlled harvesting of alligators. Both groups seek a set of workable rules that will protect the species while at the same time allowing for its controlled harvest. Because these rules are expected to differ considerably

from those set up in Louisiana, you should check with each state's game department prior to attempting a 'gator hunt.

Hunting Tips/alligator

The Louisiana Department of Wildlife and Fish prohibits all nighttime hunting of alligators and the harvesting of any alligators under four feet in length. "Headlighting" and "gigging" are also illegal methods of taking an alligator in Louisiana. In headlighting, a light is projected at night over the swampy waters of an alligator's natural habitat. When struck by the light, the creature's eyes reflect an eerie red color, thus exposing its presence to the hunter. Gigging involves the use of a barbed and deadly harpoon attached to a rope.

Most of the alligators harvested legally in Louisiana are caught on a baited hook, which is suspended at varying heights above the surface of the water. A hook that is hung close to the water will attract the smaller alligators, whereas a hook suspended higher over the water's surface can be reached only by the larger specimens. Some hunters resort to "snagging," which involves the use of three hooks on one leader. These snag the alligator as it swims through the water. If the alligator is to be taken alive, the hunter will sometimes slip a noose around its neck and pull it to land.

The next priority is to wrap some tape or rope around the captured reptile's jaws. Once that has been accomplished, the legs and tail must be tied firmly to the body. This operation is much like hog-tying, and it is certainly just as hard to do! Once the alligator has been properly secured, it can be transported safely in the back of the truck or the trunk of a car.

If it is not necessary to take the alligator alive, a shot to its head will cause instant death. Another quick, humane method of killing an alligator is to thrust a sharp knife into its neck, just behind the bony plate of the skull. See *Figure 2-67* for location of this vulnerable area. A quick, accurate slice here will sever the cord of the central nervous system and bring about immediate, painless death. Any blood that has spilled onto the hide should be washed off at once; then the alligator should be turned over on its back and kept in a shady place for about one hour. After that, the alligator carcass can be bled, skinned, gutted and placed in a cooler at 45° F. (7° C.) or less. All this must take place within four hours of the kill to avoid spoilage and contamination.

Skinning/alligator

When cutting the hide for removal, start at the vulnerable area (letter "A" in *Figure 2-68*) and circle around each side of the neck to point "B" just below

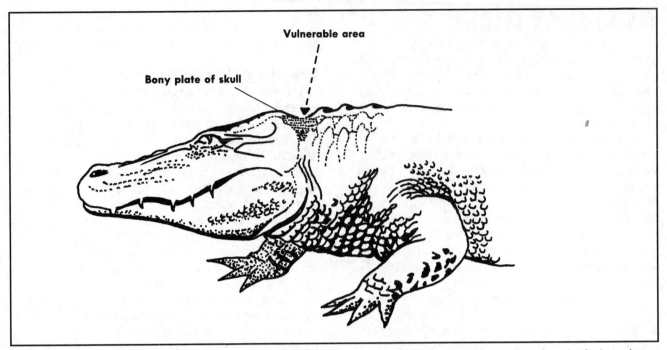

2-67. An alligator's most vulnerable point is located at the back of its neck, just behind its bony skull. A sharp knife thrust here will cause instant death.

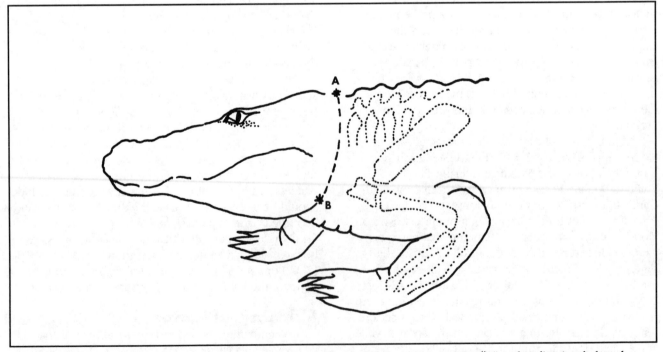

2-68. The first step in skinning an alligator is to make a cut around its neck, starting at point "A" and ending just below the lower jaw (point "B").

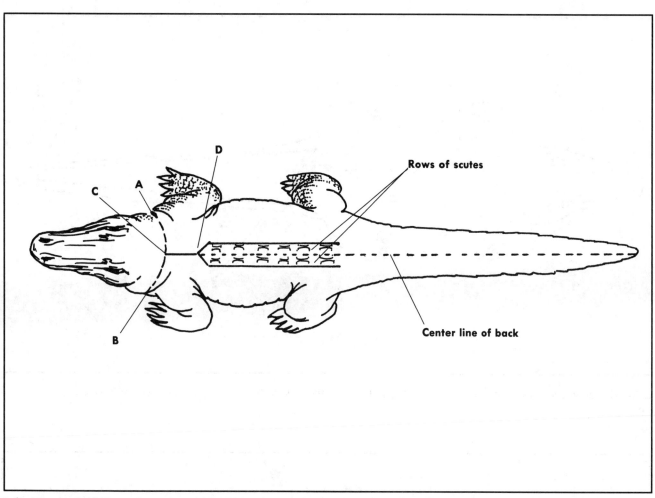

Rows of scutes

Center line of back

2-69. From point "C" cut down the middle of the neck to the base of the shoulder "D," make a small "Y" cut, and continue cutting along each side of the scutes to the tail section.

the lower jaw as shown. Do not completely encircle the neck.

Refer now to *Figure 2-69.* Cut from point "C" at the middle of the neck toward the tail, stopping just before the base of the shoulder (D); then make a "Y" cut as shown. Next, visualize a center line extending from "D" down the length of the back, shown here as a dotted line. Keeping one row of scutes (the spiny projectiles located along the back and tail) exposed on either side of the center line, extend the "Y" cut on both sides all the way down to the area just behind the rear legs.

The third step is to cut along both sides of the tail which are fairly round and smooth *(See Figure 2-70).* Begin cutting just below the top of the tail (E) and continue all the way down to the tip. Cut off the tip and discard it (F). Repeat this cut on the other side of the tail. The upper surfaces of the head, back and tail

are seldom used by tanners for any purpose and can be discarded along with the section containing the scutes.

Now make a "V" cut on the top of the alligator's head. The point of the "V" is at the tip of the snout. Extend the cutting lines as shown from the tip to the neck line at "C," just above the eye of the alligator.

Step four involves cutting around the wrist area of the rear legs *(See Figure 2-71,* point "G"). Grab each leg firmly and pull it forward, turning it in toward the body. This move unfolds the creases of the "arm pit" and exposes the back side of the legs. Now commence cutting at the heel of either foot (H). Continue up the back of the leg, cross over the back as shown and continue down the back line of the opposite leg. Both cuts should end at the heel of the foot.

In step five you'll cut the front legs in preparation for skinning *(See Figure 2-72).* First, cut completely around the feet at the junction of the wrist (I). Then

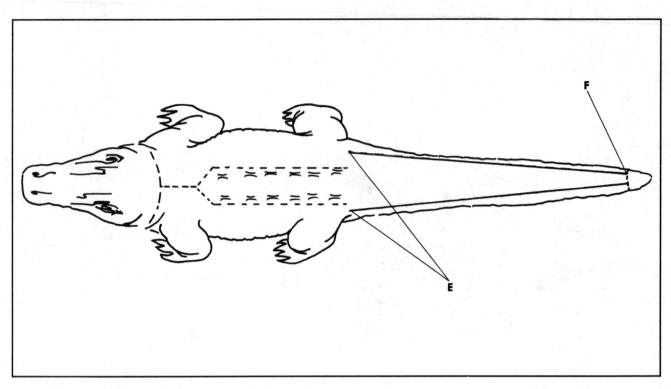

2-70. The tail is cut along both sides, beginning at points "E" all the way to the tip "F". The upper tail surfaces can be discarded.

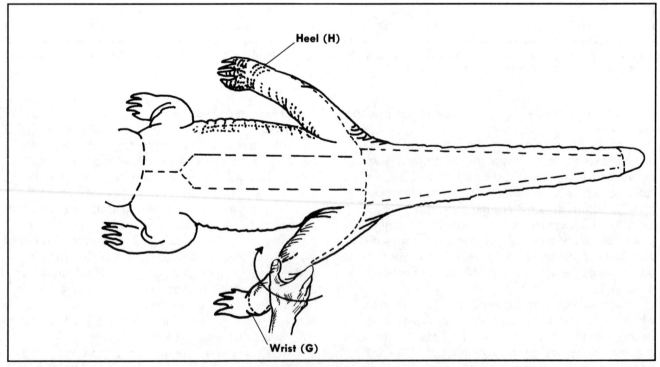

2-71. The rear legs are removed by first cutting around the wrist area "G." Then, after twisting the leg forward, cut a line all the way across the back of the legs to the opposite wrist, starting at one heel "H" and ending at the other.

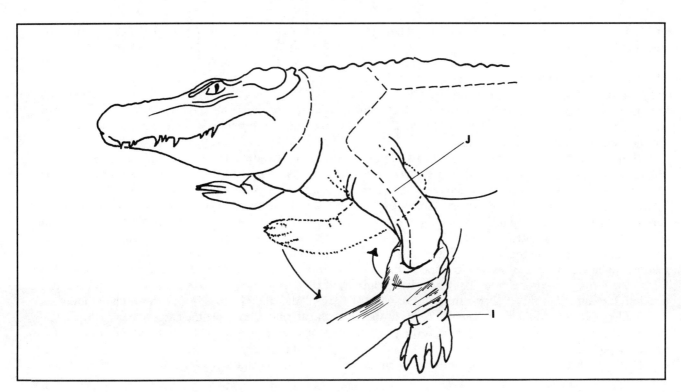

2-72. To skin the front legs, cut around feet at wrists "I," pull leg backward, and cut up front of leg along "J."

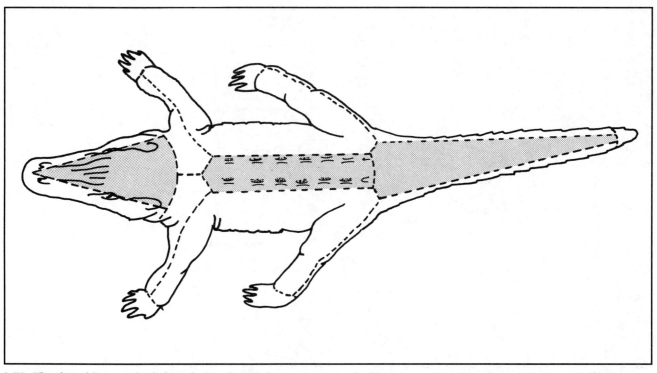

2-73. The dotted lines on both front legs indicate where cuts are made. Note they end at the same point where the "Y" cut ends. Shaded areas are those seldom used by tanners.

grab the front leg, pull it backward and cut up the middle of the leg (J).

Important: on the rear leg, a line is cut up the *back* of the leg; but on the front legs, the line extends along the *front* of the leg. Once each cut is completed, continue up and over the shoulder area to connect with the original "Y" cut on the back. Refer to *Figure 2-73* for the exact location of these cut lines.

In removing the hide, it may be easier to skin one side at a time. Start at the upper neck and shoulder area on either side, pulling and cutting when necessary *(See Figure 2-74).* This task can be made less difficult by repeated pulling on each leg to straighten the creases and folds *(See also Figures 2-71 and 2-72).*

Continue cutting on the rear legs in the same manner, pulling them out as needed to smooth the folds so that the skin can be more easily detached from the flesh beneath. *Figure 2-75* shows the alligator with its front leg and side skinned out. The rear leg is in the process of being skinned; as one hand graps the leg, the other pulls off the hide.

Next work on the tail, loosening the sides as far as possible without turning over the alligator *(See Figure 2-76).* Once one side has been completed, repeat each step on the other side. Then turn the alligator on its back.

Now, with the alligator on its back, cut through the area of the lower jaw *(See Figure 2-77),* following the line of the jaw bone. Refer back to the cutting line from "A" to "B" in *Figure 2-68.* The line you cut around the lower jaw will stop at point "B."

Start removing the skin of the lower jaw, being sure to remove the hide from the cheek and neck areas as well. Continue removing the skin from the bottom side until you reach the vent (anal) area. Encircle this area with your knife and carefully cut away the muscles holding the hide to the body. Once completed, the entire skin of the belly and underparts should pull off freely.

After the hide has been completely removed, gut the alligator and place the carcass in a cooler at a temperature of 45° F. (7° C.) or less. *Figure 2-78* shows how the alligator is gutted.

Start by cutting through the upper layer of flesh at

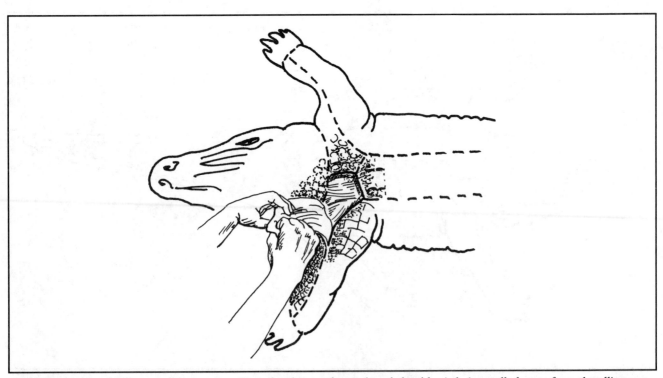

2-74. Remove the skin on one side at a time. Here the skin on the neck and shoulder is being pulled away from the alligator carcass.

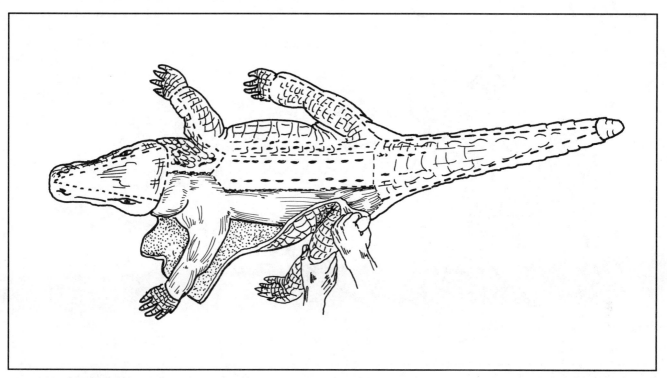

2-75. The skinning operation proceeds down the front leg and continues to the hind leg. Note that one hand holds the hind leg while the other pulls back skin.

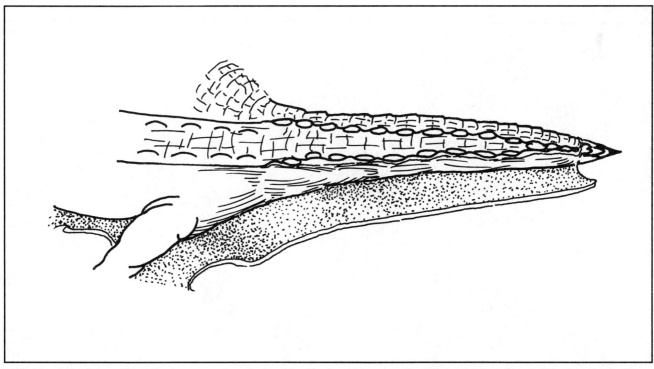

2-76. The skin of the tail section is removed as shown (the tip should be cut off earlier). The top skin of the tail is not used for tanning.

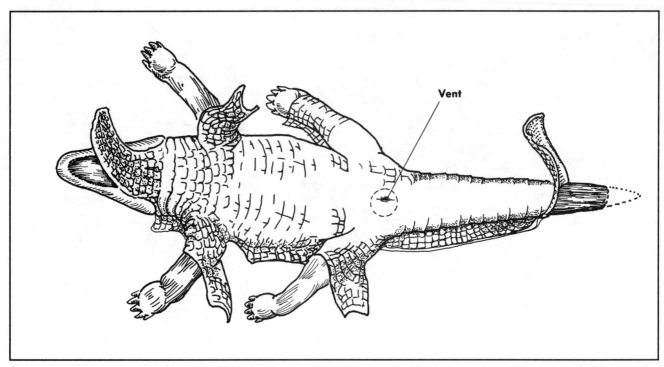

2-77. When removing the skin of the lower jaw, include the cheek and neck areas. Cut around anal area (vent) and remove bottom skin section.

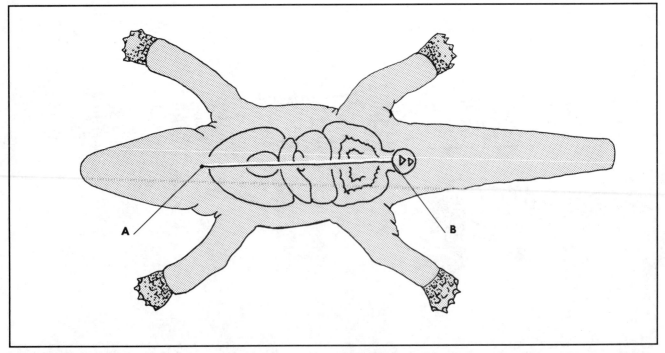

2-78. To gut an alligator, cut through upper layer of flesh from point "A" to point "B" and remove all organs. Clean cavity with cloth and store carcass in cool place prior to butchering.

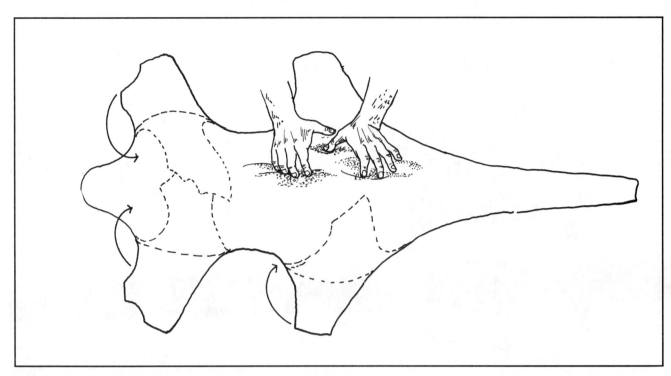

2-79. After rubbing the hide with salt and merpin, fold in all four legs as indicated.

point "A" and continue down to "B," which is the anal area. Cut around this vent and remove all internal organs and other material. Wipe the cavity clean with a cloth and store the skinned and gutted carcass at 45° F. (7° C.) or lower. Do not commence butchering until at least four hours have elapsed.

Curing the Hide

Curing the hide in preparation for the tanner involves first laying the hide out flat, fleshy side up, and carefully scraping away any remaining tissue or fat with a knife. Remove all foreign matter completely so the preservative will be able to do its job properly.

Once the inner side has been scraped clean, it must be treated chemically. With the hide spread out flat on a clean surface, rub in a thick layer of one part merpin to 20 parts salt. Merpin is added to the salt because it helps retard the growth of bacteria. Many different forms of bacteria will attack an improperly treated hide, the most prevalent and damaging being "red meat." Unless properly treated, this bacteria will turn the inside of the hide red and ultimately cause the outer layers of skin to slip off.

After every part of fleshy surface has been rubbed

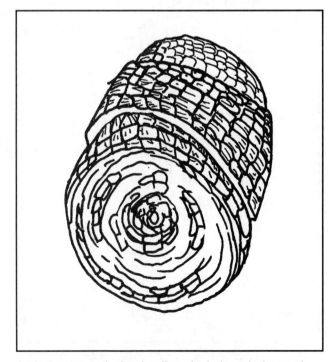

2-80. Starting at the head, roll up the hide with the tough leathery side out.

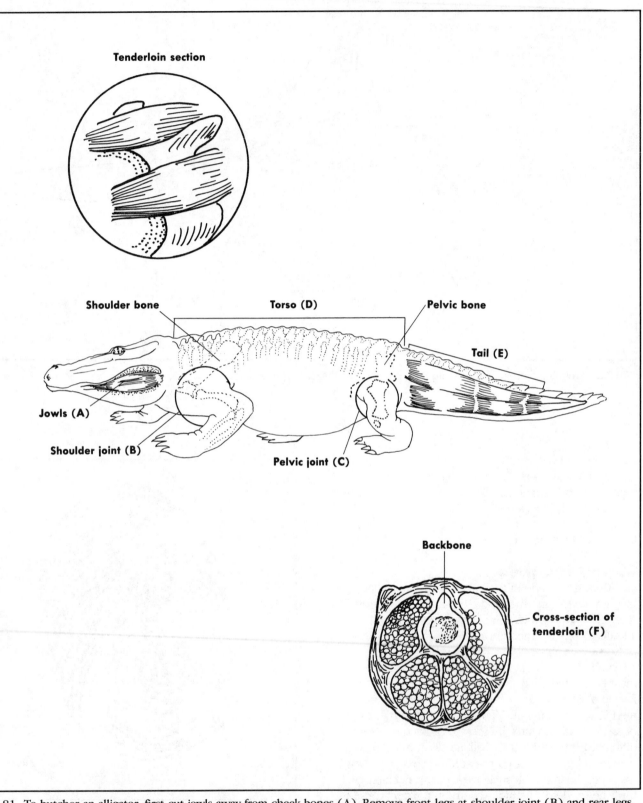

Tenderloin section

Shoulder bone

Torso (D)

Pelvic bone

Tail (E)

Jowls (A)

Shoulder joint (B)

Pelvic joint (C)

Backbone

Cross-section of tenderloin (F)

2-81. To butcher an alligator, first cut jowls away from cheek bones (A). Remove front legs at shoulder joint (B) and rear legs at pelvic joint (C). Remove tenderloin strip from backbone (D and E). Tail contains meat (see cross-section F) from which delicious scallops are made.

thoroughly with the merpin and salt mixture, fold in the legs (as shown in *Figure 2-79*) and roll up the hide, fleshy side in (*See Figure 2-80*). Allow the hide to set for one to three days in a cool, shady place. At the end of this period, unroll the hide, shake out the chemicals, and repeat the rubbing process with a fresh mixture of salt and merpin. More than 100 pounds of salt may be required to do a complete job on one hide, so don't stint.

After a thorough rubbing, fold in the legs as before and roll up the hide, starting with the head. The tough leathery side should be on the *outside* of the finished roll. The rolled hide can be stored in a cool, dry place for as long as six months. Most hides are sold "as is" to a tannery, which will then crust tan and finish the hide into leather. The highest quality hides average six feet in length and can sell for as much as $20 per foot.

Butchering/alligator

Alligator meat is easier to butcher after it has been chilled for about 12 hours at a temperature of 45° F. (7° C.) or lower. Four main cuts of meat are available: jowls, legs, torso and tail. Starting with the *jowls,* locate the bone of the lower jaw and carve the jowls away from the cheek bones (*See Figure 2-81*). Using a sharp, slender knife, carve the jowl muscle from the bony housing by scraping close to the bone so that none of the meat is wasted. Jowl meat contains more protein than any other cut of the alligator. The quality of texture varies with the size of the specimen—on a smaller alligator this muscle is more tender than that of a larger one. Marinade can always be used to tenderize a tough cut of meat.

Next come the *legs.* Remove each one by slicing through the joints where they are attached to the body ("B" and "C"). The front legs are removed at the shoulder joint; the back legs are severed at the pelvic joint. Then separate the bundles of muscles that are attached to the leg bones. Sometimes this meat will pull away easily; if not, use a long, sharp boning knife. Hold the blade parallel to the bone and cut around the circumference of the bone. Leg meat is usually darker and stringier than the rest; it is very tasty, however, when boned, chopped or diced for stews, chowder and soup.

The meat of the *torso* extends from the lower neck to the end of the rib cage, where the pelvic bone lies. One of the delicacies of this area is the tenderloin cut— a section of muscle extending from neck to tail—which fits into a groove along each side of the backbone ("D" and "E"). Tenderloin is removed in one long strip, which can be sliced into individual cutlets for broiling

or frying. Prior to cooking, the outer white sheath of fat and gristle must be stripped away, or else they will impart a sour, rancid taste to the meat. The remaining meat in the torso section can be carved away from the skeletal structure and used in a variety of ways. For example, rib meat is ideal for recipes calling for diced or ground alligator meat (see also recipes at end of this chapter).

The last meat-rendering section of the alligator is the *tail.* It's composed of four long bundles of muscle, surrounded and held together by sheaths of tough, white connective tissue resembling fat or gristle. These are actually ligamental bands that must be stripped away prior to cooking. To obtain the meat of the tail section, cut across the base of the tail, just behind the rear legs (See "C" in *Figure 2-81*). This will separate the tail from the body. To make alligator steaks, simply slice the tail into one- or two-inch slices, making sure to remove the bone from the center (See "F" a cross-section of an alligator's tail). Delicious scallops can be made from this section by pounding out a slice of tail and cutting out round pieces with a cookie cutter. These scallops are ideal for fondue, deep frying or sautéing.

Cooking/alligator

Overall, the meat of the alligator contains more protein than beef or pork and is extremely low in fat content. In fact, alligator meat has become quite a gourmet treat at many fine restaurants around the country. It is versatile and can be served in a variety of ways as you would red meats and fish; try it as a delightful substitute for the red meat in any of your favorite dishes. Several excellent recipes using alligator meat are included below, compliments of Jean H. Picou and Windell A. Curole.

Microwave Alligator
(Serves 2)

2 alligator tail chops, ½-inch thick	1 medium onion, sliced
1 teaspoon Season-All® or lemon pepper	

Season alligator chops with Season-All® or lemon pepper and place in an uncovered 1½ quart glass or ceramic dish. Cook in microwave on high for 5 minutes. Arrange onion slices over chops, cover with Saran Wrap™ and microwave on low for 20 minutes. Allow to stand 5 minutes before serving.

Alligator Balls
(Serves 4 to 6)

1 pound alligator meat, ground
1 egg, slightly beaten
1 tablespoon onion, finely chopped
2 tablespoons celery, finely chopped
1 tablespoon parsley, finely chopped
2 tablespoons shallots, chopped
2 teaspoons lemon pepper
½ teaspoon salt
¼ cup bread crumbs
flour
1 cup vegetable or peanut oil

Combine first 9 ingredients and form into 1-inch balls. Refrigerate for 1 hour. Dredge with flour and fry in batches in oil until brown. Serve immediately with hot buttered noodles or boiled white rice.

Fried Alligator I
(Serves 2 to 3)

1 pound alligator meat, thinly sliced
1 cup vegetable or peanut oil
white cornmeal

Batter:
1 12-ounce can beer
½ cup flour
1 teaspoon Season-All®
1 teaspoon black pepper

Add 4 batter ingredients to a blender and blend well. Coat alligator meat with batter and dredge in cornmeal. Fry in batches in hot oil about 15 minutes, turning often until golden brown.

Fried Alligator II
(Serves 2 to 3)

1 pound alligator meat, cut into bite-size pieces
1 cup sherry
1 tablespoon lemon pepper
1 teaspoon Season-All®
¼ cup lemon juice
½ cup Italian salad dressing
flour
¼ cup vegetable or peanut oil

Marinate alligator meat in sherry, lemon pepper, Season-All®, lemon juice and salad dressing for 2 hours. Drain and dredge with flour. Fry meat in hot oil for about 15 minutes turning often until brown. Drain and serve immediately.

Smothered Alligator
(Serves 4 to 6)

2 onions, finely chopped
¼ cup vegetable or peanut oil
1 green bell pepper, finely chopped
½ cup celery, finely chopped
2 pounds alligator, cubed
1 bay leaf
¼ teaspoon dried basil
salt and black pepper to taste
¼ cup parsley, finely chopped
¼ cup shallots, finely chopped

Sauté onions in oil until golden brown. Add green pepper and celery and sauté until tender. Add meat, bay leaf, basil, salt and pepper, and simmer, covered, for 40 minutes. Add parsley and shallots last 5 minutes of cooking time.

Fried Alligator Italian Style
(Serves 3 to 4)

1 pound alligator meat
½ cup Parmesan cheese
½ cup Italian bread crumbs
¼ to ½ cup vegetable or peanut oil

Cut alligator meat into thin finger strips. Thoroughly mix cheese and bread crumbs in a paper bag. Add meat in batches and shake until well coated. Fry in hot oil for 2 minutes.

Alligator Dip

½ pound alligator meat, diced
½ teaspoon liquid crab boil
1 teaspoon salt
½ lemon
1 tablespoon teriyaki sauce or soy sauce
2 tablespoons shallots
2 tablespoons celery
2 tablespoons green pepper
2 tablespoons onion
2 tablespoons parsley

In a mixing bowl combine first five ingredients. Finely chop shallots, celery, green pepper, onion and parsley and add to mixture. Blend well. Chill and serve with your favorite crackers.

'Gator Sauce Piquant
(Serves 4 to 6)

2 cups onion, chopped
⅓ cup vegetable or peanut oil
1 green bell pepper, chopped
½ cup celery, chopped
1 16-ounce can peeled tomatoes
2 8-ounce cans tomato sauce
2 tablespoons Worcestershire sauce
¼ teaspoon dried basil
1 bay leaf
¼ teaspoon oregano
salt and black pepper to taste
1 6-ounce can sliced mushrooms
2 pounds alligator meat, cubed
¼ cup shallots, chopped
¼ cup parsley, chopped

Sauté onions in oil until dark golden brown, stirring often. Add green pepper and celery, and sauté until tender. Add peeled tomatoes, tomato sauce, Worcestershire sauce, basil, bay leaf, oregano, salt and pepper, and simmer for 10 minutes. Add mushrooms and alligator. (If meat was marinated in wine, drain before adding.) Cover and cook for 40 minutes, add shallots and parsley and cook uncovered for 10 minutes more. Serve with boiled white rice.
(Note: Alligator may be marinated in red wine 1 hour before cooking.)

BUTCHERING AND PRESERVING GAME

There's a great amount of satisfaction to be gained in doing your own butchering. In the first place, you'll learn in a hurry that it's not as difficult as it may seem; and second, you'll be sure of getting the same animal you shot—not someone else's as so often happens at a processing plant or even your local butcher's. *Figure 2-82* shows the inner skeletal structure for each cut of meat, as represented by the pronghorn (antelope). Knowing the location of an animal's bones can make the butchering job much easier. Besides, do-it-yourself butchering affords a good education about where the various cuts of meat originate. To do all this properly, though, you'll need a meat cleaver, a long sharp knife, a short knife and a good bone saw. All set?

Start butchering your smaller-size big game animal by cutting it in half as it hangs *(See Figure 2-83)*. Do not cut the vertebrae in half; instead, choose one side of the backbone and saw flush up against the attachment of ribs to vertebrae all the way down the back. That way, you can get chops from at least one side of the carcass (the one that includes the complete backbone column). For big game, cut the vertebrae down the center.

Once the carcass has been sawed through completely, take one side down and, using strips of packing tape, outline the areas of meat you intend to cut. Use *Figure 2-82* as a guide. Have available some good freezer wrap, some self-adhesive tags and a marking pen. You'll need to mark each section as it's wrapped for identification, weight and date (See "Preserving Game" later on in this chapter).

In the following pages, you will find detailed drawings and instructions for butchering bear, deer and pig. Since these are representative of most big game, this information will enable you to cut up and package the choice cuts from any large animal you are likely to bring down.

Butchering/bear

To prepare for butchering a bear, you must first hoist the carcass up to a level that is comfortable to work with. A very strong tree limb or wooden rafter should support a hanging bear.

The butchering process begins by removing the

neck. Cut through the spine at a point immediately in front of the shoulder *(See Figure 2-84)*. The meat and bone of the neck, together with the lower sections of the front and hind legs, can be used later in several ways. Now remove one half of the carcass and place it on a table for quartering into fore, middle and hind sections.

The forequarter is composed of the shoulder, brisket, limbs and perhaps one or two ribs. Begin your cut just behind the front leg and continue on up until you have severed the spine about three inches behind the shoulder *(See Figure 2-84B)*. Next remove the leg by cutting through the joint at which it attaches to the shoulder bone *(See Figure 2-84C)*. The remaining shoulder section can be sliced into two or more sections by cutting in the same direction in which you severed the neck from the body. These will become the blade pot roasts.

The middle section, which begins just in front of the hind leg and terminates in front of the pelvic (or hip) bone, contains most of the ribs *(See Figure 2-84E)*. This middle section may be further divided into rib roasts, chops or ribs only. To do this, chop the ribs in half by cutting at right angles to the direction in which the ribs run. In other words, cut horizontally across the length of the carcass. The underside of this section produces short ribs and flank, while the top section takes the form of a rib roast. This can be converted into chops by slicing between each vertebra at right angles to the direction of the spinal column.

To obtain the hindquarter, remove the hind legs by cutting through the joint attachments at the pelvic bone *(See Figure 2-84F)*. The meat surrounding this last section of the vertebral column and pelvic bone is called the rump *(See Figure 2-84G)*. Depending upon the size of the bear, you might obtain two separate rump roasts from this area by slicing it in half. Again, cut through the spinal column at right angles.

When separating the hind legs, the top portions will be considerably wider and meatier than the lower parts (toward the shank). On a small bear, you can use this whole top section as a roast without any further butchering—save that of optional boning, as illustrated in *Figure 2-85*. Should you desire some additional cuts from this section, simply slice it as many times as size allows and in the thickness you desire *(See Figure 2-84H)*. Again, these cuts are made at right angles to the bone which runs the length of the thigh.

One other possibility for the midsection is to remove the strip of meat which runs along the length of the backbone, inside the rib cage *(See Figure 2-86)*. In an average bear, it measures about four inches wide

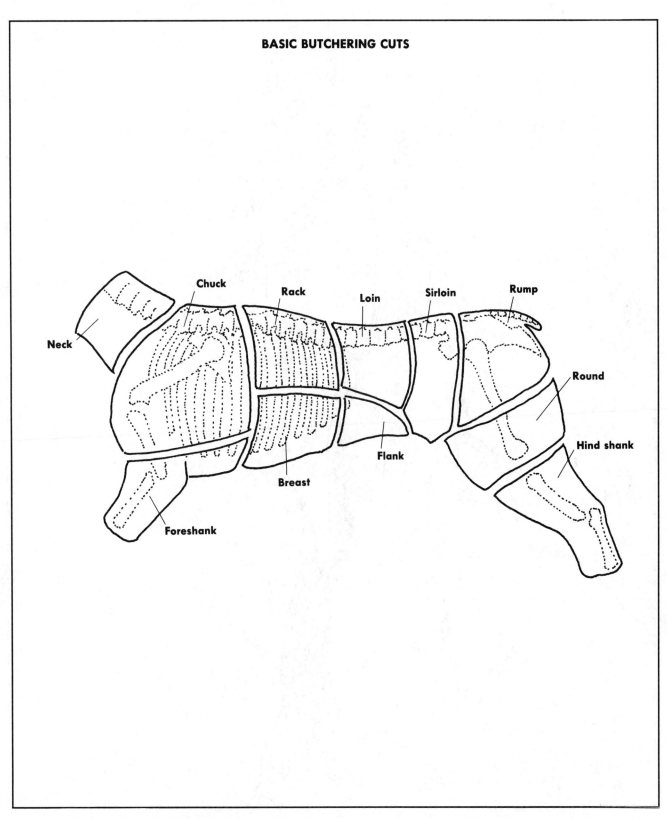

BASIC BUTCHERING CUTS

Neck

Chuck

Rack

Loin

Sirloin

Rump

Round

Hind shank

Flank

Breast

Foreshank

2-82. This butchering chart for the pronghorn indicates where each basic cut of meat can be found in most big game animals. Study it carefully before starting the butchering process for any of them.

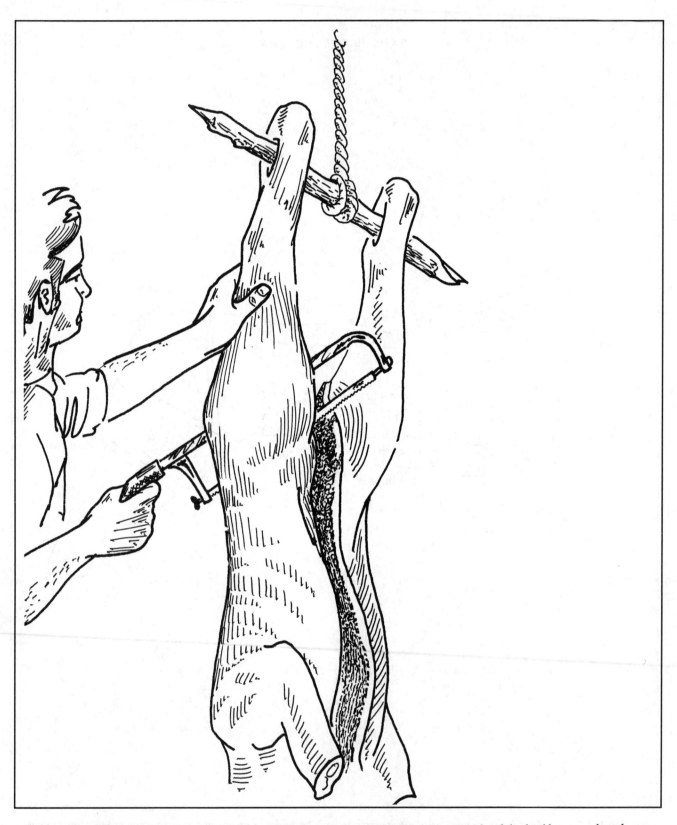

2-83. Hang big game upside down as shown above. Saw the carcass lengthwise along one side of the backbone so that chops can be cut off easily.

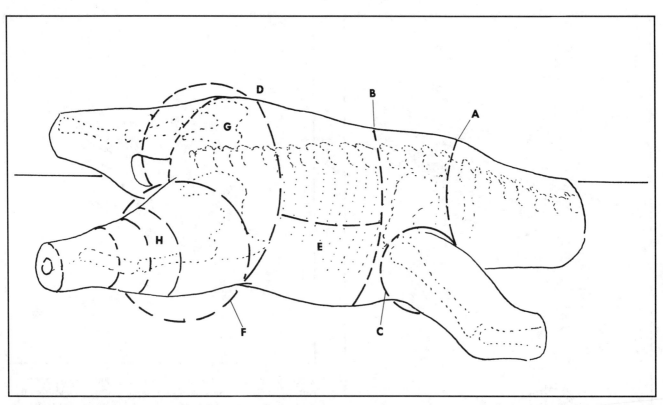

2-84. When butchering a bear, first remove the neck by slicing through spine along line marked "A". Cut fore section along line "B", severing spine about 3 inches behind shoulder. Remove forelegs at shoulder joint (line "C"). Ribs are carved from middle section extending between lines "B" and "D". Remove hind legs by cutting along line "F" at the pelvic bone. The rump (marked "G." above) yields excellent roasts.

and two feet long. This tenderloin section tastes great when rolled, tied and roasted. It also makes a delicious rib eye roast.

Other edible parts of the bear include the heart, liver and paws. In cooking bear meat, remember that, like pork, it may contain the trichinosis larvae. This can be killed by cooking at temperatures of 137° F. (58° C.) or higher for two hours, or by freezing at 5° F. (−15° C.) or lower. Bear meat, which is dark in color, can be marinated or parboiled to remove the gamy taste and improve its tough texture.

Butchering/deer

For quartering a deer, follow the same general instructions provided in the bear section. See also *Figures 2-87 and 2-88* for the inner skeletal structure and butchering sections of the deer. The small drawings in *Figure 2-89* offer suggestions on what meat can be obtained from each of the five main cuts of the hind-quarter. *Figure 2-90* shows the divisions of the fore-quarter with accompanying drawings suggesting possible uses for each of the six main portions of the forequarter.

One excellent way to butcher deer meat is to create what we call "butterfly chops." Let's say you've killed a white-tail deer. Cut about four to six inches, depending on the size of the animal, lengthwise in the same direction as the backbone and through the rib cage on each side of the backbone. Then cut across the backbone to make your double butterfly chops. In most cases, you cut down the center of the backbone and remove the tenderloin strip beneath the backbone; but with a small deer, you can saw a few inches away from the backbone and through the small ribs on each side of the backbone, then cut across in different thicknesses to create these beautiful butterfly chops.

Butchering/wild boar

Compared to butchering deer, bear, moose, or other big game, a wild pig, boar, or javelina presents some important and obvious differences. For example, its head can be used for making head cheese (as

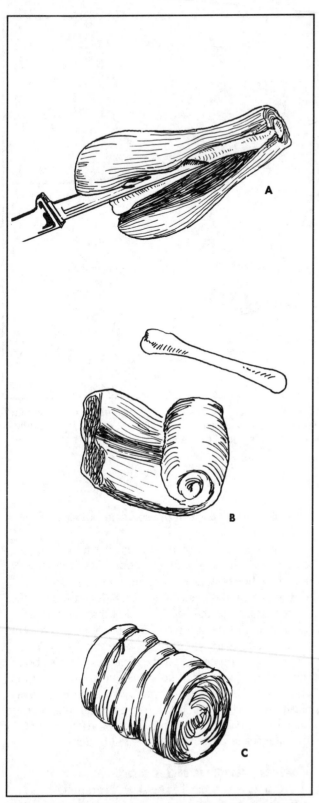

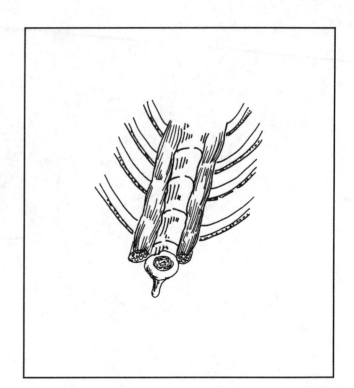

2-86. To make delicious tenderloin cuts and roasts, bone out the strip that runs along the length of the backbone. In most bears, it measures about 4 inches wide and 2 feet long.

described on page 112. Other differences can be observed in the Wild Boar chapter. Note that in addition to the five basic sections, a pig's forelegs are cut into three pieces, one being the foot, which is pickled and consumed by many food fanciers. Ham hocks come from the middle section of the front leg, and the well-known "picnic shoulder" is obtained from the top section. All these cuts are shown in the detailed drawing (*See Figure 2-91*). The front section of the wild pig also yields the shoulder butt (upper back).

The midsection can be cut into pork loin, spareribs and bacon (except the javelina, which has very little body fat, hence no bacon). The pork loin is derived by cutting through the ribs at right angles. This section can be sliced down between the ribs to produce pork chops, or it can be rolled and tied for use as a roast. Bacon from this section is cut into strips running in the same direction as the ribs. You can also leave the lower section of ribs in one piece for barbecuing or broiling.

The hindquarter contains the ham and the hind foot. The ham section is obtained by cutting through the joint of the upper thigh and pelvic bone.

2-85. To make a succulent roast from the bear's hind leg, split lower portion as shown (A). Then roll flattened meat into a roast (B) and tie with string for roasting (C).

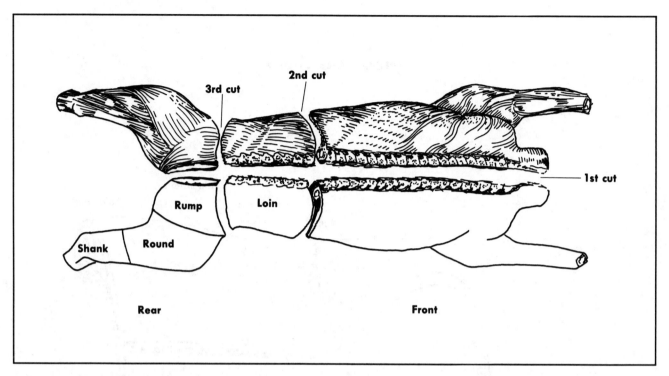

2-87. A deer carcass must first be cut up into fore-, middle and hindquarters. This diagram indicates each major section as it looks after the initial butchering stage.

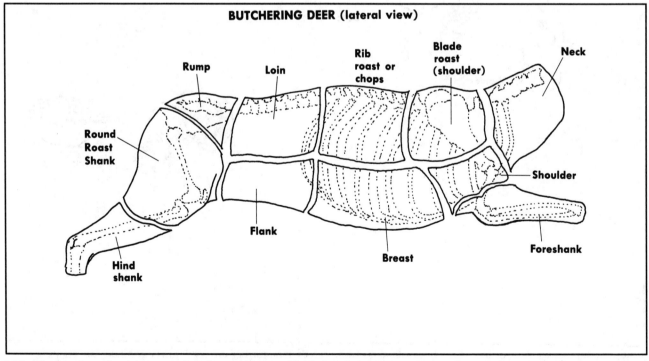

2-88. The location of various cuts taken from a deer are detailed in this diagram. Almost all parts of the deer are usable.

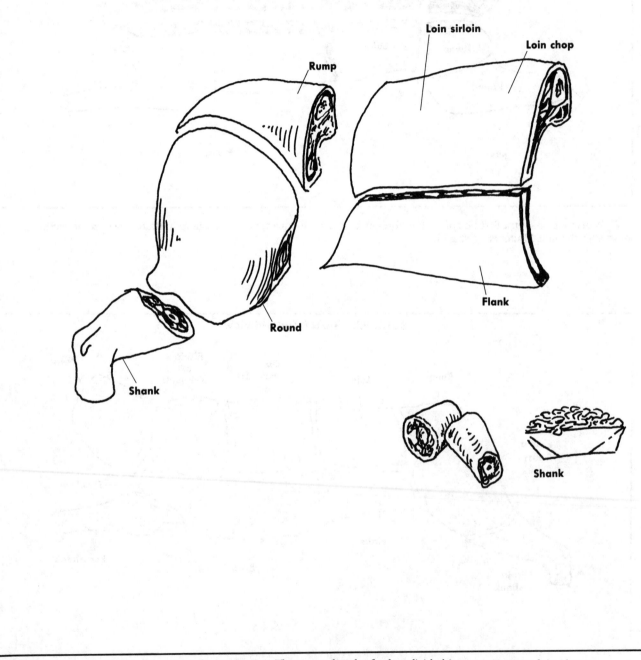

HINDQUARTER OF DEER

Loin sirloin

Loin chop

Rump

Round

Shank

Flank

Shank

2–89. The hindquarter of the deer yields five main cuts. These can then be further divided into rump roasts, loin chops, steaks, etc.

CUTS OBTAINED FROM HINDQUARTER

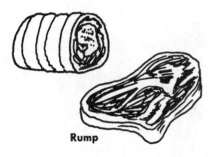

Rump

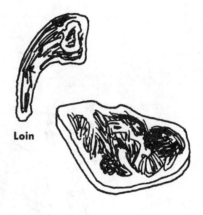

Loin

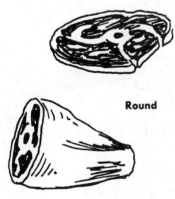

Round

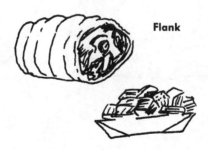

Flank

BUTCHERING DEER (forequarter)

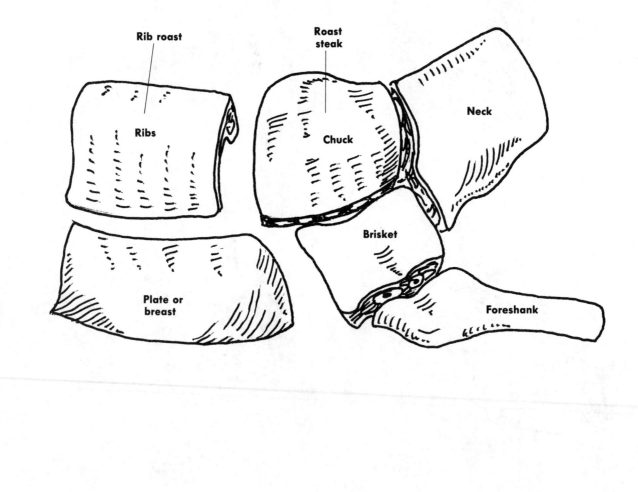

Rib roast

Roast steak

Neck

Ribs

Chuck

Brisket

Plate or breast

Foreshank

2–90. The forequarter of the deer is divided into six major portions as indicated above. The various cuts and dishes derived from these areas are depicted within the drawings at right.

CUTS OBTAINED FROM FOREQUARTER

Chuck

Steak

Roast

Neck and shoulder

English cut

Rolled roast

Ground meat

Foreshank

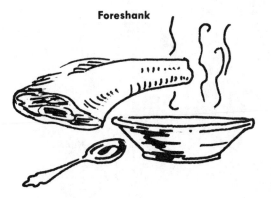

Brisket

roast

Arm chops

Ground meat

Ribs

Ribs

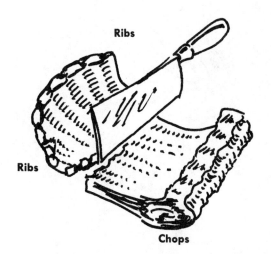

Chops

Plate

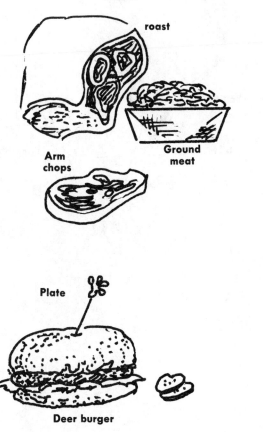

Deer burger

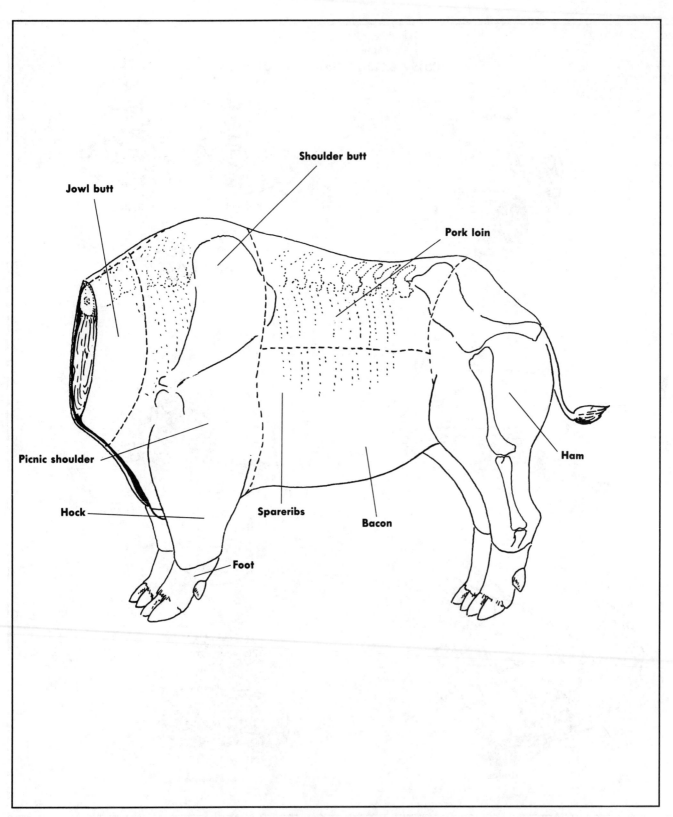

Jowl butt

Shoulder butt

Pork loin

Picnic shoulder

Hock

Spareribs

Bacon

Ham

Foot

2-91. A wild boar or pig presents different butchering needs from those of the deer or bear. For example, bacon is derived from the lower middle section; and even the head is utilized for making head cheese.

SOME COMMON NAMES OF CUTS FROM BIG GAME

Chuck Steak: located adjacent to the neck.

Cube Steak: any thin steak which must be tenderized with a block hammer or ground up.

Stripped Tenderloin: represented by the small center cuts from the shoulder roast, sometimes referred to as the eye of the roast.

Rib Steak: located on the rib section next to the short loin.

Delmonaco Steak: comes from the rib and is actually the eye portion of the rib steak.

Club Steak: located at the end of the short loin next to the ribs; it is the least desirable of the T-bone steaks.

Porterhouse Steak: that portion next to the top of the loin, or the first portion of the short loin. It contains the largest portion of the delicious tenderloin that runs along the backbone.

New York Cut Steak (or Kansas City Steak): this cut represents the tenderloin portion of a T-bone steak, found in the short loin.

T-Bone Steak: the bone is left in and not removed as with the New York or Kansas City steak. It is also found in the short loin.

Tenderloin Steak: a portion of a T-bone steak located at the top part of the rib cage, next to the short loin. It is found in the loin, sometimes called top of the loin, or loin end.

Filet Mignon: choice first steak derived from the tenderloin section along the backbone.

Chateaubriand Steak: the center and choicest steak derived from the thickest part of the tenderloin.

Tournedos: from the narrowest part of the tenderloin strip.

Sirloin Steak: found on the loin end next to where the rump begins. It is known as the loin or top of the loin.

Rump Steak: cut from the rump, next to the loin and in front of the round.

Round Steak: comes from the widest part of the hind leg, called the round (next to the rump on the top side).

London Broil: the most tender steak from the round. The top round comes from the inside of the back leg; because the muscles in this area are used less, they become more tender and therefore tastier.

Teriyaki Steak: located about halfway through the top round, where the muscles become a little tougher. Steaks from this section must be sliced very thin.

Swiss Steak: least desirable of the round steaks. It must be pounded and cooked slowly before it will become tender.

Preserving Game

By far the easiest and most practical method of preserving game for eating at a later date is by freezing. But several other equally good, time-tested ways should be mentioned, including smoking, curing, pickling, and the use of a brine solution. These all take much more time in preparation than freezing, though, and for that reason most busy hunters choose to freeze their kills.

Before wrapping and freezing any meat, however, it is strongly recommended that all fat and tallow be cut off from your game. These ingredients attract bacteria quickly and do not last as long as the meat itself even after it is frozen.

Freezing means simply placing your cuts of meat in an environment where the temperature is low enough to preserve the meat and halt the breakdown of tissue caused by bacteria or other microorganisms commonly found in fresh meat. Bacteria are *not* killed by freezing, but they are slowed down to a minimum. This obviously enables the hunter to keep his meat much longer than if it were not frozen. Since water is contained in the juices of all meat, it will freeze also and form ice crystals within the meat. The faster the meat freezes, the better chance there is of retaining its color and flavor; moreover, the texture of the meat will remain the same as it was when freshly killed, whether it be several weeks or even months later. A good point to keep in mind is that you should not put any more meat into the freezer than can be frozen in 24 hours or less. Most freezer instructions will explain how much food can be safely frozen at one time.

The more time it takes to freeze the meat, the more time the bacteria or enzymes have to begin breaking down the meat tissues. Enzyme action starts to work on the outside of the meat first, causing what is known as *oxidation of the fat.* Gases that are present within the freezer itself combine with the air in the freezer to destroy the outside layer of meat. "Freezer burn" occurs when the ice in the freezer turns into a gaseous state without ever becoming liquid. This gas is then attracted to the meat, accelerating the breakdown of its tissues and adversely affecting its color, texture

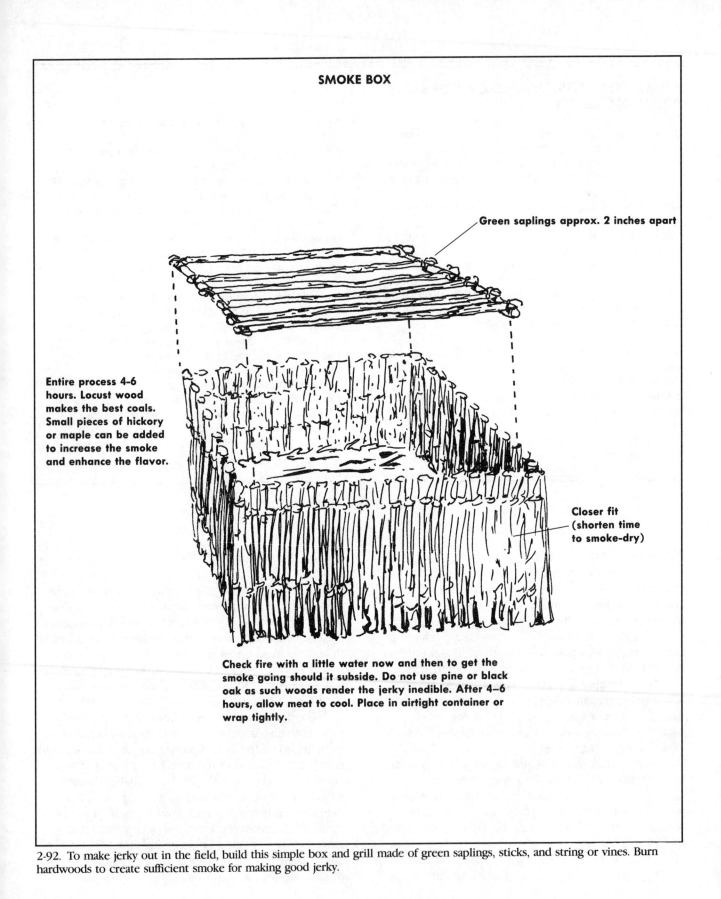

SMOKE BOX

Green saplings approx. 2 inches apart

Entire process 4-6 hours. Locust wood makes the best coals. Small pieces of hickory or maple can be added to increase the smoke and enhance the flavor.

Closer fit (shorten time to smoke-dry)

Check fire with a little water now and then to get the smoke going should it subside. Do not use pine or black oak as such woods render the jerky inedible. After 4–6 hours, allow meat to cool. Place in airtight container or wrap tightly.

2-92. To make jerky out in the field, build this simple box and grill made of green saplings, sticks, and string or vines. Burn hardwoods to create sufficient smoke for making good jerky.

and flavor. Freezer burn can cause a fine piece of meat to become hard and dry, unappetizing and unfit for consumption. This should be kept in mind, therefore, when packaging meat and even in moving packages from place to place or from shelf to shelf in the freezer.

It is also very important that game meat be chilled prior to freezing. If your kill is a large deer, for example, and the outside temperature is around 34° F. (1° C.), you can safely chill the meat in the field. Many sportsmen like to age their deer by hanging them up for several days, but this can work only if the temperature is low enough. In warmer weather, bacteria can quickly ruin the meat from a hard-earned kill. When meat is frozen slowly, the action of the water and the juices within grow in size, resulting in much larger ice crystals and increasing the breakdown of cells. Meat that is quick-frozen eliminates this cellular damage and helps preserve the flavor and texture. So, when weather conditions prove improper for hanging a big game animal for several days, it would be wise to quick-freeze your kill at a local freezer locker.

Assuming that you have the facilities to chill, package and quick-freeze your own meat, these basic rules should be followed.

Basic Freezing Steps.

1. Always use good freezer paper for wrapping meat. Buy the best kind possible—this is not the time or place to economize with bargain brands. A quality paper will have good tensile strength, be easy to handle and provide good resistance to water and gases. This holds true for most freezer foil as well; but be sure to use aluminum that is meant for freezing (it will have a different thickness and quality).

2. Plan meat menus ahead and wrap the quantities and cuts of meat in your freezer accordingly. This will lessen the time spent moving packages around and keeping the freezer door open. Constant moving can also cause edges to tear, exposing the meat to freezer burn; and keeping the freezer door open creates unwanted temperature variations.

3. Use enough freezer paper to cover the meat at least one and one-half times. Then place meat in center of wrap, bring ends of wrap together, fold over about one inch and crease along the fold. Keep folding until wrap is tight against the meat. Press wrap down at both ends to squeeze out excess air, and fold each end in about one inch to form seal. Fold ends under, tight against the package and seal with freezer (or masking) tape.

4. If you plan to have stew meat from your kill, cut the chilled pieces in small cubes about three-quarters of an inch in size and place in a container,

making sure all air has been pressed out. Mark the cut of the meat, the date and the weight in large letters. Ground meat should be kept in airtight packages. Organ meats such as liver, kidney, heart and tongue should be placed near the front of the freezer (or on the top shelf), because they are the most perishable. Again, plan ahead and avoid the cardinal sin of filling the freezer haphazardly, for that can only result in your having to empty half the freezer just to reach one piece of meat. A stand-up freezer is convenient, but I know a few people who partition their chest-type freezers for fish, fowl, roasts, steaks and chops, using cardboard laminated on the sides with freezer tape.

5. To save money on freezer containers, you can use empty milk cartons for small game such as squirrel, rabbit or cut-up fowl. Wash the containers first with lukewarm water and a teaspoon of vinegar, then wipe dry. Fill the containers with water, leaving about two inches of space at the top to force out the air.

Another popular storage area is to use the freezer section of your refrigerator, particularly if your meat is cut into small sections. Place these in a container, add water (or whatever packaging method you choose), force out the air and make a good seal on each end. If you decide to double-wrap the package, use cheaper paper only as an outer wrapper, never next to the meat. Since your frozen meats should be kept at 0° F., I would recommend using your refrigerator freezer only if the meat is to be used soon after it is placed there; otherwise, for long periods of freezing time, use only a standard freezer that you know maintains its 0° F. consistently.

Drying and Smoking.

As far as drying and smoking game goes, you can try making jerky. It consists of drying strips of meat over a smoke fire (or just leaving it out in the sun). Most hunters prefer to smoke and dry the meat over a hardwood fire slowly, then hang it in the sun.

You can make strips from 8 to 10 inches long and ½ to 2 inches wide. Jerky is especially good with a little red and black pepper, some thyme and other favorite spices beaten into it, then reheated over a fire on a stick. Never use pine or cone-bearing trees for smoking jerky—only hardwoods will do. Also, the longer you cook and smoke it, the better it will taste.

Another secret to making jerky is to extract all moisture from the meat as soon as possible. This will hasten the drying process and reduce spoilage. *Figure 2-92* shows how to build a box out in the field. Make the dimensions according to how much meat you plan to smoke at one time. Construct the walls out of green saplings tied together with string or vines. Make a grill to fit over the top as shown. The spaces between the sticks of the top piece should be about two inches. Fill the inside of the box with locust wood or other hardwood. These woods burn slowly and produce a lot of smoke; they also last for the entire smoking period, which is usually four to six hours. Small pieces of hickory or maple will help increase the smoke quantity.

Here's another good way to use jerky. After blanching some deer meat for 10 seconds or so in boiling water, marinate each slice in a mixture of one part vinegar and two parts water for about 24 hours. Marinate for another five to six hours in a mixture of ½ teaspoon Worcestershire sauce, a dash of liquid smoke, salt, chili powder and enough water to cover. Remove the slices from the marinade and drain on paper towels to remove the liquid. Put the slices on racks in a warm oven for about 12 hours and salt again about midway through the drying. Once dried, the jerky slices can be stored indefinitely until needed.

Still another delicious use of jerky is in making pemmican cakes. The Indians and early settlers used pemmican as an emergency food, mostly because it can be stored indefinitely without refrigeration. As long as you keep pemmican dry and wrapped in aluminum foil, it will retain its taste for over a year. The Indians used to keep it in tallow or beeswax which they let harden.

To make pemmican, pound out about four strips of dry venison (or beef) jerky into a powder. Add to this any types of dried fruit you like, such as dates, apricots, raisins, prunes, even sunflower seeds (about one-half cup). Thoroughly mix together with a little sugar or honey and pour tallow or beef suet over the mixture. Form these ingredients into squares and let dry in a warm oven at about 170° F. (77° C.) overnight. Then wrap in aluminum foil and keep in a dry place.

section 3

section 3

Upland Game Birds

MOURNING DOVE

Of all the upland game birds, the mourning dove is harvested in the most numbers. Despite a natural, annual mortality rate in the vicitnity of 70 percent, it is estimated that in the fall there are as many as 400 to 500 *million* in total population. And, while hunters bag an estimated 50 million doves each year, it barely depletes their numbers. This harvest is seconded only by that of the bobwhite quail, which reaches about 20 million yearly. What accounts for the dove's multitudinous numbers is its mating habits. Doves will nest up to 10 times in a given season, with five to seven nestings the more common figure.

Doves can be found in every state in the continental U.S., in Canada, and in Mexico. Those that reside in the northern areas will migrate to warmer southerly regions during the winter months, while doves indigenous to the southern areas will remain in the same territory year round.

Few people in the whole of North America are unfamiliar with the dove's distinctive cry or *coo*. A sorrowful yet soothing sound, from which the mourning dove derives its name, it is easily identifiable and most often heard in the spring when the first mating takes place.

A member of the family *Columbidae,* which includes the pigeon, the average length of the male dove is approximately 12 to 13 inches, with the weight ranging between 4 and 6 ounces. The female is somewhat smaller, weighing 3 to 4 ounces. The dove sports a small head with a slim neck. Although the upper parts of the bird appear to have a shiny metallic cast, they are actually a sooty brown, with the top of the head being grayish in color. The wings and neck are somewhat spotted and, when seen in flight, the whole body looks grayish blue.

Besides its enthusiastic mating practices, the dove differs from other fowl in its drinking methods. *Columbidae* birds sup without lifting their beaks out of the water, using a type of suction to ingest the liquid. Otherwise, their mode of eating and their diet are familiar, consisting primarily of seeds and grains (and occasional snails). Feeding time usually occurs in the early morning hours and again at dusk. Although many other birds will return to the same area year after year, the dove will alter its nesting spots during periods of migration solely because of the available food supply.

Contrary to what many people believe, doves are not monogamous. The male can mate with any female who is willing to mate with him. In some cases, he has even been known to mate with another male! However,

Mourning dove

many people still believe in this bird's monogamous nature, so it will remain a subject of some controversy.

Once the dove has mated with a female, however, each "spouse" remains quite devoted to the other during the nesting and brooding period. But beware the male that infringes upon another's territory or competes for the attention of a female. Many a winged battle has resulted in bloodshed, with feathers aflutter in the wind.

During courtship the male will fly upward in excess of 100 feet and then glide slowly back to the ground, circling slowly with his wings pointed straight outward. Once on the ground he will strut, coo, and bow with his tail pointed upward.

The dove is not a very discriminating nest builder. While the male supplies the twigs and branches, the female constructs a fragile platform-type nest located between limbs of a tree. She does not seem to care whether the nest is built at any particular height, and many times the new home is left accessible to ground predators. The female usually lays two white eggs, which are incubated by both parents, each taking their turn. Unfortunately, there are occasions when both leave the nest unattended at the same time, resulting in many dove eggs being lost through negligence.

After approximately two weeks of incubation, the squabs that hatch are not a particularly pretty sight. With no feathers and scant down, they are scrawny-looking, pathetic little creatures. But within the first week, they feather out nicely. In nine to 10 days, they start to flap their wings and could fly if they had to; in two weeks, they fully take to the air. Regardless of their rate of growth, the dovelets usually cling to their parents until they are completely weaned and on their own. The parents then immediately begin to work on the next brood.

Although the dove's normal life expectancy can reach six to seven years, many never see a second year, hence the high mortality statistics. Their predators are many: hawks, owls, crows, blue jays, snakes, squirrels, raccoons, opossums and, in suburban areas, even the backyard cat. Not to mention storms that destroy doves' flimsy nests, and man himself. So perhaps the dove's continual nesting is nature's way of replenishing their population.

Hunting Tips/mourning dove

As fall approaches—and with it the fateful hunter—doves become instinctively skittish. Hunting them then becomes true sport as they employ evasive tactics to outmaneuver the hunter. While they normally do not fly at top speeds, doves can attain speeds of 50 to 60 miles per hour when they are being flushed. The hunter, therefore, can hardly predict exactly what direction the doves may take or what acrobatics they may perform. It requires great skill, then, to bring home these birds. • Dogs are not usually used to hunt doves, only to retrieve them. • Also, keep in mind that if you plan to dine on breast of dove, you'll need to catch about three or four birds per person; if you use the whole bird, one or two will be sufficient.

For proper field dressing procedures, please refer to page 171.

Cooking/mourning doves

From a chef's perspective, unlike larger game birds, doves suffer from a lack of fat. If they are cooked too long or improperly, the finished meat may be tough, stringy, and dry. Keep this in mind when preparing the following recipes.

Poor Man's Feast

Try this "Poor Man's Feast" if you are on a camping trip, hunting small birds, particularly doves. It will be a great reward for your strenuous day in the field.

Use only birds that have been shot within a half hour of cooking time. The internal temperature of an undressed bird is 100° F. (38° C.) plus; and, since this cooking technique eliminates the field dressing, it must be begun rather quickly. Birds taken just around dusk before the close of the hunting day are best.

Of the birds you've caught, field dress the ones you want to keep and store. Take the remaining ones and, rather than draw them, simply cut off the heads, legs and wings, but leave the feathers, entrails, etc., intact.

Collect some mud (yes, mud) from a nearby stream or lake and cover each bird entirely, forming a round ball. Immediately place them in the hot coals of your campfire and let them cook for an hour or so. Take them out of the coals and break them open. You will find that the rising steam will carry an aroma of the fowl that will be positively irresistible.

Sprinkle them with a little black or red pepper, and eat them with a fork right out of the mud shell. The viscera will have shrunk up into a tight ball, with the inner cavity perfectly "clean." This method of steaming produces meat that is juicy and truly delicious; try the liver and heart for a pleasant surprise. On a chilly fall night sitting around a campfire with your hunting buddies, this dish can hardly be equalled.

Breast of Dove with Sesame Seeds
(Serves 2)

8 dove breasts	sesame seeds
½ cup butter	4 tablespoons honey

In a medium skillet, sauté breasts in hot butter. Remove from pan just before breasts are thoroughly cooked and roll in sesame seeds. Return breasts to skillet and drizzle ½ tablespoon of honey over each, then sprinkle with water. Cook, covered, over low heat until meat is tender, and steam from the water has thinned and spread the honey.

Broiled Doves
(Serves 4)

6 doves	freshly ground black
half a lemon	pepper, to taste
1 cup tart apple, finely chopped	¼ teaspoon nutmeg
¾ cup onion, finely chopped	4 tablespoons butter, melted
1 teaspoon salt	6 thick slices bacon
	½ cup dry sherry

Clean the doves and wipe out cavities with the lemon half, pressing the pulp against the cavities so they are well coated with lemon juice. Combine apple, onion, salt, pepper, nutmeg and butter, and spoon mixture into each bird. Top each dove with one slice of bacon.

Place doves on broiling rack and broil, turning often until evenly browned and tender. Transfer doves to roasting pan, add sherry, cover the pan and roast in 250° F. oven for 10 minutes until the liquor has lost its bite and blended with the fowl. Remove from oven, pour sauce over birds and serve with rice.

Band-tailed pigeon

BAND-TAILED PIGEON

The band-tailed pigeon makes its home in the western part of North America—from British Columbia through the western U.S. to as far south as Panama in Latin America. The pigeons who dwell in the northern reaches of their range tend to migrate, while those that reside in the warmer climates seem to be happy enough to stay put.

Band-tailed pigeons are not among the most popular of the game birds in North America, and only 500,000 to 600,000 birds are harvested annually. At one time, so many bandtails were taken by the early settlers of the West that the species came close to extinction, as did its now non-existent cousin, the passenger pigeon. However, as conservationism and level-headedness prevailed, they have again become abundant in the territories they inhabit.

Another member of the *Columbidae* flock that drinks without lifting its bill out of the water, the band-tailed pigeon is larger than the mourning dove, with an average length of from 14 to 16 inches and a weight of about twice that of the dove. The head of the bandtail is large and both its head and breast are purple in color. The nape of the neck is barred with a white stripe, followed by an iridescent green. The lower belly is light, while its back is dark gray. The tail is squared and banded in black, hence the name "band-tailed."

During the mating season, the male will call to the female with an owl-like sound, although ordinarily it coos in a manner similar to that heard by the dove. To prepare for nesting, the male retrieves the twigs, while his mate struggles, usually for as long as a week, to construct a nest that, when finished, appears barely habitable. Haphazardly thrown together, it is usually perched high in a tree to protect it from predators. However, nests have been found in lower branches and sometimes, although rarely, at ground level.

Breeding usually occurs between April and June and, while one brood per year is common, two and occasionally three have been known to hatch in the warmer climes. At the appropriate time, the female lays one shiny, white egg in the nest and both parents share in the incubation, which requires a period of about 18 to 20 days. The band-tailed squab that hatches, like the dovelet, is bereft of down and feathers.

Feeding is performed by both mother and father, who see to it that their new arrival receives enough of the pigeon's milk that is stored in their crops. The young bird then graduates to nuts, seeds and berries; acorns, if available, later become a staple food. By the third week, the squab is amply covered with feathers and, by the end of a month, starts flying and can pursue life entirely on its own.

If not killed by predators (eggs and squab are vulnerable to crows, jays, squirrels and the like; adults, primarily to hawks and owls), the average life span can reach five or six years.

After the breeding season ends, the pigeons tend to group together in flocks and, much like the swallows that perennially come back to Capistrano, the bandtails habitually seek their favorite nesting and feeding areas. Hunters who, in turn, seek their delectable carcasses knowingly await them and, unfortunately, they are easy prey when in large numbers at this time.

Hunting Tips/band-tailed pigeon

An excellent place to hunt band-tailed pigeons is near mineral springs. It seems they fulfill their dietary salt intake by drinking these waters. • Bandtails are swift flyers. In most cases, unlike their dove cousins, they will take direct flight paths rather than evasive action or erratic patterns. But, regardless, to catch one on the wing is the delight of any hunter.

For field dressing techniques, please turn to page 171.

Cooking/band-tailed pigeon

A culinary note—while the flesh of the plump young squab makes excellent eating, the older bird can be tough, due to the muscles formed in the stomach that aid in the digestion of the acorns they ingest.

Another point worth mentioning is that when bandtails feed on acorns they are usually so bitter that they are not suitable for eating. On the other hand, birds that feed on berries are fine tasting.

Over-the-Coals Pigeon with Butter Sauce
(Serves 4)

4 pigeons, cleaned, skinned and split in half	⅛ teaspoon cayenne pepper
Butter Sauce:	⅛ teaspoon paprika
1 cup butter	freshly ground black
1 tablespoon Worcestershire sauce	pepper to taste
	a.f.g. salt, if desired

Sauce: In a saucepan melt the butter, but do not heat to boiling. Add remaining ingredients and blend. Remove from heat.

Place birds on grill over medium-hot coals and

baste with sauce. Grill for about 5 minutes, then turn and baste again. Keep turning and basting for a total of 15 to 25 minutes until legs are tender, depending upon the size of the birds.

Rather than baste with a brush, I sometimes prefer to dip the birds right in the sauce; that way I'm sure they will be well coated and full of the sauce flavor.

Pan-Fried Pigeons
(Serves 4)

4 to 6 pigeons, cleaned and ready to prepare
1 cup flour
1 cup crackermeal
¼ teaspoon freshly ground black pepper
¼ teaspoon garlic powder

¼ teaspoon dried oregano
¼ teaspoon crushed dried basil
2 eggs, beaten with a little milk
½ cup or less vegetable oil

Combine flour, crackermeal, pepper, garlic powder, oregano and basil. Dredge the bird halves in the flour mixture, dip them in the eggs, then return them to the flour mixture, thoroughly coating each half. Heat oil in a large heavy skillet on medium high heat. Place coated pigeon halves in the heated oil and fry about 15 minutes on each side until fully cooked, crisp and tender. Drain on paper towels.

This is a nice dish served with Italian-style rice mixed with peas, prosciutto and lots of parsley.

Easy Baked Pigeons with Rice
(Serves 4)

4 to 6 pigeons, cleaned and ready to prepare
1 10½-ounce can cream of mushroom soup
1 10½-ounce can cream of celery soup
1 cup evaporated milk

1¼ cups chicken stock
salt and freshly ground black pepper to taste
1 teaspoon parsley, chopped
2 cups uncooked white rice

Combine soups and evaporated milk in a mixing bowl. In a large baking dish, evenly sprinkle the rice and cover thoroughly with the soup mixture. Place birds in dish, gently pushing them down into rice/soup mixture; pour the stock over the birds. Salt and pepper them and sprinkle with parsley. Place in a moderate (350° F.) oven and bake for 1 to 1½ hours until meat is tender and rice is fully cooked.

WOODCOCK

Both the woodcock, and the common snipe discussed in the next chapter, are similar in general size and weight to the dove and pigeon. But that's where the likenesses cease. As members of the *Scolopacidae* family of "shore" birds, the woodcock and snipe both bear slender bills of up to three inches—unusually long compared to their overall length of one foot. And, although not classified as waterfowl, yet unlike most other upland birds, these fowl prefer the water-laden areas of marshes, wet woods and meadows. (The woodcock likes a little higher, drier ground than the snipe.) Their beaks help them adapt to their environment by enabling them to extract from the soggy soil the earthworms that constitute the bulk of their diet.

The woodcock makes its habitat east of the Mississippi River and can be found as far north as New Brunswick, Canada, and as far south as the Gulf States. It is constantly moving to new locations within its range as encroaching urban development destroys its natural home. As other feathered migrants, the northern birds winter in the warmer states.

In terms of overall appearance, it would be difficult to describe the woodcock as an attractive bird. It has neither the colorful plumage nor the distinctive profile of other game birds. But Mother Nature has her reasons. If survival is a primary one, then the woodcock is well equipped. Its bulbous eyes are perched extremely far back on the bird's head—the better to spot predators with while feeding. The variegated patches of brown, black and white on its back provide perfect camouflage in its woodland environs. And its unusually tapered bill of course helps it to obtain food as well as to carry its eggs or chicks, if necessary, away from intruders. The male of the species is smaller than the female, which is most unusual in the bird kingdom. The male weighs approximately 6 ounces, and the female about 8 ounces. Otherwise, both sexes appear uncommonly similar.

The song of the woodcock is heard only during the mating season, at which time the male is something beautiful to listen to as he woos the lady of his desires. The rest of the year the woodcock does not produce any particularly distinctive call and is relatively quiet as birds go.

Mating acrobatics are quite spectacular, with the

Woodcock

male flying from the center of a clearing, spiraling almost straight upward, attaining altitudes of 300 feet or more. He then flutters back to the ground, where he will remain for about four or five minutes before beginning his upward ascent again. After this display has been repeated several times, the female will usually enter the clearing. Copulation occurs and the male departs.

To prepare for the nest, little is required of the female. She merely picks a soft, dry spot on the ground (often padded with leaves), but one that is close to a source of water. This allows her to leave the nest to drink, but provides for a quick return to her eggs. The eggs, ordinarily four to a clutch, are positioned point-end down in the nest for stability. And, like the birds themselves, they have been painted shades of splotchy brown by nature's palette to blend in with the surroundings. Both mother and eggs are so well disguised, in fact, that it is almost impossible to detect the nest with the naked eye. This affords ultimate protection for the eggs while the female briefly flits from the nest, and relative peace from would-be predators for the female while she is incubating the eggs.

Of the parenting pair, the female seems to be the stalwart member. She is the Protector Of The Eggs and under no circumstances will she leave them if she thinks they are in danger. She may move them if need be, but abandon them to save her own feathers—never. Man, for example, has been known to come upon her in the woods while she has sat motionless on her clutch and, miraculously, she has given him silent consent to stroke her—truly a rare ornithological phenomenon. Whether she feels resentment, terror or is really a gutsy creature, we'll never know. But perhaps this instinctual protectiveness is one reason why she is larger than the male—Mother Nature again defending the species.

After approximately 20 days of incubation, the newly born, because of their protective coloration, stand a much better chance of survival than do many other birds. However, if the eggs are destroyed prior to hatching, the female will nest again, but produce a lesser number of eggs. Almost upon shedding their shells, the chicks are capable of leaving the roost. Within three to four weeks of hatching, the young birds are quite adventuresome, although they will flock around the mother to seek shelter and warmth during the night.

Mature woodcock are secretive, nocturnal birds that even migrate during the twilight hours. Like bats, you can see their shadows flutter at dusk, when they are engaged in much activity, or at dawn when they can most often be observed probing for worms and insects.

At maximum maturity, the woodcock may be five years old, although most do not live beyond two. Its natural enemies are raccoons, skunks, opossums and other small animals that prey on ground-oriented birds, as well as owls and hawks. The chief threats to survival, however, are cold weather and snow, which prevent many woodcock from adequately finding food.

Hunting Tips/woodcock

The woodcock harvest is small—perhaps less than one million a year—when compared to that of other game birds. • Some autumns result in better woodcock hunting than others. If a mild fall is experienced, the birds migrate south in much smaller numbers and will be more difficult to locate. On the other hand, if a sudden downward plunge of the thermometer is the sign of an early fall, they will begin migrating in great numbers and the hunting will be more fruitful. Many times woodcock will be lured to the same site on either their spring or winter migration. Try to find out where that is. • Low, marshy, bush-filled woodlands are most productive for hunting woodcock. Search for areas where there is a likelihood of earthworms in abundance and look for borings in the ground, evidence that they have been feeding. • It might be wise also to become acquainted with a woodcock hunter in a particular region. Once a friendship is established, he just might let you in on a well-kept secret: where the woodcock are. • Special guns are made for woodcock shooting, but because of their delicate skin and small bones, the birds can be easily bagged with pellet as well as with skeet shooting equipment. • Woodcock usually fly straight up and out without the zigzagging deviations known of snipe; therefore, if you aim directly at one, you will have a good chance of hitting it. However, woodcock tend to keep fairly low and close to timber if there is any around. This is why hunting the little bird is such a challenge. It's supposedly a slow flier, but darting through an obstacle course of trees, it certainly appears fast and erratic.

Once, in fact, when I was bird hunting in Louisiana, a pair of woodcock flushed and seemed to circle like fighter pilots, zigzagging every few feet. I was with two friends, real "enthusiasts" like most other Louisiana bird hunters. We were walking along a thicket. There were trees behind us, with a small stream emptying into a large marsh just in front of the trees. My friends had dogs, but I preferred hunting without them. When the birds went up, it looked like a Pac-man video game. I fired both barrels of my over and under 20 gauge, but to no avail. If you think skeet shooting is something, you should have seen these birds. The same thing was happening to my hunting partners; the dogs would get the birds up all right, but they seemed to pair off and fly in a Z pattern, not a straight line. Most unusual—and frustrating. We never did bag anything that morning, only later on in the day when things began to "normalize" again.

Please see page 171 for field dressing instructions.

Cooking/woodcock

Creamed Woodcock with Grapes and Sesame Seeds
(Serves 4)

4 woodcocks, cleaned
  and split in half

Cream Sauce:

2 tablespoons cornstarch	salt, if desired
½ cup heavy cream, cold	freshly ground black
1 cup chicken stock	pepper
3 tablespoons butter or	1 cup green seedless
margarine	grapes, sliced
¼ cup dry white wine	¼ cup sesame seeds

Sauce: In a small saucepan, place the cornstarch and slowly add the cream, stirring well. Gently pour in the chicken stock, blending thoroughly, and heat until mixture begins to bubble and thicken. Remove from heat and add the butter and wine; mix well.

Place birds in a roasting pan; lightly season them and cover with the sauce. Bake for 1½ hours in a moderate oven, basting often.

Mix together the sliced grapes and sesame seeds and sprinkle over the birds for the last 15 minutes of baking. This is particularly tasty served with wild rice.

Woodcock Roasted in Foil
(Serves 4)

1 egg	½ teaspoon dried thyme
1 cup milk	salt and freshly ground
bread crumbs, freshly	black pepper to taste
ground	8 whole woodcocks
1 teaspoon rosemary	8 tablespoons butter
½ teaspoon sage	peanut oil

Beat egg with milk. Mix together bread crumbs, herbs and seasonings. Dip birds into the egg-milk mixture, then roll in seasoned bread crumbs. Place one tablespoon butter into the cavity of each bird. Grease aluminum foil with peanut oil and wrap each bird separately. Place on a cookie sheet or roast as is on rack in preheated 350° F. oven for 20 minutes.

Fried Woodcock

8 whole woodcocks	peanut oil
1 cup milk	
flour seasoned with	
poultry seasoning and	
salt and pepper to taste	

Dip woodcocks in milk, then dredge in seasoned flour. Do this twice.

In a large, deep skillet, heat enough peanut oil to completely cover the birds. Deep fry until golden brown.

Common snipe

COMMON SNIPE

The common snipe. Common perhaps in the late 1800's but perilously close to extinction around the turn of the century because of overhunting, this bird could hardly be considered "common" today. However, through preservation and hunting restrictions, it has slowly been brought back to flourishing numbers, although its population will probably never be as prodigious as before. Many people enjoy eating and hunting the common snipe—it is a challenge in the woods—but current statistics on approximate harvest are not readily available. It does not seem to be sought after, however, as avidly as the pheasant, quail or grouse.

The common snipe can be seen throughout much of North America—from Alaska to Labrador, southward to California, eastern Arizona, northern Colorado and the midwestern states of Iowa and Ohio. It can also be found in the eastern part of the U.S. as far south as New Jersey. When the weather starts to turn cold, it predictably migrates to more southerly regions.

The common snipe is similar in size and shape to its *Scolopacidae* cousin, the woodcock, weighing about a half pound and measuring close to a foot in length. The female of the species, however, tends to be smaller, not larger, than the male. Of the other shared characteristics, the common snipe also has an extremely long, slender bill compared to its relative size, and its eyes are set far back in its head.

So how can you tell them apart if they are so much alike? The tail. While the common snipe is colored with the shades of autumn—its head and upper body are striped with broken bands of brown and buff and the underside is white streaked with brown—its tail is extremely short and displays a wide bar of burnt orange, which virtually flashes when the bird is in flight. Both male and female are colored similarly.

Also, the common snipe tends to be noisier than the woodcock. It not only emits a special call during the breeding season—a lyrical *wheat, wheat* sound—but gives off a separate alarm call as well as a distinct flight call whenever the bird is flushed.

During the mating months, the male puts on quite a spectacular exhibition for the female. The snipe spirals upward to nearly 500 feet and quickly plummets to earth, creating a strange strumming noise with its wings to attract the female waiting below. Without lighting on the ground, he takes off again, repeating the ritual until he hears the female's call, which perhaps acts as her applause and ultimately her approval.

Once the couple has finished with nature's embrace, the female will usually lay four drab olive-colored brown-spotted eggs in a ground nest that is grass lined and near water. The snipe, it should be noted, prefers marshy areas and other locations for nesting and general habitat that are somewhat wetter than those selected by the woodcock. Because neither the parents nor the eggs possess the excellent camouflage of the woodcock, the female snipe will repeatedly, as needed, build a roof out of leaves and such to serve as a shroud. The eggs are incubated by both sexes for approximately 20 days, after which both male and female will care for the young in a very protective fashion.

As other *Scolopacidae* chicks, the young snipes are instantly active upon hatching, but do require about 14 days of growth to reach normal flying capability.

The diet of the common snipe, although it consists primarily of worms, differs from the woodcock's in that it encompasses many crustaceans found in coastal areas, insect larvae that dwell in or near water and wet grasses and weeds.

If it survives to maximum maturity, the snipe can reach about four years of age. To try to combat the life-threatening forces of nature, the snipe will move about mostly during the shadowy hours of dusk and dawn, flying—even migrating—from one site to another at night. It also is a master at contriving an erratic flight pattern, deviating at oblique angles both laterally and vertically to escape predators. Because of this unique ability, few birds or animals could consider the snipe their prey.

Hunting Tips/common snipe

A hunter must be a skilled, experienced shot to be able to shoot a common snipe on the wing because of its clever flying capabilities and because, when flushed and frightened, the bird can attain a flight speed of approximately 45 to 50 miles per hour. • Excellent table fare, the snipe is a small bird, which means it would require several to satisfy the average person's appetite.

Turn to page 171 for field dressing procedures.

Cooking/common snipe

Perhaps because shellfish constitute some of their diet, snipes, according to some experts, tend to taste similar to oysters and lobsters. Whether that is to your liking or not, keep in mind that when preparing them, you'll need more than one per person and that cooking time should be kept to a minimum.

Sautéed Snipe with Mushrooms
(Serves 4)

4 snipes, cleaned and split in half
4 slices bacon
2 cloves garlic, sliced
4 scallions or 1 small onion, sliced
½ pound mushrooms, thinly sliced
freshly ground black pepper
sweet paprika
1 cup flour
¼ cup vegetable oil
¼ cup butter
½ cup dry white wine
1 tablespoon parsley, chopped

In a large skillet, fry the bacon until crispy and all the fat has been rendered into bacon grease. Remove bacon slices. Add to the pan the garlic, scallions or onion and sauté lightly until onion has turned golden. Mix in the mushrooms and heat through, but do not overcook; they should still be firm. Remove onion/mushroom mixture from pan and keep warm.

Sprinkle the snipe halves with the pepper and paprika and dredge in flour.

In the same skillet, heat the oil and butter. Sauté the floured snipes in it about 10 to 15 minutes on each side. You should not be deep frying here so if you have too much oil/butter, remove some of it. You do not want the birds to be saturated in it, merely sautéed.

When the birds are tender, cover them with the onion/mushroom mixture; add the wine and parsley and heat rapidly until all the ingredients have blended together, about 5 minutes or so.

Snipe Orientale
(Serves 4)

4 snipes, cleaned, skinned and split in half

Orange Sauce:
1 6-ounce can frozen orange juice
2 tablespoons lemon juice
½ cup pineapple juice
1 fresh orange, thinly sliced
2 tablespoons honey
2 tablespoons vegetable oil

Mix all sauce ingredients together. Arrange birds in a large roasting pan, pour the sauce over them and marinate at least 2 hours, turning occasionally.

Preheat oven to 350° F. Bake in same pan in a moderate oven for approximately 1½ hours, until tender. Baste frequently during roasting. This is delicious served with stir-fry vegetables and rice.

Roast Snipe
(Serves 4)

8 snipes with entrails intact
½ cup butter, melted
salt and freshly ground black pepper to taste
1 tablespoon dark rum
4 tablespoons dry sherry
8 slices white bread, toasted

Put snipes in a roasting pan and coat with ¾ of the melted butter. Place in a preheated 450° F. oven and roast for about 20 minutes.

Remove cooked birds from the pan, finely chop the entrails and season with salt and pepper. Skim off half the pan juices; then add the entrails, rum, sherry and remaining butter to pan. Simmer the gravy until reduced by about one half. Place birds on toasted bread and ladle the sauce over them.

Snipe Entrails Hors d'Oeuvres
(Serves 4 to 6)

4 tablespoons butter
1 snipe, meat and entrails removed and minced
3 scallions, chopped
salt and red pepper to taste
1 tablespoon flour, or more as needed
1 tablespoon sherry
1 egg yolk, beaten

Melt butter over medium heat. Add snipe and entrails, scallions, salt and red pepper and sauté over medium heat for 20 minutes. Remove from heat and set aside.

In a large bowl, combine flour, sherry and beaten egg yolk and mix well. Add the snipe mixture. Spread on toasted party rye rounds, place on greased cookie sheet and bake at 350° F. for 10 to 12 minutes.

DRESSING OUT DOVES, PIGEONS, WOODCOCK, SNIPE

Because doves, pigeons, woodcock and snipe are all very small in size and light in weight, you would field dress them the same way. In general—and this applies to all birds—your two most important field-dressing objectives are: first, to remove the viscera immediately; and, second, to pluck the feathers if the birds are going to be cooked or frozen.

To eviscerate a bird—and of course you would do this in the field—simply make a straight incision with one of your sharp knives from the vent, or anus, to the base of the breastbone; make a crosscut under the breast, making a "Y" shape; insert one or two "hooked" fingers and pull out all the internal organs. Study *Figure 3-1* to familiarize yourself with bird anatomy and *Figure 3-2* to get a basic idea of the general skeletal formation of birds and the placement of the cuts. This will help you do a better job of removing the viscera.

Carefully check to make sure you have removed all the innards and, if any remain, pull them out. If necessary, you may slit the neck to reach and remove the windpipe and crop. Wipe out the cavity with paper towels or dry grass, then prop it open with a stick for cooling. This entire process takes literally seconds because the birds are so small. It should also become a rather routine part of your bird hunting experience.

Depending on whether or not you are going to eat the birds immediately upon bagging, it may not be necessary to field dress them at all. See, for example, my recipe for "Poor Man's Feast," page 161. However, if you are eventually going to freeze them, or if the weather is warm, or even if you simply have a long drive home, the entrails must be removed immediately. Do not discard them, though, because they can be made into excellent appetizers as in my recipe, "Snipe Entrails Hors d'Oeuvres," on the preceding page. And if nothing else, the liver and the heart are good eating by themselves.

Removing the feathers—the next step—can be done anytime after the birds are killed, although the best time to pluck them is when the bodies are still warm. So after you return from the field to your campsite, for example, is an auspicious time.

First, with game shears snip off the wing feathers and of course at this time you can opt to remove the feet if you haven't already done so. Head removal (simply pull it off) should wait until you are finished depluming.

Begin plucking by pulling the large feathers out by hand at the neck and work downward. The feathers should always be pulled downward in the direction in which they grow to avoid tearing the skin. The smaller feathers can be removed with pliers or tweezers if you can't grip them with your fingers, or they may be singed off with a candle, a gas flame or even a flaming roll of newspaper. If you use the singeing method, make sure you are outdoors; burning feathers give off a very strong odor that takes forever to dissipate. More elaborate feather removal methods involve scalding and waxing the carcass, and are discussed in later chapters dealing with larger birds. With the smaller birds, however, I prefer to perform the feather removal completely manually.

Some birds, such as the mourning dove, are so small that many people feel the only salvageable meat is the breast meat. In this case, it is not necessary either to field dress the birds or to remove the feathers, since you'll be recovering only the breast section. In *Figure 3–2* you can see that the bones of the wing attach to the breastbone, or sternum. Because of this, it is necessary to detach the wing in order to remove the breast successfully.

Wing removal is relatively simple. Grasp a wing in your hand and twist it off as shown in *Figure 3-3*. You can see that it is being torn off right at the joint. Next, cut into the belly in a V-shape below the breastbone, as shown in *Figure 3-3*. Insert your fingers into the slit and pull upward as indicated in *Figure 3-4*. Note that the fingers are curved under the breastbone as they pull upward. The cracking sound you'll hear will be the ribs separating from their attachment to the breastbone. Once you've snapped the bone away from the ribs, use a small pocketknife to finish removing the breast meat from the bird, shown in *Figure 3-5*.

The final step is to peel the skin and feathers away from the meat, which amounts to little more than a mouthful, but does make a great addition to any breakfast, lunch or dinner when sautéed in butter.

When preparing smaller birds, it is usually advisable to leave the skin on because it serves as a natural wrap that retains the moisture often lost during the cooking process. With doves, however, when only the breast meat is used, you will find that removing the skin is preferred.

Another way to remove the breast meat involves taking the feathers off first and is usually done in the field. Begin by plucking the breast clean from the base

INTERNAL ANATOMY OF THE BIRD

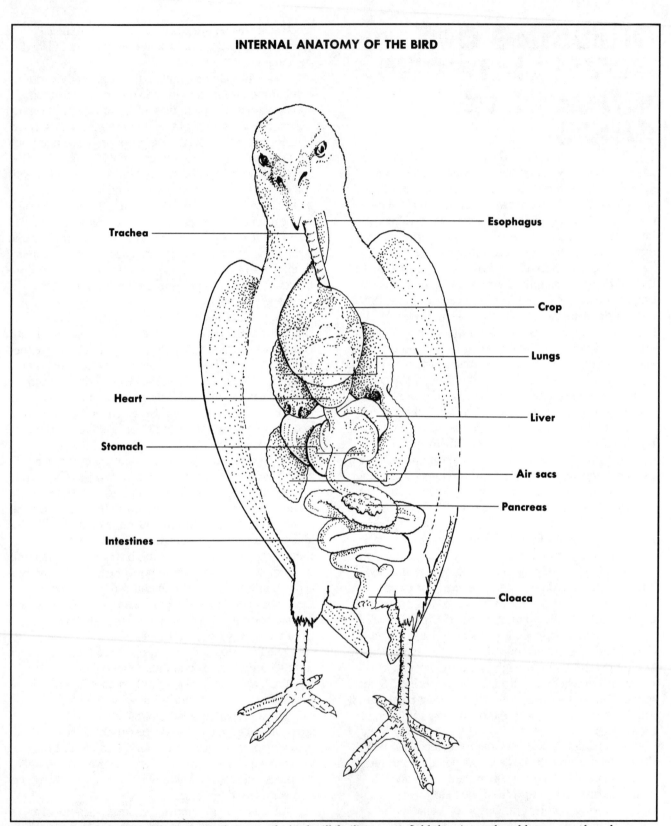

Trachea

Esophagus

Crop

Lungs

Heart

Liver

Stomach

Air sacs

Pancreas

Intestines

Cloaca

3-1. Familiarizing yourself with the internal organs of a bird will facilitate your field dressing and enable you to select the parts you want to keep.

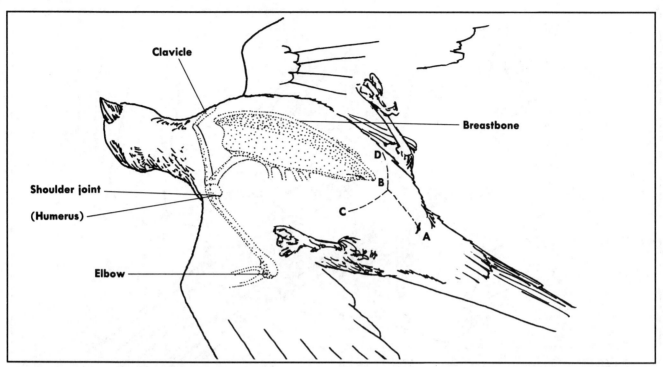

Clavicle

Breastbone

Shoulder joint

(Humerus)

Elbow

D

B

C

A

3-2. To field dress small birds, such as the dove, pigeon, woodcock or snipe, start at the vent, or anus (point "A"), and cut upward to the bottom of the breastbone (point "B"). Then make a crosscut from points "C" to "D" to allow your fingers to get inside the bird. Remove the entrails by simply pulling them out. If necessary, slit the neck to reach and remove the windpipe and crop. While you are still in the field, dry out the cavity with dried grass, a cloth or paper towels, if available.

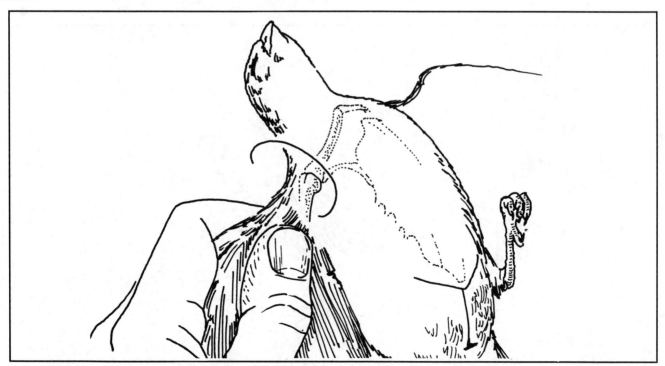

3-3. Many hunters keep only the breast meat on these smaller birds and throw the rest of the bird away. To remove the breast, refer to *Figure 3-2*; note that the wing bones are attached to the breastbone, or sternum. Remove the wings first by taking one, then the other in your hand and twist each off at the joint. Now make a crosscut under the breastbone as shown above.

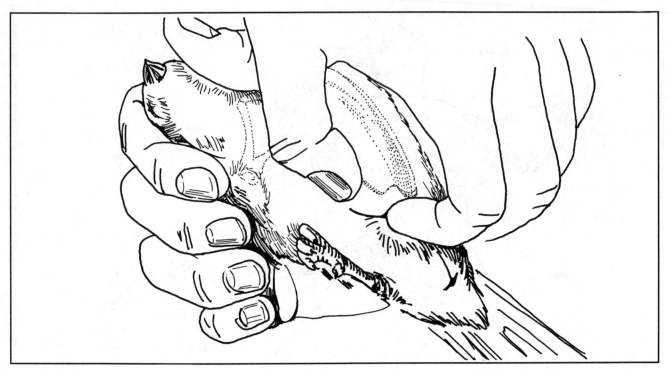

3-4. The next step in breast removal is to insert your fingers into the cut you have made, shown in *Figure 3-3,* and pull upward, lifting the entire breast out, feathers and all.

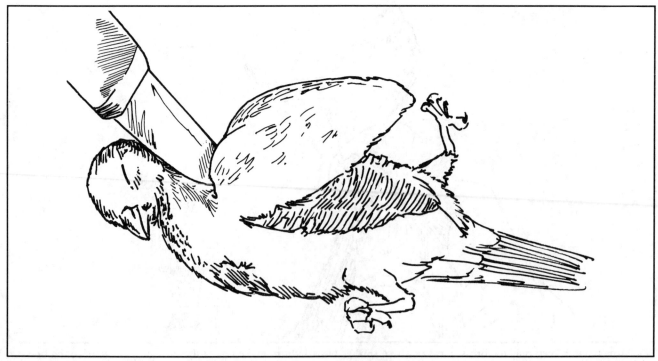

3-5. The final step is to take your pocketknife and separate the meat at the joint at the top of the sternum. Prepare the breast for cooking by taking your knife and gently lifting the skin with feathers from the meat.

of the neck down to the tail and on either side down to the wing bone and thigh of each leg. Remember to pluck in the direction of the growth of the feathers.

Now, to skin the breast area, stretch the skin tightly across the breastbone and make a slit with a very sharp knife from the crop down to the tail, being careful not to cut into the flesh. With your thumb and forefinger, fold the skin back, gently tugging downward toward the wing and the tail of your bird until the breast is exposed. As you work downward, you will be able to hold onto the skin more tightly.

Using the center ride of the breastplate as a guide, cut the meat to the bone from the base of the neck to the tail. Cut as closely as possible to the breastbone on each side. You should now be able to remove the breast meat and prepare it for cooking.

If the freezer is the ulitmate destination of your birds, be sure to rinse them out with cold, salted water first to rid them of any foreign matter, feathers and blood; also to freshen the flesh. Extract any pellets you may find. Here is a trick—quick and easy—that will facilitate their storage and ensure a longer stay under ice: take a clean, plastic half-gallon milk carton, place a bird or two in the carton, cover it with water and freeze. This will prevent freezer burn, since the small sharp bones will not penetrate the carton (as they might more fragile freezer paper). However, if you prefer freezer paper, aluminum foil or plastic bags, do double wrap. Don't forget to label the carton or package with its contents, including the weight and the date you put it in the freezer. Indelible markers on masking tape work well, also wax crayons.

Finally, remember that the birds should be thawed out and then enjoyed using any of the various recipes I have included here. I recommend using them within about six months of the freezing date; three months is preferable and nine months the definite maximum for whole birds. Be sure that if you plan to keep them frozen for any length of time, the birds should be stored at 0° F. (−18° C.) in a standard freezer (not the freezer compartment of your refrigerator, since that low temperature cannot be maintained).

BOBWHITE QUAIL

Of the various types of quail hunted in North America, the bobwhite is the most well known for its unforgettable mating call, the sound of its own name. The bobwhite resides chiefly in the eastern half of the U.S., with heavy concentrations in the southeast, but has also been sighted in the northwestern states of Washington, Oregon and Idaho.

The species indigenous to the West—the mountain quail, the largest member of the quail family, also called the plumed quail because of the thin feathers protruding straight back from its crest; the California, or valley, quail, perhaps the most outstanding in appearance with its forward-curving plume; the desert-dwellers—the scaled, or cottontop, quail and the Gambel's quail; and the smallest member, the harlequin or Montezuma quail—are found in lesser numbers and are all variations on a main theme, that, for all practical purposes here, being the bobwhite. In other words, since many of the characteristics of the bobwhite are common to the other quail, I am going to stick to a discussion of the bobwhite only.

Quail are desirable to hunt. They are elusive, to say the least, and can hide in areas that even dogs won't venture. Statistics claim that about five million or more people take to the field each year, harvesting about 20 million birds, half of which are bagged in the southern states. And although they can be small in size (the male weighs between 5 and 9 ounces), these plump little birds of the *Phasianidae* family satisfy many a gourmet's palate. In addition to enjoying my own recipes, I had the pleasure of eating roast quail in South Carolina one time, with quail eggs served in a "nest" of shredded potatoes and topped with a brown gravy; it was just out of this world.

Quail, as all the remaining wildfowl discussed in this section, are gallinaceous birds (*gallinaceous* is presumably derived from the order *Galliformes* of which quail, pheasant, grouse and turkey are members). It means they are exclusively ground denizens that eat, roost, mate and nest on good old Mother Earth. Not that they don't fly—they certainly do, often with great bursts of speed of from 40 to 50 miles per hour. But if given a choice, all prefer scurrying—safely under cover—on a sound surface. This, of course, adds to the hunter's and bird dog's challenge.

In most cases, both the male and female of each species of quail are similarly marked, with the male carrying the brighter, deeper colors. With the bobwhite, the breast, back, wings and tail are predominantly a reddish-brown, accented in black. The head, which gives the bird its physical distinction, bears a white stripe above the eyes curving from the bill to the back of the neck and a white patch under the bill, both white areas being separated by a dark-brown band. In the female, these white sections show up yellowish and, overall, her coloring is softer and lacks the distinctiveness of the male's. She is also smaller in size and lighter in weight.

The familiar bobwhite call is heard in the spring when these quail are engaged in mating. It is the male's call to the female before actual mating takes place and to the rest of the animal world afterward, announcing his territorial claims. Beyond that, both sexes share a danger cry and perhaps more important from man's point of view is the *quoilee* or *whoilkee* sounds used to regroup a covey that has scattered. In fact, in the fall many a hunter has tried to imitate that call, attempting to reconvene a flock.

Quail breed in large numbers. The average clutch contains about 15 white eggs, almost all of which will hatch if left undisturbed by bad weather, lack of cover (in addition to natural ground cover, the male, who builds the nest, adds a roof for protection) or the predatory birds and small animals that enjoy dining on eggs. The parents usually breed only once a year, but if their efforts have been thwarted by disaster, they will nest as many times (up to four) as is required to produce a family. Some pairs have even been known to mate in the fall. Although the annual mortality rate is about the same as that of doves, approximately 70 percent, quail can reach a maturity of four to five years. While rain and cold are particularly injurious, if not fatal, to the chicks, accidents from automobiles and farm equipment, as well as disease also take a considerable toll.

After the chicks have grown, which requires several weeks, the family remains together until late summer and fall, when it joins with other quail families to form a covey. Bobwhite are not migratory birds and usually spend most of their lifetime within a quarter-mile radius of the "homestead," especially if the seeds and plants of their diversified and predominantly vegetarian diet are close by. As cooler autumn weather approaches, the range expands due to a diminishing food supply and less protective ground cover.

Behavior of the covey should be of particular interest. At night quail almost always roost in a circle on the ground with their tails pointing inward. This not only affords warmth, but also protection against predators. If a raccoon, for example, is stalking a grassy field, his chances of being detected are greater the more birds there are. At least one is bound to be awake. The excitement really starts once the danger alarm is sounded. All of a sudden the bobwhite will burst into flight, scattering every which way, with their short wings flapping noisily. During the day in hunting season, you might witness the same occurrence if a covey is disturbed. It's almost like Old Faithful burping birds instead of water out of the earth. It's certainly a dramatic sight—one that will startle you and set your heart pounding.

Hunting Tips/bobwhite quail

Since bobwhite roost in a circle, look for bird droppings in a similar pattern. Look also for tracks in dusty ground areas, because quail, like many other birds, dust to relieve themselves of insects and parasites. • Quail are incredibly clever at finding hiding places, which is why the bobwhite is one of my favorite birds to hunt. To be successful, you've got to be as resourceful as the species. • As a ground dweller, bobwhite will run far longer distances before they will flush or hide. And I certainly find dogs invaluable when trying to flush the birds. In fact, says Charles Waterman in *Hunting Upland Birds,* "Bobwhite are probably the best of all birds for dog work, and I know of no pointing breed that will not handle them if properly trained." • Although quail appear to flush fast, the astute hunter realizes that they are not nearly as fast as they seem. Therefore, more deliberateness will bring better results. • Be aware that on hot, sunny days, snakes will often seek shade in the same areas as the bobwhite. If you're going to hunt in the South, in particular, be prepared and don't hunt without proper snake-proof footgear.

To field dress your quail and prepare for the savory meal you'll enjoy, see page 183.

Bobwhite quail

CARE OF BIRD DOGS

Just as it is the hunter's responsibility to use the proper hunting gun and ammo, it is also, in my opinion, the hunter's obligation, if he uses dogs in the hunt, to select the appropriate breed and care for the dogs in a responsible way so they will adequately fulfill his hunting requirements.

The breed of dog you select will naturally depend on what you are hunting and to some degree your individual personality: the dog can be one that points, one that flushes, one that fetches, one that trails or others that are bred to accomplish specific tasks. To name only a few, the English pointer and the English setter are always being argued over as to which is the better breed that points. Some hunters will pick the Brittany spaniel, the Weimaraner or the German short-haired pointer and say that these are the favorites. There are also the cocker spaniel and the English springer spaniel that flush; and the retrievers, such as the well-known Labrador, the Chesapeake and the golden. All have their work cut out for them and share an honored place in bird hunting.

Regardless of the breed of dog you prefer, here are a few important rules concerning care of your animal that you should follow before and after the hunt, as well as the time between seasons when you are not working him.

1. Your dog should at all times wear a good collar with a name tag bearing your phone number.

2. Depending on what you are hunting and what time of year it is, get the dog in good condition, and also start your own conditioning program well ahead of the season. There is nothing worse than for a dog to be holding point and you not be able to get there to release it from its position.

3. When transporting a dog in a car, truck, station wagon or other vehicle, keep him caged or in a confined area. Allowing him to run around loose may only lead to trouble, possible injury or an accident for both of you.

4. During the hunt, do not overwork your dog in extreme weather conditions.

5. Check the condition of your dog each time you take a break. Don't wait until the hunt is over. This will prevent many small injuries from becoming major ones. Specifically, check:

—The foot pads first for cuts, thorns and other foreign matter, such as small stones or splinters, that may have worked between the toes. Treat these first because, after all, a dog does travel on its feet.

—The eyes for thorns, splinters, grass and bits of branches that may have snapped back into the eyes. Treat these immediately because the dog himself may make the injury worse by rubbing with his own paw.

—The entire body thoroughly, scanning for cuts and other out-of-the-ordinary things that may be potentially injurious.

You can wait until after the hunt to dry your dog off and rub him well. This is the time you can repay him for all the work he's done for you. By this I mean that you can get to know your dog better during this rubdown and drying time and you will be able to inspect the animal much closer for any injuries he may have sustained and treat them accordingly.

6. Carry first-aid equipment with you, such as hydrogen peroxide, commercial foot ointment, tweezers and eye lubricant. Also, consult with your veterinarian beforehand about what he advises you to take with you for emergency treatment. Good care of your dog will yield better results.

7. Feeding habits differ from animal to animal but, if a dog does not get carsick, I prefer to feed him about a third of his meal before the hunt. Some hunters will wait until they have taken a break for lunch and then feed a dog half his meal to replenish the energy burned up in the morning, then feed again after the hunt. This would again depend on what type of hunting you are engaged in and what the weather conditions are, as well as how much work the dog has accomplished.

In addition to the above points to keep in mind, if you are the owner of a hunting dog, training, conditioning and habits are all important and should be worked out on an individual basis throughout the course of the year.

I realize that controversy looms over whether or not a hunting dog should be kept outside the home and never shown any particular familiarity, except when you are on a hunt. But I know many hunters who own bird dogs and, believe it or not, they care for those animals as though they were part of their family, even to the extent of letting them live inside and function as house pets. How many dogs you can keep and handle and how you care for them will depend on what you hunt, where you live and the kind of person you are. Any further comments about indoor versus outdoor care I will leave to your own preferences and your own good research on the subject.

Cooking/bobwhite quail

Roast Quail
(Serves 1)

4 tablespoons butter
1 quail
salt and freshly ground
   black pepper to taste

crushed tarragon leaves to
   taste

Place 2 tablespoons butter inside the cavity of the quail and season cavity with salt, freshly ground pepper and tarragon leaves. Arrange quail on rack, spread 2 tablespoons of butter over bird, sprinkle with salt and pepper.

    Roast at 450° F. for about 20 minutes, basting well once during roasting time. Remove from oven and let rest in a warm place for 5 to 6 minutes before serving.

Fried Quail
(Serves 4)

6 quails
½ cup flour, seasoned
   with salt and freshly
   ground pepper to taste

6 to 9 thick slices bacon
parsley sprigs

Split quails lengthwise down the backs and shake in plastic bag with the seasoned flour. Fry bacon until crisp and keep hot in oven. Over medium-high heat, sauté the quails in the bacon fat until golden brown. Reduce heat to low and let cook, turning once or twice, until fork-tender. Transfer to hot platter and top with bacon slices. Garnish with parsley and serve with Gravy.

Gravy:

2 tablespoons flour
1 cup milk
salt

black pepper, freshly
   gound
Tabasco sauce

Remove all but 3 tablespoons of fat and pan juices from the skillet and add flour. Mix well over medium heat and stir until smooth. Gradually stir in milk and continue to stir until mixture is smooth and thick. Season to taste with salt, pepper and Tabasco sauce.

Quail Cooked in a Bag
(Serves 4)

1 tablespoon flour
1 large oven cooking bag
6 quails
salt and red pepper to
   taste
1 cup onion, chopped
½ cup green pepper,
   chopped

1 pound fresh
   mushrooms, sliced
1 bay leaf
1 cup dry sherry
juice of half a lemon
1 cup water

Grease a large roasting pan. Put flour in oven cooking bag and shake, making sure that the inside of the bag is evenly coated.

    Split birds lengthwise in half, and sprinkle flesh with salt and red pepper. Place birds in the bag and add the onion, green pepper, mushrooms, bay leaf, sherry, lemon juice and water.

    Tie the bag and punch 12 holes in the top of the bag with a large two-tine fork. Roast at 350° F. for 45 minutes.

    This method of roasting creates its own gravy and bastes the birds at the same time.

CHUKAR PARTRIDGE

The chukar is one partridge you won't find in a pear tree. The mountain goat of birds, this extraordinary species seeks the steepest, craggiest mountain slopes it can find. And no wonder. Indigenous to the Himalayan foothills, from where it was successfully imported in the 1930's (a few aborted attempts were made prior to that), the chukar is no stranger to the precipitous cliffs, canyons and neighboring arid regions it now enjoys in the Rocky Mountain reaches of the U.S.

Perhaps because of its relatively localized range or the fact that it inhabits remote terrain or perhaps because just not too many gunners are aware of its existence, the chukar is harvested in relatively small numbers. But it is worth the hard work, time and patience involved in hunting it, not only because of the satisfaction of victory you'll experience after the chase, but that its approximately 1½ pounds of flesh affords mighty fine eating.

From a distance, the head of the chukar, with a dark band running through its eyes, resembles the bobwhite. On closer inspection, however, the band is black and runs unbroken from the top of the bill down, around and under the neck. The overall coloration of the bird appears a grayish-brown. Its distinctive features are the bold black-and-white stripes of the flank feathers, which sharply contrast with the red accents of the bill, feet, legs and rings around the eyes. Although the female is slighter in size and weight and has no spurs, she is otherwise identical in appearance. As you can imagine, in flight, chukar are quite an out-of-the-ordinary sight.

The chukar is similar to the bobwhite in other respects: the male has a call which sounds like its own name; as a ground dweller, it prefers the safety of being on foot and will flush only if there is absolutely no alternative; it enjoys the companionship of birds of its own and other game-birds species, and happily and noisily gathers in coveys; it breeds in comparably large numbers; and it is not a migratory bird.

Although their winters are spent at lower altitudes in search of food, chukar seek higher elevations as spring breeding season approaches. Unlike the bobwhite in this respect, the chukar males will battle each other violently to settle territorial claims and to acquire a mate. After an elaborate courtship, in which the males proudly ruffle their feathers, droop their wings and lower their heads, mating takes place. The females lay approximately 15 buffy, well-spotted eggs in a nest that is built near some type of brush the female has hollowed out of the ground and filled with both grasses and breast feathers. Incubation can take up to 25 days, for which the female is solely responsible. She is also in charge of rearing the young.

Almost immediately after they have dried off, the chicks rapidly depart the nest. They feed primarily on insects for protein, but soon turn to the grasses and seeds of various weeds and plants that, as adults, constitute the bulk of their diet. As mature birds, they do maintain some intake of grasshoppers, beetles and the like.

While chukar usually feed in the cool of the evening and prefer shade during the day, they can often be found near a watering hole during the daytime hours when the sun is high. Incidentally, when the water supply is abundant, the coveys tend to be much larger than when water is scarce. Only if extreme drought has hit an area will they travel great distances in search of water; otherwise, they can survive quite well on barren, arid lands.

In addition to drought and the usual menacing animals and large birds of prey, deep snow will destroy the chukar's maximum longevity of seven years the fastest. Here again, we see survival dependent on a species' ability to cope with the elements. While light snowfall does not completely cover their source of food, a storm with deep drifts can force chukar to comb vast areas, often with futile and fatal results.

The gray partridge, another member of the partridge family and imported from Hungary (hence, the nickname the "Hun" or "Hungarian" partridge), is uniquely able to withstand the cold and snow. It is found in North America in almost all the Canadian provinces and the states of the U.S. that border Canada. It is equally good eating as the chukar.

Hunting Tips/chukar partridge

Because of its ability to hide in rocky crevices and difficult-to-get-to terrain, the chukar is a particular challenge to the hunter. So first of all, wear appropriate walking and climbing gear. • If you are not a native to the area you're going to hunt, I definitely recommend that you find someone to guide you through what may be unfamiliar and dangerous territory. • Here is a tip I came across a long time ago which has proven true on my own hunting trips—that chukar "walk up and fly down." That is, as long as there is ground for them to scurry up, they'll stick to it; they'll only flush at the top of a slope when they run out of real estate.

For dressing out techniques, turn to page 183.

Chukar partridge

Cooking/chukar partridge

Chukar Partridge à la Mushroom Sauce
(Serves 4)

2 partridges, halved
½ cup butter
1 10¾-ounce can cream of mushroom soup
2½ tablespoons flour
2 tablespoons bacon bits
2 tablespoons Worcestershire sauce
salt and freshly ground black pepper to taste
4 slices of your favorite bread, toasted and cut diagonally to form toast points

Melt half the butter (4 tablespoons) in a skillet and brown the meat until tender, about 20 minutes. Remove from pan, drain on paper toweling and let cool. Remove meat from the bones and cut into bite-size pieces.

While meat is cooling, in a saucepan place the mushroom soup and flour, stirring until well mixed. Add the remaining butter, bacon bits, Worcestershire sauce, salt and pepper. Heat until thickened, stirring constantly.

Return skillet to stove with meat pieces in it; add mushroom sauce and simmer over low heat until mixture begins to bubble. Stir often.

Serve over toast points.

Quick and Easy Partridge
(Serves 4)

This recipe is great for those who like to save time in the kitchen, and still come up with a delicious meal.

2 partridges, split in half
½ cup butter
1 package dry chicken soup mix or your favorite dry soup mix, such as onion
½ cup water
1 teaspoon celery seeds
1 teaspoon fresh parsley, chopped
½ cup sour cream (optional)
salt and black pepper to taste

Melt butter in a large skillet. Add the four partridge halves and brown for approximately 20 minutes over medium heat.

While they are browning, in a separate bowl mix the soup packet with the water to make a sauce. Add the remaining ingredients and salt and pepper to taste.

Pour the sauce over the birds and reduce heat to low. Cover skillet and stir often with a wooden spoon, basting the meat with the sauce. Let cook for approximately 30 to 45 minutes or until meat is tender (check the thigh meat as it takes the longest to tenderize).

Serve over rice, or noodles cooked according to package directions.

DRESSING OUT QUAIL AND PARTRIDGE

You may be asking yourself, "How many ways can there be to field dress a bird?" As I've said before, there is no one right way, but there are more ways than one. I'll describe these as we go along, and you can choose whatever techniques you feel most comfortable with. As the wildfowl get larger, you'll see that the techniques become more elaborate.

With the previous group of small birds (doves, pigeons), I recommended that you make the Y-shaped incision in the breast area and proceed from there. The principle of eviscerating as soon as possible applies to all techniques and situations, of course. The method explained here using the quail or partridge as examples requires that you place the bird on a flat surface, holding back the wing and leg on the side you are going to make the opening.

Begin by first pinching off the feathers located near the anal opening. You can use a knife and your forefinger, as shown in *Figure 3-6*, and pluck them off in the direction in which they seem to be growing. I prefer to use just my thumb and index finger. Either technique is effective.

With your knife, make a slit from point "A" at the anus to point "B," indicated in *Figure 3-7*. Be careful not to cut into the entrails.

With the incision facing you, reach in with two fingers and remove the innards as shown in *Figure 3-8*. Now you can reach farther into the craw area and take out any foreign matter there. Your bird should then be propped open with sticks and placed in a cool, dry place away from sunlight where it can cool down.

If you want to save only the breast meat, hold the bird at arms' length in one hand, with the bird's feet facing downward and its head under your thumb. The breast should be facing you. Then, as I recommended with the dove, make a slit from the anus upward to the base of the breast and make two small slits to either side of the breast, like the letter Y. By placing your fingers into this incision, you can lift up and pull the breast out with very little effort, feathers and all. You may need to use your knife at the top of the breast to cut it away from the body. (With this technique, it's

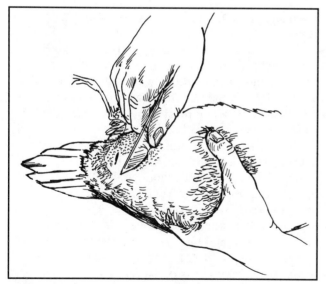

3-6. First, remove the feathers from the anal area with a small, sharp knife and your forefinger. I prefer to use just my thumb and index finger and pluck the feathers off in the direction in which they grow. Either method is effective. If you are going to take the breast only, this is a good time to pluck the entire breast area, or simply skin it, feathers and all.

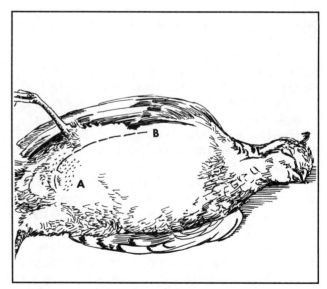

3-7. With the bird on a flat surface, hold back the wing and leg of the bird on the side you are going to make the incision. Take your knife and make a cut from point "A" to point "B." Be careful not to cut too deeply or you will damage the entrails.

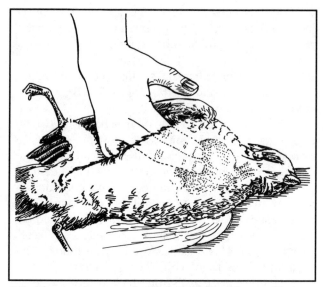

3-8. After you have cut the bird, reach in with your fingers and remove the entrails. You can now move up into the craw and take out any foreign matter in this area. Wipe the bird out with paper towels, a cloth or dried grass. Prop open the cavity with a small stick and allow the bird to cool down by letting air circulate in it. This takes a little extra time, but makes for a better eating bird. Remember to keep the bird in a shady, cool, dry area until you get back to camp or home. Do not place it in a plastic bag—it generates too much heat which would only spoil the meat.

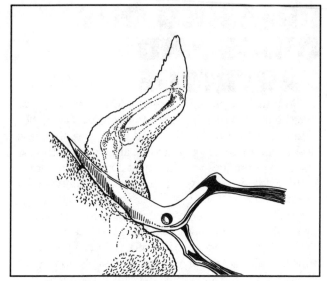

3-9. Unlike a chicken, a quail or partridge has very little meat worth saving on the wings. So before you begin plucking the bird, take your shears and clip off the wings where they join the body. You may also shear off the feet at the knee joints at this time. (If you have elected to snap or twist off the wings in your initial field dressing, you of course need not do the above at plucking time.)

probably a good idea to remove the wings first by twisting or snapping them off.)

What you can also do—and I've seen a few hunters do this—to remove the breast section, they simplify the whole procedure into three swift steps. First, with the aid of a small, sharp knife, they make an incision at the anal area and in virtually one motion skin the breast, keeping the feathers on. They then pull out the breast with their fingers, and, finally, cut it away at the sternum. Done.

If you're saving the whole bird, you'll want to deplume it once you get back to camp or home. You can begin by pulling off the tail feathers. Clip off the wings close to the body, using your game shears rather than your knife; it's much easier this way (*See Figure 3-9*). Then continue plucking by pinching the feathers between your thumb and index finger and pulling the feathers at the same angle in which they lie. Remember

it requires less effort to pluck a bird when it is still warm.

The final step in preparing the bird for eating is to clean the bird thoroughly. Remove any pellets, if possible, and clean thoroughly around any wounds in your bird. Wash the bird inside and out with cold, salted water. It is then ready for you to try some of the recipes included in this book.

If you are going to freeze the bird, wrap it for freezing. Place it in a plastic bag as the primary wrapper; then wrap in aluminum foil, followed by a heavy-duty plastic freezer bag. Make sure you squeeze the bags before sealing to ensure that all the air is expelled. Label your freezer packet with the species of bird, the weight and the date. It can then be kept frozen at O° F. (−18° C.) up to six months without worry of spoilage or loss of flavor.

RING-NECKED PHEASANT

Of the gallinaceous game birds, the ring-necked pheasant is the most popular to hunt. Its exotic plumage, in my opinion, certainly creates an allure hunters find irresistible. Moreover, a mature rooster, for example, can be one of the wiliest, challenging creatures imaginable. And, of course, the white meat of a pheasant, when properly prepared, makes tantalizing table fare.

The ringneck is also a relative newcomer to North America. Although George Washington reportedly kept pheasants at Mount Vernon in the mid-1700's, this game bird was successfully imported only a century ago from both the Orient and the British Isles. The pheasant's recorded history dates at least as far back as pre-Christian times, about 250 B.C., when it was described in ancient Greek and Roman writings. During the Middle Ages, the bird slowly and gradually made its course through Europe perhaps the same way it arrived here—via interested parties who found it a fascinating phenomenon.

Today in North America, this hardy, adaptable bird flourishes in many regions, particularly in Washington, Oregon, the plains states, the Midwest, the East Coast, sections of New England and Canada. While it cannot survive in mountainous woodlands or forests, the pheasant thrives in a habitat of pastures and brushy edges.

Although there may be 15 million or so pheasant hunters, the annual harvest is a rather misleading figure. The overall take is actually influenced more by the number of pheasants that hatch and survive rather than the total number of hunters. In 1976, for example, a good harvest year, the yield was close to 14 million, while the following year, it dropped by about half. The

Ring-necked pheasant

amount of food, cover and the weather conditions are the pivotal factors. The pheasant will keep dropping in population unless more wildlife management areas are set aside, and proper food and cover are left for the birds to live and reproduce.

The rooster, a bird of striking appearance, weighs about 5 pounds and measures up to 36 inches in length, two-thirds of which is tail feathers. Its head, neck and ear tufts are a dark metallic green with crimson cheek patches around the eyes that grow more brilliant during the mating season, and a yellow-white bill. Ringed in white, the neck, from which the bird's name is derived, separates the Christmas-like colors of the head from the light and dark shades of brown on the back wing feathers. The breast and belly plume is dark red-brown, almost brick-colored, with spots of black. The base of the back and tail are aqua-tinted, while its exceptionally long tail feathers are tan barred in black. Quite a rainbow, wouldn't you say?

Not surprisingly, the 2½- to 3-pound hen is colored much more modestly than her male counterpart, in a blend of light and dark brown markings. She bears a considerably shorter tail and her overall length reaches about 25 inches. (How could she possibly compete?)

While both the male and female can make a chicken-like clucking sound, it is the primary call of the female. When flushed, however, this clucking is also voiced by the male.

In the spring the male develops a high call similar to the common crow. The ringneck's overall coloration becomes brighter and, like many other animals, it will fight for its opportunity to mate. Each cock tries through combat to acquire a harem of four to seven hens. The battle, a violent exchange among the males, will continue until one of the opponents is killed or gives up and flees. Although the female pays little attention to this wildfowl warfare, she will never attach herself to the loser of a fight, should he live.

After breeding, the hen selects a nesting area on the ground in a hay, grain or heavily weeded field. From the weeds and grasses she finds there, she then shapes a nest with her body. Drably shaded to provide camouflage from such predators as crows and snakes, the eggs she lays are produced at a rate of one each for 10 to 12 days. Incubation, which commences after the entire clutch is laid, requires 23 days. This she tends to alone, assisted only by her own drab coloration for protection.

The chicks are on their feet within an hour of being hatched and, although they seem extremely adept, they must be safeguarded against the elements by the mother for the first few days after birth. The fledglings attempt to fly by the end of one week and are fairly capable of flight by the time they are two to three weeks old. True to their nature, the new brood pecks and scratches—primarily for insects, the protein of which their young bodies need for proper growth— and they will use their beaks to pick up just about any object that rouses their curiosity.

A physical characteristic that distinguishes a young pheasant from an older one is the spurs. While these small back-of-leg projections on the young pheasant are dull in color and blunt, those of the older pheasant are extremely dark, shiny and sharp as a finely honed blade. Additionally, in contrast to the grouse, for example, the legs of the pheasant are not fully feathered.

Although they do ingest some animal matter, the primary diet of mature pheasants consists of corn, soybeans, milo, wheat, oats and buckwheat. This is why the birds are frequently found near farm land, much to the distress of farmers whose fields are invaded by hunters during open season. And since corn is a particular favorite, the pheasant population thrives especially well in the midwestern cornbelt. If their preferred foods are not available, the ringnecks will make a meal of berries and fruits. The animal portion of their diet includes earthworms, snails, ants, grasshoppers, crickets and beetles.

Despite the fact that the pheasant is not a migrant, it may change residences with the seasons when snow, ice and cold deprive it of protective cover. At this time it will seek temporary shelter in marshes and swamps, where food is more readily available and the tall grasses furnish warmth.

If the pheasant can survive the harsh winters, the hunters and the many small animals and larger birds that prey on it, it could potentially live about eight to ten years. On the average, however, its life span reaches half of that.

Hunting Tips/ring-necked pheasant

Because the ringneck feeds mainly on grains and seeds, as a hunter look for this game bird near cultivated farm lands. I had an interesting experience one time when I hunted in the northwest section of Kansas, which is rich in cornfields and pheasants. There were five other hunters and myself, and we had only one young dog, which belonged to my old pal Perkins. We got into the cornfields at about dawn and Perkins' inexperienced dog began barking at everything. Perkins kept yelling at the dog, so I decided to move away from the group and hunt in an adjacent field against the wind.

The sun hadn't come out that day and it was cold and hazy. All of a sudden about a hundred yards straight in front of me was a large coyote. He was stalking and moving extremely slowly along the same cornfield line that I was walking. I'm sure he was hoping for a bird just as much as I. I've seen and killed many coyote at my ranch in Colorado and other places, but I never saw one that was challenging me for hunting rights. This one was not excited—he just kept staring at me; he didn't move or try to run. He looked normal, that is, no signs of being ill; he wasn't sluggish, frothing or dripping saliva from his mouth.

I wondered what to do. At first I thought it must be someone's pet coyote. Then I thought about shooting him, but I soon forgot that. I couldn't kill him at this range with No. 6 shot; it would only wound him and cause any birds that might be in the area to scatter quickly.

Well, the answer came soon enough for both of us. Before he had a chance to make up his mind or move, two cock pheasants and a hen broke straight up ahead of us and flew toward the coyote. I was carrying a Browning over-and-under 12 gauge and I immediately swung through as the birds hit their peak. Down came both cocks.

In all the excitement, I had forgotten about the coyote. I spotted and mentally marked the site where the birds fell and began to move through the low cornfields. Just as I picked up the first bird, which was a large one, I saw a movement through the field in the direction of the other downed bird. You guessed it. The coyote had the bird in its mouth and was making tracks away from me—right down the center of the cornfield with *my* bird. I stood there for a moment and said to myself, "I don't believe what I'm seeing!" In all my years of hunting, I've never seen that before, nor have I heard of it.

The story doesn't end here, though. At the edge of the cornfield next to me where my fellow companions were, Perkins' dog abruptly stopped barking. Suddenly, about 30 birds went up in every direction, which resulted in a round of gunfire that sounded like WW II. And running in a big circle was the coyote, still holding my pheasant in his mouth. No doubt he was scared to death. I think what had happened was that between my buddies' movements, my shots and the coyote's stalking, along with the dog's constant barking, we had unknowingly driven the birds into one area. All the commotion must have been too much for them, because they all broke at once.

I had bagged a fine pheasant, my friends had gotten five nice birds and the coyote had made out like a bandit. Like I said, try the cornfields.

- If you are accustomed to shooting birds on the wing, don't be surprised to learn that the pheasant prefers to, and will more often than not, stay on the ground. To avoid danger, it would rather run away—not fly, for in flight perhaps it senses it is an easier target. On occasion, I've seen pheasants meander across country roads in Connecticut totally oblivious to any threat, including the automobiles that barely miss running them over. Not so during hunting season, though, when they turn into the cleverest, craftiest escape artists, capable of outsmarting even the most experienced hunting dogs. The ringneck will often circle a hunter, always making sure it is behind him; better yet, it can camouflage itself, brilliant coloration and all, head down in a protective spot, literally undetected and free from the dangers at hand. Perhaps you could call that his 'possum plan, and it works.

- Although a ground runner, the pheasant is capable of remarkably rapid bursts of flight of from 40 to 50 miles per hour. Once airborne, the bird can glide for a half-mile or so and, if necessary, will flap its wings, gathering speed or gaining altitude, only to glide again. If you should encounter this, the best time to take your shot is just at the point when the initial climb has been topped out because, for a fleeting second, the pheasant almost becomes a still target. Aim for the ring on the neck, as this will likely cause the bird to drop immediately.

- I'd advise you not to hunt pheasant in rainy weather. If you think they're tough to flush under ordinary circumstances, it's virtually impossible when it's raining and they are sheltered under brush.

Dressing Out/ring-necked pheasant

To keep your pheasant (or any other bird or animal you've bagged) in the best possible condition for when you're ready to make a meal of it, you should always dress out the bird while you are still in the field.

The process begins by making a cut from the anus of the bird about one-quarter of the way up the belly; then reach in and remove the entrails with your hand *(See Figure 3-10)*. If the weather is about 45 degrees F. (7° C.), or above, it is a good idea to remove the crop or craw to avoid spoilage. You can do this by making a small (maybe one-inch) cut at the top of the breastbone in the direction of the neck. Reach in with your fingers and with one hand firmly gripping the craw, cut it away with your other hand. The giblets

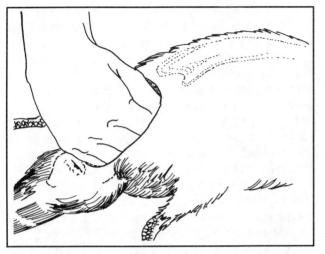

3-10. To field dress your pheasant, make an incision from the vent about a quarter of the way up the belly. Reach in with your hand and remove the entrails. If the weather is above 45° F. (7°C.), it is a good idea to remove the craw. To do this, simply make a cut at the top of the breastbone up toward the neck. Reach in and firmly grip the craw with one hand as you sever it with the other. Use dried grass or a cloth to clean out the cavity while in the field.

should be reserved and the remainder of the innards discarded.

Upon returning to camp or home, you should prepare the bird for cooking. Begin by placing it on its side; grip the legs tightly with one hand and with the other pluck the feathers from the breast in the direction in which they seem to be growing *(See Figure 3-11)*. Try to pluck in firm, gentle tugs to avoid ripping the skin. After the bird is completely deplumed, cut away the flight feathers from the edge of the wings *(See Figure 3-12)*. The remaining pin feathers can be removed with tweezers. Any other difficult-to-remove feathers or hairs may be singed off with a candle, a gas flame or a cigarette lighter. Just remember, if you have to singe the feathers, do so in a well-ventilated (preferably outdoors) area, because burning feathers give off a particularly strong odor.

With the breast down, remove the head; you can pull it off or chop it off with a cleaver. Slit the skin encasing the neck *(See Figure 3-13)*. Pull the skin away from the neck and cut the neck off as close as possible to its base, reserving it for preparation of stock or gravy. Insert your fingers into the neck cavity and

3-11. Some outdoorsmen wet-dip pheasants like waterfowl, but most pheasants are dry-plucked. To dry-pluck, lay the bird on its back and begin to pull the feathers from the breast in the direction in which they grow. Pull firmly, but do not pull hard enough to tear the skin. Have newspaper or something under the bird to catch the feathers that fall.

remove any foreign matter that may have remained there and in the rib cage. Cut through the legs just under the joints and twist off the feet.

With pheasant and other larger game birds, some people remove the uropygial gland, commonly known as the preen, or oil, gland. This gland is the double button-like protuberance located at the base of the tail; it varies in size, depending on the size of the bird *(See Figure 3-14)*. Not all birds have this gland however; pigeons, for example, do not. While preening itself, a bird will poke at the gland with its bill, releasing an oil that aids in waterproofing the feathers. If you are going to remove it—not all people do—it is important to cut around it carefully and not let the oil touch the knife, the surrounding meat or your hands. If this happens, wash the affected parts before continuing. The reason that many people don't remove it is that you rarely cut into or eat that section of the bird. However, be forewarned that if punctured, the oil that the gland secretes has a very pungent odor and taste.

Finally, carefully examine your bird for shot and cut any meat that may be spoiled. Then wash the bird inside and out with cold, salted water. Your pheasant is now ready to be roasted whole or cut up for other recipes. If you're going to freeze it, follow the instructions for freezing quail and partridge, page 00.

Disjointing the Bird. If you want to proceed immediately to the stove, here are some tips for cutting up the bird for, let's say, a pheasant casserole. With the breast side up, insert a very sharp knife (a regular boning knife is good) at the point where the thigh connects with the body of the bird, between the ball and the socket joint *(See Figure 3-15)*. Then slice off the entire leg; repeat on the other side. Take a heavy-bladed knife and make a cut along either side of the backbone *(See Figure 3-16)*. This will free it from the rest of the carcass; use it for stock or merely discard it (I throw very little away—however light, the stock made from the back and feet is delicious).

Turn the bird over and again with your boning knife, gently cut away the fine meat on either side of the breastbone *(See Figure 3-17)*. Add the breastbone to the stock you're going to make or discard that. Finally, cut each side of the breast sections in half, one of which will contain a wing *(See Figure 3-18)*. You should now have two legs, two thighs, two wings and two breasts for making your casserole. Should you have a particularly large bird, you could also separate the wings from the anterior breast section as you did with the thighs. This would give you two additional pieces, although pheasant wings are not known for their abundance of meat. In any event, good eating.

3-12. Remove the flight feathers from the edge of the wings by cutting them off with game shears. With tweezers remove the remaining pin feathers. You can singe off any really difficult-to-remove hairs with a candle, a gas flame or even a cigarette lighter. Preferably outdoors hold the bird in one hand extended at arm's length and face downwind, so you will not be burned.

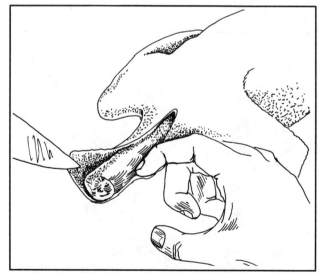

3-13. Sever the head from the neck and slit open the skin encasing the neck. Pull the skin away and as close as you can to the base of the neck cut the neck off; save for making gravy or adding to the stockpot. With your fingers, extract any foreign matter in that area you may have missed before.

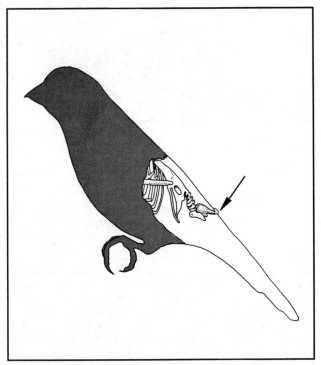

3-14. The preen, or oil, gland, located at the base of the tail, should be removed after the bird has been plucked.

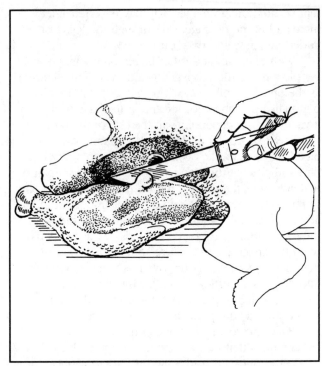

3-15. To cut the pheasant into pieces, first remove the thighs. With the bird on its back, insert a sharp knife where the thigh connects to the body. Place the blade between the ball and the socket joint and cut straight through.

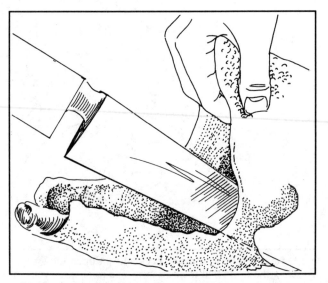

3-16. Take a heavy-bladed knife and make a cut along each side of the backbone. Remove the backbone and save it for soup, or discard it.

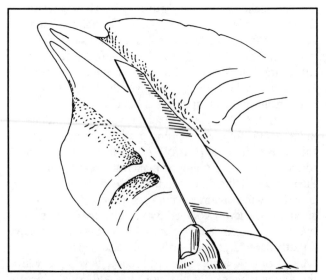

3-17. To remove the breastbone, take a boning knife and gently cut away the meat on either side of this large bone. Cut straight down and slice it out; it should remove easily.

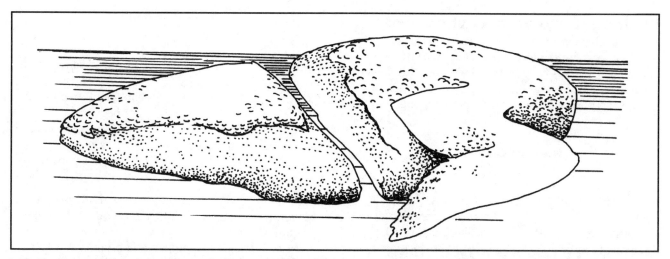

3-18. Finally, cut each breast section in half, one of which will contain a wing. When finished, you should have two legs, two thighs, two breasts and two wings; also, a neck, back and a breastbone for stock.

MOUNTING YOUR BIRD

You've done it. You've bagged the ringneck of a lifetime. It was an exhilarating chase, a difficult shot and now you're plumb proud of your accomplishment.

You throw it in your game bag, pack up your gear and hop in your Scout for the drive back. Wait till they hear about this back home. Yes, maybe you'll even have it mounted. You've got to save this one—and show it off.

Unfortunately, contemplating mounting the pheasant *after* you've shot it may be too late. You may have damaged some feathers, ruined it with blood or have blown out a section with too large shot.

My advice is to think about taxidermy *before* the hunting season draws near. And while home taxidermy may be challenging and rewarding, it requires study, patience and considerable skill. So seek a professional— one who is experienced, reputable and reliable. And don't wait until the last minute. Take some time to look at his work before going on your hunt. Check on his charges and how he wants the animal brought to him. After hunting season, you can usually not make satisfactory arrangements because all good taxidermists are extremely busy.

Most taxidermists will tell you, however, that the chief thing to remember with game is to keep it as clean and in as perfect condition as possible. To do that, keep these points in mind:

1. Birds should be taken with the smallest shot possible, so any holes can be camouflaged with feathers during the mounting process.

2. Do not field dress the bird; you do not want any large incisions or breaks in skin that can't be properly repaired by the taxidermist.

3. Wipe the mouth clean with cotton and place cotton in it so that blood will not run out and ruin feathers or skin. Try to do some preliminary clean-up of other affected parts by dabbing with cotton also.

4. Do not allow the bird to become bent or out of shape in any way, as this could lead to a more difficult job for the taxidermist, and you wouldn't have as nice a finished product.

5. Wrap each bird individually in newspaper, smoothing the feathers and generally keeping the bird as undisturbed as possible. Do not use plastic bags because the heat that generates within them results in rapid deterioration of the bird.

6. If you have an ice chest, place the bird in there to transport it; then transfer it to the freezer if you can't get it to the taxidermist immediately. If you don't have a cooler with you, make sure to keep the bird in the shadiest, coolest place possible and make tracks getting home.

If you would like to try your own hand at taxidermy, there are many books devoted to it in which you will find much good instruction. You will also discover a whole new world in the art of taxidermy if you decide to go into it. Not only will it bring financial rewards, but personal satisfaction as well. Some hunters say that taxidermy is the "final dimension" to hunting.

Cooking/ring-necked pheasant

Most chefs recommend stove-top stewing for pheasant, because the lean white breast meat tends to dry out. However, I have come up with my own recipe variations that add roasting and frying to the cooking process, and I'm sure you'll find them tempting.

Pheasant Casserole
(Serves 2)

1 pheasant, cut up	1½ cups heavy cream
flour	2 tablespoons minced
salt, black pepper and	fresh tarragon or 1½
paprika to taste	teaspoons dried
5 tablespoons butter	tarragon
3 tablespoons oil	¼ cup brandy

Dredge pheasant in flour that has been seasoned with salt, pepper and paprika. In a 5-quart flameproof casserole, brown the meat well in butter and oil, turning several times to ensure even browning. Transfer meat to a platter and keep warm.

Remove all but 2 tablespoons of oil from the casserole. Add cream and bring to a simmer, stirring well. Add tarragon and brandy, and stir. Add pheasant, cover, and bake at 325° F. for 1¼ hours or until fork-tender. Serve with noodles.

Braised Pheasant with Sauerkraut
(Serves 3 or 4)

2 pounds sauerkraut, preferably fresh	1 or 2 pheasants, cleaned and singed
2 cups chicken broth	1 teaspoon salt
8 juniper berries, crushed	1 teaspoon freshly ground
4 tablespoons butter	black pepper
3 tablespoons peanut oil	parsley sprigs (garnish)

Wash sauerkraut; combine with chicken broth and juniper berries in a Dutch oven. Simmer, covered, 1 hour on top of stove.

Heat butter and oil in heavy skillet and brown the pheasant on all sides over medium-high heat. When golden brown, sprinkle with salt and pepper and place in Dutch oven on top of sauerkraut.

Cover and roast in 375° F. oven for 45 minutes, or until the birds are tender. Arrange on a platter with sauerkraut and serve with buttered new potatoes. Garnish with parsley sprigs.

Roast Pheasant I
(Serves 4)

2 pheasants	1 10½-ounce can chicken gravy
salt and black pepper to taste	½ cup green onion, chopped
flour	1 cup fresh mushrooms, sliced
½ cup white wine	3 tablespoons parsley, finely chopped
1 10¾-ounce can chicken broth	

Cut pheasant into quarters and wipe with a damp cloth; dry thoroughly. Mix salt, pepper and flour and dredge birds in mixture.

Place birds in roasting pan and broil until golden, turning once. Add wine, chicken broth and gravy to pan. Roast, covered, for 40 to 45 minutes at 300° F., basting frequently.

Remove birds from pan, place on a serving platter and keep warm. Add onion and mushrooms to drippings in roasting pan and simmer on top of stove until tender. Pour drippings and vegetables over pheasant, sprinkle with parsley and serve.

Roast Pheasant II
(Serves 4)

2 pheasants	½ cup cooking sherry
salt and black pepper to taste	1 10½-ounce can beef gravy
seasoned salt	4 large green onions, finely chopped
flour	3 teaspoons parsley, finely chopped
2 to 4 tablespoons peanut oil	1 10½-ounce can mushrooms
1 10½-ounce can consommé, or more	parsley sprigs (garnish)

Halve pheasants lengthwise, clean with a damp cloth and dry thoroughly. Sprinkle with salt, pepper and seasoned salt and dredge in flour. Heat oil in Dutch oven, add pheasant and brown on top of stove until golden brown.

Add consommé, sherry and beef gravy to Dutch oven. Cover and cook in oven at 300° F. until tender, approximately 40 to 45 minutes. Baste frequently.

Remove birds from pan and add green onion and parsley to the drippings. Simmer on top of stove until onion is tender, then add mushrooms and additional consommé, if more gravy is needed. Serve pheasant garnished with parsley sprigs.

Fried Pheasant
(Serves 2)

1 young pheasant	a.f.g. thyme
½ cup plus 3 tablespoons flour	2 tablespoons butter
	2 tablespoons peanut oil
salt and freshly ground black pepper to taste	½ cup white wine
	1½ cups light cream

Cut pheasant into serving pieces. Combine ½ cup flour, salt, pepper and thyme in heavy brown paper bag. Add meat and shake until well coated.

Heat butter and oil in a heavy skillet over high heat and brown pheasant until golden. Reduce heat to low and add wine. Cover and simmer until tender, then uncover and cook until done. (Remove white meat pieces as soon as they are tender; let dark meat cook slightly longer.) Transfer meat to platter and keep warm.

Remove all but 3 tablespoons of fat from the pan juices and add 3 tablespoons flour, blending well. Cook, stirring constantly, scraping up any browned bits clinging to bottom of pan. Add cream and cook over high heat until the mixture thickens, still stirring constantly. Strain into gravy boat, correct seasoning and serve over pheasant.

GROUSE

Grouse, the next group of ground-dwelling game birds, come in a remarkable assortment of shades and colors, ranging from gray to black to beige to brown. They are members of the large *Tetraonidae* family, which includes the various ptarmigan and the prairie chicken. And what they all have in common, unlike their gallinaceous relatives, is fully feathered legs. Ptarmigan even have feathered toes.

Grouse in general have a wild, ragged sort of look—much more primitive than the other game birds. In fact, if you can get a glimpse of a sage grouse, for example, strutting "in rut," it bears an uncanny resemblance to a lizard, perhaps its evolutionary ancestor.

Grouse range the mid- to upper altitudes of North America. The dusky blue and sooty grouse inhabit the deciduous woodlands of the Rockies from northern Canada clear down to southern California; the spruce grouse combs the forests of Canada from Atlantic to Pacific and dips into the states along the Canadian border, especially the upper New England states; the sharp-tailed grouse prefers brushlands, which limits its range to parts of Alaska south into the non-coastal provinces of Canada and the northern midwestern states of the U.S.; the sage grouse of course can be found only in the western Canadian provinces and the states of the U.S. where sagebrush grows in abundance; and the ruffed grouse, which enjoys the greatest numbers, covers the North American continent from coast to coast, primarily the northern reaches along woodland edges. It is to this last species—the "king of the game birds"—that we will turn our attention.

The average ruffed grouse measures close to 20 inches in length and weighs from 1½ to 2 pounds. In terms of coloration, the grouse is basically a muted blend of browns and grays with black and white accents. However, depending on the locale and the camouflage necessary, some appear more gray or beige, while others wear a darker brown or black plumage. The male and female do not differ in appearance much, although the female is somewhat smaller. Both bear a rather long tail—about a quarter of their total length—and the only difference is that the male's tail is edged with a wide unbroken black band, while the female's band is interrupted midway by several brown feathers. In winter, both also sprout comb-like growths on their toes which help them adapt to walking on the snow.

One of the most distinctive characteristics of the male grouse is his "drumming" during the mating season. The sound is created by the bird's wings beating back and forth and upward as he sits on a favorite log, rock and stump. Not an action he does automatically, rather one that must be learned by trial and error, this drumming is a perpetual sound that can be heard throughout the entire year, during both daytime and evening hours. It is not nearly as loud nor as continuous as during the mating season, however, when it signals the stirring of procreative juices.

During this season, the ruff circling the neck, from which the bird's name is derived, is proudly puffed out as the male struts, spreads its tail and suspends its wings, all part of his attempt to attract the female. Should his territory be trespassed by another male, a bloody struggle will occur, with the loser abandoning the region. While the male is going through all these contortions, the female remains unimpressed by the display and only when the male decides that she probably really isn't worth the effort does she become interested in him.

The female habitually positions a loosely constructed nest close to a tree trunk, a stump or a bush, near a clear patch of land or roadside. Usually, it will be a mere depression filled with whatever material is at hand. She then lays one egg per day until approximately 10 to 12 light brown eggs have been deposited in the nest. The average incubation time is roughly three weeks, for which she is totally responsible. If for any reason the nest and eggs have been destroyed, she will renest, producing a smaller clutch. Controversy reigns over whether the leaves that cover the hen while she is nesting fall on her by accident or are purposely placed by her to camouflage the nest and eggs from such predators as racoons, opposums and the like. In any event, it is a trick that seems to provide some protection during the breeding season.

Another measure the entire family takes to protect themselves from ground-roving grouse lovers is that once the young can fly, they roost in trees rather than on the ground. This habit is contrary to that of all other gallinaceous birds, except the turkey. And, unfortunately, it does not save the grouse from their chief winged enemy, the great horned owl.

Probing grouse demographics reveals some interesting facts. Although the average life expectancy is between three and four years, the general population is kept down by several factors. As many as 70 percent of the brood never hatch and of those that do, 50 to 60 percent will fall prey to accidents and predators. Many times only one or two chicks will be raised out of a hatched brood. In addition, as many as 75 percent of the young grouse become fatalities before the autumn months.

Ruffed grouse

Sharp-tailed grouse

Now in the fall, many young grouse die as a result of a very strange phenomenon. They will fly from their regular territory in an almost crazed fashion, traveling anywhere from two to nine miles out of their normal range and flying directly into window panes, fences and other objects that get in the way of their frenzied flight path. Many a hunter has returned home from a fruitless expedition only to discover an injured or dead ruff under his dining room window.

Another strange event takes place in mountainous areas and the northernmost regions. Every 10 years, there is a slow buildup in the grouse population, reaching a peak every third or fourth year of the decade, followed by a decline. As of yet, there is no proven explanation for this trend. And hunting, incidentally, in no way influences these population fluctuations.

Why do grouse hold such fascination for the hunter?

All the game birds provide some sort of challenge to seasonal gunners, but the grouse is the master of evasion, the mogul of escape—in short, he's not the "king of game birds" for nothing. On the ground or in the air, he will flee—silently, gracefully, and completely. If he is on the ground when danger strikes, he will try to walk away, picking a circuitous route under brush and bramble. After all, as a ground dweller he does prefer the cover of familiar terrain. If he happens to be roosting in a tree, he will jump down and fly low and silently at a speed of between 25 and 35 miles per hour. If he is flushed, he will create a frightening racket that could startle even the most seasoned hunter. And although he is not a long-distance flyer, he can attain a rate of 50 miles per hour, which can give him plenty of a head start. He is an impossible target at best, because in flight he is able to dart erratically, putting all sorts of obstacles in his wake. Easy hunting? Hardly.

Hunting Tips/grouse

Hunting with a good, experienced dog is a must. • Grouse prefer areas where they can obtain the buds and fruits they like so well; aspen buds, in particular, are one of their favorites. They inhabit areas populated by young trees and saplings and open fields, so the best place to hunt grouse is in areas where the brush is dense and their favorite foods are readily available. • Be aware that grouse and whitetail deer coexist in the same habitat and compete for the same food. • Grouse can usually be found in a given area in a ratio of one grouse to every four acres of land. • Although primarily a solitary bird, grouse will congregate for protection in groups of two to eight

during the colder months. So if you're hunting in the winter with the snow crunching under your boots, who knows, maybe you'll get lucky.

The grouse is a delicious eating bird and well worth the rigors of hunting its habitat. It is somewhat larger than the quail and therefore tends to go farther. In the section on cooking, I have given you several different recipes, one of which is a scrumptious combination of game birds that is truly fit for a king.

Field dressing techniques begin on page 204.

Cooking/grouse

15th Century King's Platter
(Serves 8)

Use any combination of grouse, partridge, ptarmigan, or large quail:

4 upland birds, halved	¼ teaspoon crushed
5 pounds rock salt	thyme
½ cup butter, melted	4 strips bacon, cut in half
freshly ground black	parsley
pepper	apple or pear sections
salt (optional)	½ cup brandy

Fill the bottom of a pan so that it is well covered with about 2 inches of rock salt (the same kind you use to melt ice with). Pepper and brush each bird with the melted butter. Place each piece breast-side up on the rock salt. Sprinkle thyme over each half and salt, if desired. Arrange bacon strips over the breasts. Preheat oven to 475° F. Pour the remaining rock salt over the birds and mound over the top. Sprinkle a little warm water over all with your hands and pat the rock salt into place.

Place pan in oven, reduce heat to 400° F. and bake for about 35 minutes. When you remove pan from the oven, the rock salt should be hard and darkened on the top and sides. If the top is not dark, place pan back in oven and increase heat to 475° F. for about 5 to 8 minutes more.

Remove from oven and place on a wooden board or other safe place. Take a screwdriver or hammer and chisel, and hit the block until the rock salt breaks into pieces. Remove the birds and brush off any rock salt that may remain. You will find that the birds have not shrunk and the juices have been sealed in. Nor does the rock salt leave any taste.

Place the cooked birds on a platter surrounded by parsley and fruit sections, such as pears or apples. Take ½ cup of brandy and pour over the birds, light a match and torch the birds. Carry the flaming platter to your table and you'll have a meal fit for a king!

Grouse Stuffed with Wild Rice
(Serves 2)

2 grouse
1½ cups wild rice, uncooked
1 quart water
¼ cup onion, chopped
½ cup pine nuts
4 slices cooked bacon, diced
½ cup mushrooms, chopped
4 tablespoons butter, melted

Cook rice in water 45 minutes to 1 hour, until all water is absorbed. Add remaining ingredients, except butter, to rice.

Loosely stuff grouse with wild rice dressing. Place on a rack in roasting pan, breast side up. Roast in 325° F. oven for approximately 2 hours or until tender and the legs separate from the body. Baste every 20 to 25 minutes with melted butter.

Baked Grouse
(Serves 1)

4 tablespoons butter, melted
¼ cup red Burgundy wine
¼ teaspoon ground sage
1 grouse, cut in half lengthwise
salt and freshly ground black pepper to taste

Combine butter, Burgundy and sage. Drizzle mixture over grouse, then rub in. Sprinkle with salt and freshly ground pepper. Wrap each half in aluminum foil and bake at 375° F. for 30 minutes. (Grouse may also be cooked over the coals of your campfire, in which case the foil-wrapped grouse should be turned every 5 minutes.)

PTARMIGAN AND PRAIRIE CHICKEN

Ptarmigan, in general terms, are northern grouse. There's the willow, the rock and the white-tailed ptarmigan, all of which enjoy the higher altitutdes and colder temperatures of North America. And despite their differences, which are few, all three have one trait in common that distinguishes them from most of the avian world: feathered legs and toes. It is no coincidence that their genus, *Lagopus,* originally derived from the Greek word *lagopous,* means hare-footed. And like the hare, their covered lower limbs enable the ptarmigan to walk on and virtually burrow in the snows of winter.

The willow ptarmigan is the largest of the trio—15 to 17 inches in length and approximately 1¼ pounds in weight. Its range is the widest, covering all of Alaska, Canada and the northern U.S. border states. It can be found at the lowest altitudes.

The rock ptarmigan is next in line, measuring about 15 inches and weighing a little more than a pound. Its range reaches across all of northern Canada, into Alaska and Greenland, and encompasses the higher altitudes where open rocky terrain prevails.

The white-tailed ptarmigan is of course the smallest, with a length of only 12 inches and weight of barely a pound. This little bird is a real cliff-hanger, most often seen at the highest levels above 5,000 feet, in the mountainous regions of Alaska, the Yukon, British Columbia and Alberta and the northwestern states of the U.S.

In appearance and coloration, these three ptarmigan look remarkably alike. With the advent of winter, their plumage turns snowy white to blend in with their hoary habitat. In fact, the feathers become so thick the birds look almost like a cross between an overstuffed pigeon and a malamute. Both the willow and rock males have black bills and tails that remain dark throughout the year, and red comb-like flesh above each eye. It is perhaps only the black stripe that runs through the eye of the rock ptarmigan that distinguishes it from its sibling species, the willow. The whitetail's tail of course is white and stays so, while the beak is black; its eye comb is orange.

The warmer months bring noticeable variations among the ptarmigan—as noticeable as they get: the willow male keeps his generally white look, although the head, breast and upper wings turn a russet color; the upper parts of the female appear more a brown and white mix. The rock ptarmigan male also retains his predominantly white appearance and even more so than the willow, especially in the breast area; the female looks identical to the willow hen. The whitetail male appears the most mottled of all, in shades of grays and browns, with the female appearing almost exactly as her partner.

As far as their breeding habits go, more is known about the willow ptarmigan because it is the most accessible of the three species. We can only assume that the other two relatively follow suit.

During mating season, the sounds of the males (which from the willow's beak sound surprisingly and unfittingly like the croaking of a toad or bullfrog) can be heard as they select their limited territory. The breeding male, whose comb has now become much more prominent, will strut and leap into the air, gracefully spiraling back to earth, certainly to attract a female's attention. While no actual to-the-death fighting takes place, the males will sometimes bump each other's breasts. When a hen is ready, she will eventually emerge from cover and mating takes place, consummating a monogamous relationship.

The female exercises great care in building a nest, which is perfectly symmetrical in shape and constructed of grasses and leaves. She will lay between eight and 13 eggs at the rate of one per day, which require anywhere from 22 to 25 days of incubation. Although the hen is entirely responsible for incubation, her mate is quite attentive and remains close by should any danger or predators approach; he will become extremely aggressive in guarding the nest. The young are as precocial as any, leaving the nest shortly after having been hatched and beginning to feed immediately on insects in the vicinity. They will later switch to a vegetarian diet consisting of leaves, berries, young twigs, buds and an occasional insect, which constitutes the adult diet, and which they often have to scratch through the snow to find.

The birds will stay together as a family unit, each family in its own territory, until the young are raised and the colder weather begins to set in. At this time, they will gather together in larger groups. Although ptarmigan are not migratory birds, they will travel short distances and change territory depending on the weather conditions and available food supply.

The average ptarmigan can live to an age of three or four years, but is vulnerable to such animals as the fox, wolverine, hawks, owls, gulls, and many other birds that inhabit their territory. Not to mention humans, who find their flesh extremely good eating. Incidentally, in the fall and summer months, when ptarmigan are consuming tender vegetation, they are

Rock ptarmigan

Prairie Chickens

excellent. However, when they are ingesting older growth during the winter months, they can taste acrid.

Hunting Tips/ptarmigan

The rock and white-tailed ptarmigan are not greatly hunted due to their inaccessibility. However, if you choose to go after any of the ptarmigan, be prepared for plenty of rugged country. Wear sturdy footgear and dress appropriately for high altitudes and wind; also, carry two knives as I suggested in Section 1 because you never know when they'll come in handy.

• Ptarmigan are curious birds, often more curious than they are afraid. Therefore, don't hunt with pointing dogs; they'll only become frustrated pointing at birds that will often amble around in the open. A retriever might be a help, though. • Ptarmigan are so well camouflaged in the winter and can sit so completely still that you can easily walk right past one and never see it. For this reason, they are very difficult to flush. • As other ground dwellers, ptarmigan prefer to stay close to the ground, and only if danger is imminent will they resort to flight. This is another reason they are a particular challenge to the hunter.

Prairie Chicken

Few people have seen a prairie chicken in the wilds—and for good reason. Until recently, this prairie grouse was a dying species, primarily because of the expanding farm lands that upset the plains ecology and eliminated the bird's natural varied diet. Even now, its population is small, relatively speaking, with only about 80 thousand harvested annually. That may sound like a lot, but it isn't compared to the millions of other game birds taken each year.

I want to mention just a few points about the prairie chicken, however, since it does seem to be coming back.

There are two varieties of prairie chicken: the greater and the lesser. The lesser differs from its larger counterpart in the range of its habitat and the fact that its throat sacs are a muted red-violet, rather than bright orange. Otherwise both chickens are very similar.

The range of the greater prairie chicken extends from the midwestern prairie provinces of Canada south into the U.S. plains states as far as northern Texas. The lesser prairie chicken, found in fewer numbers, also suffers a limited range, embracing only the southern prairie states of New Mexico, Texas, Oklahoma and Kansas.

In general appearance, the prairie chicken, at about 1½ feet in length and 1½ to 2½ pounds in weight,

looks remarkably like the sharp-tailed grouse, and only the experienced eye can tell them apart. In fact, they appear so similar that even the birds themselves have a difficult time sorting out one from the other, and interbreeding is common. The distinguishing feature is the black "bars" that stand out against a light-brown background on the greater prairie chicken as opposed to a more mottled and less defined pattern on the sharptail.

When it comes to courtship rituals, grouse are particularly creative, and the prairie chicken is nonpareil. Paralleling the tribal dances of the Sioux and Cherokee, who roamed the same plains (in point of fact, the Indians, down to their feathered dress, probably imitated the fowl), the male prairie chickens begin to converge on their "booming grounds" in late winter. There, at dawn and dusk, usually about a dozen birds display, and stamp their feet in "dance," making a booming sound to beckon the females from afar. This they faithfully do every day, engaging in occasional squabbles and establishing the pecking order, until the hens are ready to receive the most dominant males in the spring.

After mating, the females retreat and prepare nests in the densest grasses they can find. Then each one lays 12 or so eggs, which are often olive in color and flecked with brown. Upon hatching—and the prairie chicken enjoys a high hatch rate—the chicks are as precocious as any grouse can be.

Prairie chickens share other common characteristics of the ground dweller: dining on a primarily vegetarian diet of seeds, berries, grains and a few insects; preferring to walk, rather than fly—but will fly rather than submit to danger; and providing the hunter with not only a challenge in the field, but also a gourmet delicacy at the table.

For field dressing techniques, please turn to page 204.

Cooking/ptarmigan and prairie chicken

Ptarmigan with Cheese
(Serves 4)

2 ptarmigans, halved	4 slices of your favorite
¼ cup butter	cheese (Velveeta or
4 slices bacon	cheddar are delicious)
½ cup green bell peppers, chopped	salt and black pepper to taste
½ cup red onion, chopped	

Melt butter in a large skillet. Add the birds breast-side up and lay one bacon strip over each; cook for approximately 20 minutes. Add the green peppers and red onion; lower heat and continue cooking for about 20 minutes more or until birds are tender.

Place one slice of cheese over each breast; cover the skillet and allow cheese to melt. Season with salt and pepper if desired.

Ptarmigan Country Style
(Serves 4)

2 ptarmigans, halved
4 slices bacon
¼ cup butter
½ tablespoon freshly ground black pepper

¼ cup onion, chopped
salt to taste
2 dashes (or to taste) Tabasco sauce or your favorite hot sauce

Melt butter in skillet; place ptarmigan halves in skillet breast-side up and top with bacon slices. Cook for approximately 20 minutes. Add the black pepper, onion, salt to taste and the hot sauce. Lower heat and cook for 15 minutes more or until meat is tender.

This recipe is great with grits, red eye gravy or sliced home-fried potatoes. Also try varying this recipe with partridge.

Baked Prairie Chicken
(Serves 2)

1 prairie chicken, cut in half lengthwise
salt and pepper to taste
4 tablespoons butter, melted
2 bacon strips, diced and uncooked

¼ cup green pepper, diced
¼ cup onion, diced
2 small cloves of garlic
½ cup dry white wine

Preheat oven to 325° F.

Season chicken with salt and pepper; then coat with melted butter. Place each half on a piece of aluminum foil large enough to wrap around each piece. Mix together the onion, green pepper and bacon bits and sprinkle over each chicken half. Place one clove of garlic on each half and close the aluminum foil. Bake in a dish at 325° F. for approximately 1½ hours or until tender.

Remove baking dish from oven and punch several holes into the foil. Now pour the white wine over the halves and let it seep through the holes in the foil. Place in oven for an additional 15 minutes. Serve with wild rice.

Prairie Chicken with Mushrooms
(Serves 2)

1 prairie chicken
¼ cup flour
½ cup corn meal
1 teaspoon onion salt
¼ teaspoon black pepper

4 tablespoons butter
4 tablespoons vegetable oil
½ cup fresh mushrooms, sliced
¼ cup water

Cut the prairie chicken into pieces (use the wings only if they have enough meat on them). In a plastic bag place the flour, corn meal, black pepper and onion salt; add the chicken parts and shake until coated. Melt the butter and oil in a heavy skillet. Add the chicken pieces and brown on all sides. Add the mushrooms and water to the skillet and cover. Cook over low heat for about 45 minutes or until the pieces are tender.

DRESSING OUT GROUSE, PTARMIGAN AND PRAIRIE CHICKENS

In dressing out any members of the grouse family, you may wish to try another method of field dressing, the *button-hook method.*

A button hook can be made right in the field from the forked branch of a tree. Find one that measures about ⅛ inch in diameter at the fork point and that extends beyond the fork six or seven inches. With your jackknife, cut off one tine above the fork and the main stem just underneath the fork. Whittle away the rough edges where you made the cuts and smooth the point *(See Figure 3-19).*

To use the button hook in removing the entrails, first make an incision at the vent, and cut part way up the stomach. Insert the pointed edge of the hook into the bird a fair distance and give a 90-degree turn. Gently pull out the stick on which the intestines should now be looped. Keep pulling gently until the intestines fall out.

If the feathers have become fouled, you can clean them on grass or leaves. When you reach a cold, running stream, you can wash out the cavity of your bird; however, do this *only* if you are going to eat it right away. Make a small cross-cut at the anus and put the tail end of the bird into the water. Pressing on the now-empty cavity will cause it to fill with water when you stop pressing. Shake the bird so the water sloshes around inside it; then drain by lifting it out of the stream and allowing the water to run out. A couple of repeat procedures should leave you with a good, clean bird *(See Figure 3-20).*

If you're going to your campsite, the bird can be hung in a cool, dry place by the legs until you are ready to pluck it and eat it.

Do not use water if you are not going to prepare the bird immediately. Rather, after opening the cavity, wipe the bird clean with a cloth and let the bird cool.

Another easy way to eviscerate a bird of this size is to hold the bird in one hand with the head under your thumb *(Figure 3-21).* With your other hand, make a slit from the vent to the base of the breast. Reach in with your fingers and remove the entrails. Then reach farther into the breast, removing the craw and the windpipe.

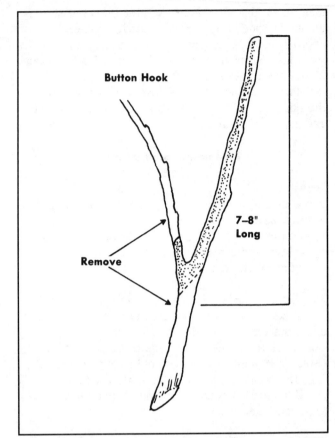

Button Hook

Remove

7–8" Long

3-19. Using a hand-made button hook is an easy way to field dress such birds as grouse, prairie chickens or ptarmigan. To make a button hook, first find a forked tree branch about ⅛ inch in diameter and about 6 or 7 inches long beyond the fork. Take a knife and cut one tine above the fork as shown; then cut below the base, making a point and smoothing out the edges with your knife. To field dress, make a cut from the vent part way up the stomach. Insert the hook end of your new wooden tool and give it a 90-degree turn inside the bird. Carefully remove the entrails, which should be caught on the hook.

Wipe the cavity clean and dry with paper towels or a dry cloth.

To finish preparing the bird for eating, you must remove the feathers. Begin plucking at the breast area, gently tugging downward. Continue this gentle tugging until you have the bird completely free of feathers, with the exception of the wing, or flight, feathers, which can be clipped off with kitchen or game shears. Any remaining pin feathers can be removed with small pliers or tweezers. Or use the singeing method described in previous dressing out sections.

3-20. If you are going to cook the bird immediately, you can rinse it out with water if you happen to be near a stream. Make a cross-cut at the vent and submerge the bird tail-end first. Allow the now-empty cavity to fill up with water. Slosh it around a little, then allow the water to drain out the bottom. Do this at least twice. Do *not* use water if you are not going to prepare the bird right away. Water, as you know, will cause spoilage rapidly.

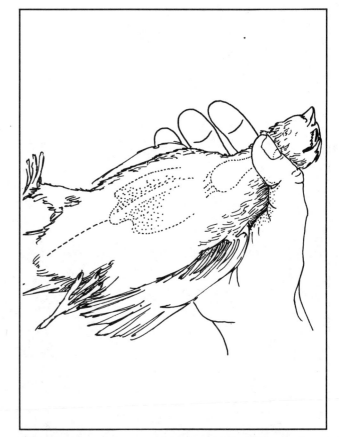

3-21. Another quick way to field dress birds of this size is to hold the bird in one hand with the head under your thumb. With your other hand, make a slit from the vent to the base of the breast. Reach in with your fingers and remove the entrails. Then reach farther into the breast and remove the craw and the windpipe. Wipe the cavity clean and dry with paper towels or a dry cloth.

Always be sure that the preen gland is removed very carefully (See page 189 in "Dressing Out Pheasant" for complete details.). Do not pierce the button-like nodules that contain the oil or the secretions will ruin the flesh of your bird. I prefer to use a second knife when I am removing this gland. This ensures that if any oil spills on my blade, I will not be transferring it to the meat of the bird when I begin working on it again.

Before trying any of the recipes in this chapter, rinse out the bird with cold, salted water to be assured of a nice, clean bird.

Wild turkey

WILD TURKEY

One spring when I was serving as Deputy Commander for the Civil Air Patrol Emergency Service Squadron for the State of Colorado, my late son, Jay, and I decided to hunt wild turkey. We picked the area south of Trinidad because this stretch in the Rockies is abundant in wildfowl as well as all sorts of other game, big and small.

Wild turkey, the last and largest of the ground-dwelling birds I'll discuss, used to enjoy a large population nationwide. But overhunting in the late 1800's reduced the numbers of this *Meleagrididae* member so much so that it nearly reached extinction. Luckily, today with better game management, it is coming back stronger and stronger. Nothing like the old days, though, I understand. Colorado in spots has a decent population—but many other states across the nation are now boasting good-sized, growing tribes. It doesn't matter where you are, however, hunting turkey is something else.

To get to Raton Pass, our ultimate destination, we drove south on Interstate 25 and passed along "Purgatory"—a vast treacherous expanse of terrain. Although the elevation in this area climbs between 7,000 and 8,000 feet, Purgatory reminds you of the moon's surface—lots of red rock and plunging canyons, sometimes as deep as 1,000 feet. You can't see Purgatory from I-25, and if you went inland not knowing where you were going, you could find yourself in a place you might not be able to get out of. Needless to say, you don't move across Purgatory at night, especially if you have been injured or are lost. My job as Deputy Commander of CAP had been to head the ground search parties trying to recover survivors from downed aircraft. And none of my crews, knowing the changing moods and fickle weather patterns of the area, would venture into it at night. For this reason, become familiar with the topography of where you're going to hunt and study local maps with your hunting buddies beforehand.

Well, Jay and I got to Raton Pass, which connects southeastern Colorado with New Mexico, but the first day, because the Governor of Colorado was hunting the area, we were prevented for security reasons from even taking a shot. We could do nothing but drive around and inquire from the locals what were good hunting spots.

Frustrated from the delay and now eager to get going, we started off really early in the morning, dressed in full camouflage gear. We stopped at a site we felt would offer good hunting—you know, a wooded area with water, near the forest edge where you'd likely find roosting places, sounds of hens, opportunities for adequate camouflage—the chief factors the gunner looks for in hopes of getting that gorgeous gobbler.

We picked a large tree and set up, hoping to blend into the forest environs. Wild turkeys have keen eyesight and if any were nearby, we wanted to make sure we stayed undetected. Hence, the camo gear we wore. Turkeys supposedly can distinguish hunter orange, which is one of the reasons why the risks are high when you hunt these wild birds. Most gobbler-getters don't wear that protective color, so accidents can happen pretty easily. Turkeys can spot your shiny gun barrels reflecting in the sun, too, and some hunters go so far as to camouflage their shotguns. We didn't, though.

By 8:30 A.M., we started to hear the hens. We sat still and waited. I sparingly worked the box call, but we saw nothing. This often happens; you'll hear them but never see them, especially if they are mature and suspicious. The flock may respond to your call, but will move farther away, rather than closer, expecting you to join them.

So about one and a half hours later, we started to track and followed the faint noises of the hens. We knew that where they were, a tom would surely be nearby, keeping tabs on his harem. We looked for signs of droppings, prints or small stones that would be turned over by scratching; they'd be wet on one side and dry on the other. The ones that were still damp would indicate that the big birds had been there not long before. I pointed out to Jay that the grassy area was bent down and only about halfway back up to its original position. The sun was fully out by this time; we decided to move through the area. As we worked our way ever so slowly and carefully for about the next hour, we crossed a dirt road and one fence.

As we walked, I got to thinking. Because it was late spring, presumably mating was over and brooding had begun. We'd probably not see the tom strutting around, fanning his tail out flamboyantly for the hens, or the wattles under his chin flaming red. Nor would we glimpse the males fighting viciously for territorial prerogatives. By this time, some of hens should have been laying their eight to 15 light brown eggs in a depression they hollowed out of the ground and maybe filled with dead leaves. If left undisturbed, most of the eggs would hatch and the poults would thrive, increasing the turkey statistics. I knew the area was rich in insects and vegetation, which made it a good feeding ground. Unfortunately, ground predators or even jealous toms had been known to destroy the eggs. It hadn't been a particularly rainy spring, so that at least eliminated one of the young turkeys' chief enemies, wet weather.

At this point, we figured and hoped the tom could still be lured by simulated female clucking, since his breeding instinct was still pretty much alive.

On we tracked, very cautiously. I didn't want to approach suddenly and see the turkeys flee from fright. Wild turkeys are incredibly wary, wily creatures. If startled, mature toms could run up to 15 miles an hour. And if they had to fly, which they would prefer not to do, they could beat their large wings, speedily reaching 45 to 50 miles an hour—and an easy escape. The hens don't seem to move quite so fast. And, incidentally, the turkey is the only upland bird that is fair game on the ground as well as in the air.

All at once our hearts began to pound. It sounded like we'd found all the turkeys in the world and not more than a hundred yards in front of us! The wind blew in our faces, Jay smiled at me and we crouched down and started to crawl. I could see several hens and one enormous, bearded tom through the tall grass. They were a sight. Their black-tipped feathers caught the light of the sun and blazed in iridescent copper and green. It was hard to tell from a distance how large the tom was, but he was one of the biggest I've ever seen. Maybe 20 pounds, a little better than average. From the long caruncle bobbing from his bald-looking forehead to the scaly spurs jutting at his ankles, he was a beauty. The hens, although smaller and less colorful, seemed to be along for the walk, but we weren't interested in them.

Peering through the grass, I couldn't believe it . . . this was just too easy. They didn't even seem to notice us. Best of all, we were in a ditch, which allowed us to lay against the bank and take our shot.

Well, turkey hunters, this is what happened: Just as Jay and I picked our toms and prepared to squeeze the triggers, a voice yelled at us in piercing tones:

"Shoot my turkeys and I'll blow you away!!"

I couldn't believe my ears. My son was holding his stomach and laughing uncontrollably. I couldn't make out what this irate stranger was saying, but I was more than ready to lower my gun. You guessed it. The tom and a few other hens had led us right to the backyard of a turkey farm.

The old man had a shotgun and I swear to this day he would have used it if I had got one of his birds. I explained to him what had happened and how we had

3-22. Before you begin field dressng your turkey, roll the bird on its side. Pluck the feathers in front of the vent, or anus, up to the pelvic arch so you have a clear area at which to make your initial incision. Cut from the anus to a point just under the breastbone. Reach inside with your hand and pull out the intestines, breaking them off as close to the anus as possible.

arrived there. His answer to us was,

"My whole road is posted up to the gate, can't you read?"

Well, what was the use of trying to explain. We had crossed almost four miles from the other direction. My son was still laughing.

"You're supposed to be a hunter who knows a lot. Why don't you put this story in a book sometime. I dare you!"

Humbly, I relate this story; but of course I went on to hunt—and bag—a few toms after that, always taking excruciating pains to know exactly what I might expect to find in an area I was hunting.

Hunting Tips/wild turkey

Because the wild tom has exceptional eyesight, be sure to hunt in complete camo gear and select a site in which you will harmonize fully with the surroundings. • Next to good equipment and an area abundant in game, patience and fortitude will be your best assets. Hunting turkey is tough. • Keep in mind that, unlike other gallinaceous birds, turkeys roost in large trees, usually one to a tree. They may return to a favorite tree nightly, or some birds will choose a different tree night after night. And although they prefer to sleep alone, they are quite gregarious once day breaks and feeding begins. • You will be more successful if you learn as much as you can about the area and the habits of the wildfowl in it. Turkeys are notorious for maintaining the same stomping grounds year after year, using the same paths and patterns.

P.S. Stay away from turkey farms.

Dressing Out/wild turkey

If you've been lucky enough to bag a big tom, before actual field dressing begins, you may want to bleed it first. Simply slit the neck above the breastbone (do not cut off the head at this point; it comes in handy later) to sever some of the veins and arteries there, hold it up by the feet and let the blood drip down and out.

You can facilitate removal of the entrails, the next step, by rolling the bird on its side and pulling out the feathers in the small area located from the pelvic arch to just in front of the vent as shown in *Figure 3-22.* Then starting at the vent, cut into the cavity to a point just under the breastbone where you have removed the feathers, being careful not to puncture the intestines inside. Reach in with your hand and pull out the intestines; break them off as close to the anus as possible. Remove the heart and the liver, which should be together and which may or may not have come out

3-23. Proper method of holding bird for wet-dipping. Use scalding, not boiling, water to about 180° F. (82° C.) Plunge the bird into the water several times to loosen the feathers, then begin plucking. This method is especially effective with larger birds.

3-24. To remove pin feathers and fuzz, you can singe them off with a candle, a cigarette lighter or a propane torch. Hold the bird horizontally in one hand, while you apply the flame with the other; turn the bird as necessary.

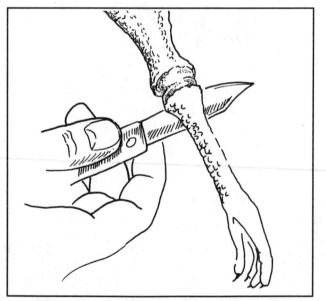

3-25. Remove the feet at the hocks by bending the legs at the first joint and slicing through the skin around the joint with a sharp knife until you can see the joint. Then simply cut straight through or use your shears to sever the tendons and remove the feet.

with the intestines. Also, you may have to go in again for the lungs, which lie against the back of the bird. Reaching farther up into the throat, remove the windpipe and crop or make a small slit at the neck above the breastbone and pull out the crop from above.

Finally, with dry paper towels or a clean cloth wipe out the bird doing the crop area first, then the entire cavity until it is thoroughly clean and fairly dry. Then you can hang your turkey head down from a tree, propped open with a stick to allow for cooling. Be sure you place it in a cool, dry, shady area away from the sun, and watch carefully to see that flies and insects are kept away.

Scalding Method of Feather Removal. Plucking of this large bird is easily accomplished by using the scalding method. In a large washtub, add scalding water of approximately 180° F. (82° C.). Make sure you check the water with a thermometer, because you do not want the temperature to exceed 180 degrees. The closer the water nears boiling point, which is 212° F. (100° C.), you'll end up with a partially skinned bird, which makes it more difficult to pluck. (Skinning, incidentally, which some outdoorsmen advocate, is a whole different process and approach to preparing wild turkey. While it may be easier than plucking, I'm not crazy about the end results or with the way the bird roasts without the skin.)

Holding the turkey by its feet, dip it in and out of the water several times in an up-and-down motion (*See Figure 3-23*). This enables the water to penetrate the feathers and skin. Again, make sure the water stays at a constant 180 degrees F. (82° C.); do not allow it to get any cooler. Dipping a maximum five times should be adequate, although fewer dunks should do it. You can check by pulling on some feathers to see if they come out easily. There should be some resistance as you pull the feathers out. This will indicate that you have properly scalded the bird.

Beginning at the breast, pull the feathers downward with your hands, pinching gently. This is when you may find that leaving the head on was a smart thing to do, because you can use the head to hold the bird more securely as you pluck away.

Once you have removed all the large feathers, some difficult-to-extract pin feathers and fuzz will undoubtedly remain. These can be singed off with a rolled-up lighted newspaper, a small blow torch or even a candle. Burn off these feathers and fuzz by holding the bird horizontally in one hand, while you apply the flame with your other hand; turn the bird as necessary (*See Figure 3-24*).

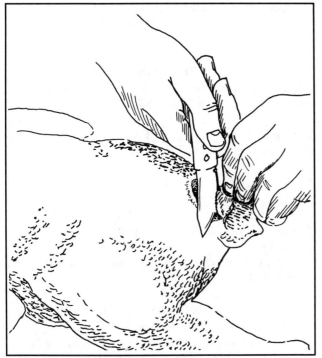

3-26. Make sure you remove the preen gland found at the base of the tail. This button-like gland should always be cut out, as it contains the odorous oil that all birds use to waterproof their feathers. Use a second knife for this process in the event some oil touches the knife.

As an alternative to simple scalding, you can also try waxing, which is discussed in the waterfowl section, page 243.

The flight feathers should now be cut off at the wings with shears. Also, remove the feet at the hocks. To do this, bend the legs at the joints and slice around the joints with a sharp knife, cutting through the skin until you can see the joints. Snip the feet off at the first joint with kitchen shears or simply cut straight through with your knife (*See Figure 3-25*). At this point, you can sever the head with the shears or chop it off with a cleaver. Finally, carefully cut off the preen gland on the underside of the bird, being sure you don't pierce it (*See Figure 3-26*).

Remove any shot and discolored or damaged flesh and soak the bird in cold, salted water for about 15 to 20 minutes to clean it thoroughly and freshen the flesh.

Your turkey is now ready for roasting.

If you are going to freeze the turkey first, remember to wrap it well, label it with the weight and date, and freeze it at 0° F. (−18° C.) in a large, standard freezer.

Cooking/Turkey

Roast Turkey with Wild Rice Stuffing
(Serves 6 to 8)

1 8- to 10-pound turkey	salt and black pepper to
4 tablespoons butter or	taste
margarine, softened	

Wild Rice Stuffing:

1 Cup wild rice	½ cup butter or
½ pound bulk sausage	margarine, melted
1 medium onion, diced	salt and black pepper to
2 cups fresh mushrooms,	taste
sliced or 1 8-ounce can	thyme, sage and marjoram
sliced mushrooms	to taste (optional)

Wash turkey, pat dry and place in a large roasting pan. Spread turkey, including cavity, with softened butter or margarine. Salt bird and cavity to taste and pepper the breast. Prepare Wild Rice Stuffing.

Wild Rice Stuffing: Cook rice according to package directions. Fry sausage with onion, drain and combine with remaining stuffing ingredients. Stuff turkey and truss with kitchen twine. (Serve any excess stuffing separately or place around turkey just before serving.)

Cover stuffed turkey with aluminum foil and roast slowly at 325° F. for approximately 3 to 4 hours. Remove foil for the last 20 minutes of cooking time to allow breast to brown. Baste frequently.

Turkey Hash
(Serves 4)

4 tablespoons butter or	1 large onion, diced
margarine	salt and black pepper to
2 cups cooked turkey,	taste
diced	1 cup evaporated milk
2 cups cooked potatoes,	
chopped	

In a large skillet melt butter or margarine over medium-hot heat. Add turkey, potatoes, onion and salt and pepper. Stir until well browned. Add milk and stir well. Cover and reduce heat to medium-low, stirring occasionally until mixture is well heated, about 15 minutes.

Wild Turkey Croquettes
(Makes about 1 dozen)

1 cup thick Cream Sauce
2 cups cooked, diced
  wild turkey
1 to 2 tablespoons onion,
  chopped
2 tablespoons parsley,
  finely chopped
2 tablespoons white wine
¼ teaspoon tarragon
dash hot pepper sauce
1 teaspoon Worcestershire
  Sauce

salt and freshly ground
  black pepper
garlic powder
flour
2 eggs, beaten and diluted
  with a little milk
1 cup bread crumbs
vegetable oil
leftover gravy

Cream Sauce: Melt 2 tablespoons butter in a saucepan; blend into it 3 tablespoons flour, cooking for about 5 minutes. Slowly pour in 1 cup milk and stir constantly until smooth and thick. Stir in 1 or 2 egg yolks until well blended and sauce is very thick.

While Sauce is still warm, add turkey, onion, parsley, wine, tarragon, hot pepper sauce and Worcestershire Sauce. Return pan to low heat; add salt, pepper and garlic powder to taste; stir until well blended. Pour mixture into greased pan and chill until cooled thoroughly.

Form into medium-sized balls or cones. Roll first in flour, then beaten egg, then bread crumbs. Let dry on a rack about 1 hour.

Deep-fry in oil about 5 minutes, turning gently until golden brown. Serve with warmed leftover gravy.

Turkey Soup
Try this fresh variation of the homemade chicken stock you used to get from Mother's kitchen.

1 turkey carcass
2 medium onions
3 whole cloves
3 cloves garlic, peeled
2 large carrots, peeled
  and quartered
2 stalks celery with leaves,
  quartered
4 medium tomatoes,
  quartered

1 whole kohlrabi, split in
  half
1 wedge fresh lemon
3 sprigs fresh parsley
paprika
freshly ground black
  pepper
a.f.g. saffron
¼ teaspoon thyme

In a large stainless steel kettle, place the turkey carcass and fill with cold water, enough to cover turkey.

Slice one onion completely; cut the other in half and insert the three whole cloves into one of the halves. Place all the onion in water.

Add garlic, carrots, celery, tomatoes, kohlrabi, lemon and parsley; bring to a boil. Reduce heat to simmer; skim; sprinkle with paprika and black pepper and add saffron and thyme.

Simmer, partially covered, 2 to 2½ hours. Serve with rice.

section 4

section 4
Waterfowl

It is truly awesome to contemplate the myriad varieties of birds and waterfowl found in North America. In this section of DRESS 'EM OUT, I have tried to highlight the ducks and geese most sought after by hunters and gourmands. The species are grouped into pond ducks, diving ducks and geese. The pond, or "puddle," ducks are usually freshwater surface feeders that merely dip in bill first with tail up. The divers actually go beneath the surface to retrieve their food. And of course the geese are a breed apart, larger and with flat, triangular bills. All the waterfowl are members of the *Anatidae* biological family.

Pond Ducks

AMERICAN WIDGEON

The first of the surface-feeding pond ducks I want to discuss is the American widgeon. Known as the "baldpate" in certain locales because of its featherless-appearing crest, the widgeon is considered a table delicacy by some hunters.

The American widgeon's range is quite wide and can cover all of the United States and most of Canada at some point during the year. It winters along the fringes of the Altantic, Pacific and Gulf coasts, but may travel as far as Mexico. Its breeding territories include the Rocky Mountains to the Mississippi River, from Wyoming through Canada's prairie provinces, British Columbia, the Yukon and Alaska. It is rarely found nesting along the Atlantic coast.

The drake measures anywhere from 16 to 20 inches and probably weighs about 2 pounds. The center of his crest is white, which greatly contrasts with the brilliant green band that runs on either side of the head, encompassing the eyes. It is this white area that when viewed at a distance gives the appearance of baldness. The cheeks and neck are stippled black on an off-white background. The back, breast and sides are pinkish brown, also accented in black but in thin waves. The belly and the foreparts of the wings are pure white. The speculum picks up the green again, bordered on the upper side in black, while the primaries are brown.

The "baldness" is not present in the hen, which instead of contrasting colors has a solid gray head, riding atop a brown body. Her belly, reaching up to her sides, bears more white than that of the male; her forewings are a marbled brown and white.

The male quacks, but his call usually consists of a three-note whistle. The female, on the other hand, has a hoarse quack.

Widgeon pair up at their breeding grounds, often arriving in small flocks. The males rival each other for the females' attention; since the ratio among widgeon is about 50/50 male to female, however, there is no excess of unmated drakes or hens during the breeding season.

During courtship the males gather around the female and whistle softly. They also twist and turn while flying at high speeds. After the female has selected her mate, the two birds swim off engaged in a head-bobbing ritual. They then go to the pothole or pond that the male has selected as his territory. There they build a nest—which is often just a depression in the ground, quite a distance from the water—and mate.

Most females lay seven to nine eggs which are incubated in 24 or 25 days. When the ducklings' down has dried, they begin to head toward the water. Though it is unproved, some experts say that the mother carries each duckling to the water in her mouth. The young ducklings spend about two months in the water before they begin to fly.

During the period when the mother is raising her young, the male goes into his molt and becomes flightless. The males gather together now, usually on a large body of water covered with ample vegetation. The female begins her molt before the young have learned to fly and completes it after they are in flight.

Widgeon do not rush to their winter grounds. Instead they make many stops along the way, gathering food and water. Although they start their migration as early as September, they don't arrive until late November. This, despite the fact that they can attain speeds of up to 60 miles per hour.

The main enemies of the widgeon are fire, drought and disease. Egg predation is done by crows, raccoons, skunks, foxes and coyotes, while owls, hawks, eagles and otters will prey on the young. If the bird does make it to adulthood, it may live to seven years of age.

Hunting Tips/american widgeon

Due to its primary diet of celery and wild rice, the widgeon is sought after for its fine-eating flesh. Many hunters are more than happy to down a widgeon, too, as the bird's quick and erratic flight patterns can often drive a shotgunner crazy. The bird is also very wary of people, and will spend its days far from shore, coming inland in the evening to feed. If hunters are spotted, you can bet that the bird will flush as quickly as any.

For dressing out techniques and recipes, see pages 241-251.

BLACK DUCK

One of the more popular sporting species, the black duck is primarily an eastern bird. Its breeding grounds range from the Ungava Peninsula in northern Quebec, southward to Illinois and Maryland, and from Wisconsin east to the Atlantic Ocean. Its wintering grounds overlap the southern portion of the breeding grounds, which extend from the Great Lakes to New England and southward to Texas and Florida.

The most common of the freshwater ducks, the black measures from 21 to 25 inches in length and weighs about 3 pounds. The crown of its head is dusky brown, while the rest of its head and neck are streaked with lighter browns. The body is a mottled dark brown, and the wings are violet bordered in black and white underneath. The male's bill is yellow, while the female's is olive-green.

Both the male and female quack, but the female is much louder than the male. Both birds also hiss and whistle.

Although the black duck pairs in the wintering grounds and migrates to the breeding grounds with its mate, it still follows a courtship ritual. The paired couple will often try to outfly each other, racing at speeds of 45 to 50 miles per hour back and forth across the length of the pond or lake they have chosen for their breeding grounds. This continues until the female decides the male is worthy of her. Mating then takes place.

The black duck usually builds its nest on the ground, hidden from view by high grasses or low, bushy growth and almost invariably located close to water. The female will form the nest with her body and then add grass, vegetation and down.

Most female black ducks lay six to 12 eggs with incubation taking approximately four weeks. After hatching, the young remain in the nest for a few hours until their down has dried and they have regained the energy they spent breaking out of their shells. Once strong enough, the ducklings follow their mother to water, where they begin eating insects.

Within eight weeks after being hatched, the young birds are on their own and are capable of short flights. They join the adult drakes at this time, and usually travel in small flocks.

Although the black duck is migratory, it doesn't begin the trip to the winter grounds until it is forced to leave by frozen waters in the North. In some cases, where the water does not freeze because of underground springs or perhaps because of a mild winter, the bird will not migrate south at all.

An extremely wary and alert bird, the black duck will often keep to the open waters during daylight hours and feed very early in the morning and again in the early evening. Almost 35 percent of its diet can consist of animal matter, such as marine life, with the rest of its food made up of vegetation.

The average life expectancy of the black duck is five to six years, although many birds fail to make it to their second spring. Marsh fires, floods and high tides take their toll on the birds, as do icing conditions that can cause food shortages. The eggs are prey to opossums, crows and raccoons, while the young may be eaten by snapping turtles and fish. Mink, otters and foxes will eat the eggs, young and adults if they can catch them. Owls, hawks and eagles also take the birds when possible.

Hunting Tips/black duck

Hunters don't cause nearly as big a dent in the black duck populations as do natural causes, but quite a few birds do fall to shotgunners each waterfowl season. Many gunners go after the birds in backcountry lakes and ponds, often setting up decoy spreads and calling them into range from blinds or concealed duck boats. Perhaps the best time to hunt for black duck is during the winter season, when the birds are found massed along the coastlines rather than in the remote areas where they are found during nesting seasons.

Please refer to pages 241-251 for field dressing techniques and recipes.

BLUE-WINGED TEAL

Found throughout the lower 48 states and almost all of Canada, the blue-winged teal has a breeding range that stretches from Nevada to Pennsylvania and New York as far as the Great Lakes, and then north to the Yukon. Although the bird does not breed along either coast, it will winter in the Atlantic coastal states from Connecticut as far south as Florida. It also likes the Gulf States of Louisiana and Texas and many of the birds even migrate to South America. This is due to the fact that the blue-winged teal is a migratory bird that prefers almost tropical weather during winter. In fact, many of the birds will stay in the southern regions all year, although those that do migrate north are among the first birds to migrate south in the fall.

The bird gets its name from the blue patch on its forewing, which is edged in white. The male's head is gray, with a white crescent that extends from the top of the head to the chin in front of his eyes. He has a brown back and is spotted underneath, while the female is mottled brown with an off-white belly. The male measures about 15 inches and weighs approximately 15 ounces. The female is somewhat smaller.

The blue-winged teal is a quiet bird in comparison to other puddle ducks. Both male and female will occasionally make twittering sounds while flying. The female has a very weak quack, while the male will hiss and peep from time to time.

Since the blue-winged teal migrates to its breeding grounds at a late date, courting takes place before arrival at the grounds. Some experts say this occurs during the actual migration. Some of it is performed in flight, with two males and one female twisting and turning in the air. On the water, the female usually starts the courting by calling to a male. The two then swim close to each other, with the male whistling softly and showing off his brightly colored legs.

Once the courtship and mating have taken place, the female will build a nest of dry grass and down. There have been occasions, however, when she has built her nest in an abandoned muskrat house. Since the nests are frequently built close to farm land or on farm acreage itself, the eggs are often lost to farm machinery. Anywhere from eight to 12 eggs are laid by the female, with incubation taking about 22 days. The mother is very protective of her eggs during this period, and makes sure they are well-camouflaged when she leaves the nest in search of food or water. The young begin to leave the nest within two to four hours after being hatched, and start feeding on insects almost immediately.

Unlike other members of the duck family, the young are capable of flight just about six weeks after hatching. This is nature's way of compensating for their late arrival to and early departure from the breeding grounds. In general, the birds reach the breeding grounds in early May and head south again around the first of August.

During the summer months many watering holes become dry and the families scatter and gather into larger groups. Ducklings often lose their families during this moving about, but will attach themselves to another female who accepts them as part of her family.

In winter, blue-winged teal prefer to make their homes in small bayous and lagoons. Although they will sometimes enter inshore saltwater bays, they prefer fresh water. They have adapted to civilization much better than many other duck species, and often nest in lakes in the middle of cities and towns.

The blue-winged teal has a maximum life expectancy of about seven years, although many birds fall prey to predators before that time. Raccoons, skunks, foxes, coyotes, crows and even squirrels will eat the eggs, while winged predators such as hawks and eagles take the adults.

Hunting Tips/blue-winged teal

If the hunter is lucky enough to shoot a few of these elusive birds, they make for excellent eating. Hunting any of the three teal ducks is basically the same. • Find their feeding grounds. • Use blocks and a blind, floating blind or skull boat. • And hope the weather isn't too sunny, as these birds are very fast and blend into the blue sky well. • The best time to hunt teal is in the early morning. • Don't be afraid of using your mallard decoys, but keep them closer together than you would when hunting diving ducks.

For field dressing methods and recipes, see pages 241-251.

CINNAMON TEAL

You can find the cinnamon teal in western North America from southern British Columbia to the southwestern part of Saskatchewan and southward to the central part of Mexico. The bird winters in Central America down to Colombia, with some remaining in the southwestern United States. The breeding range encompasses British Columbia and Alberta and all the states of the U.S. south of those Canadian provinces.

The cinnamon teal is a puddle duck and prefers to make its habitat on shallow streams and ponds. The male is generally 15½ to 16 inches long, and attains a weight of about 12 ounces. His head, neck, shoulders, breast, belly and flanks are a warm cinnamon color, while the back and rump are mottled brown. The tail is brown. Both the male and female have a distinctive patch of blue on the front wing. The speculum is green, edged in white, and the underlining of the wing is off-white. The female's coloration is primarily mottled brown, with the exception of the blue patch. The female has a louder voice than the male, but these are relatively quiet birds.

After a brief courtship display that revolves around a head-bobbing ritual, the female will choose a mate from among the many trying to win her favor. She will then build a nest that consists of grasses and is well-lined with down. The nest is normally constructed on dry land, but close to the water. After an incubation period of 22 to 23 days, anywhere from six to 12 ducklings are hatched.

The most unusual aspect of this period is that unlike other ducks, the cinnamon teal male does not abandon the female during incubation. There have been times when the male has even assisted with the rearing of the young ducklings. They will use the pretense of injury to lure danger from their young.

After hatching, the young cinnamon duckling embarks upon a steady diet of insects. It begins to fly in about six weeks, a comparatively short period for ducks. When it reaches adulthood, the bird will be able to attain speeds of up to 50 miles per hour.

Cinnamons tend to stay together and fly together as a family until migration, when they begin to gather in small flocks. They start to go south at the end of September and beginning of October, and do not return to their breeding grounds until April.

Not a particularly gregarious bird, the cinnamon is rarely found in large flocks or in the company of other duck species. It prefers the shallow edges of ponds, obtaining much of its food from grasses and other vegetation growing about the water line. It also eats seeds and some animal matter.

If able to live its life to the fullest, the cinnamon teal can attain an age of seven to nine years. Coyotes and crows are its greatest enemies, in addition to the other predators inveterately feared by land-nesting ducks.

Hunting Tips/cinnamon teal

Cinnamons are not heavily hunted, and figures on the numbers harvested are not readily available. However, since the diet of the cinnamon is primarily vegetarian, the flesh is considered excellent table fare. All teal ducks are surface or puddle ducks, and they can be found roosting in shallow water, potholes, ponds and along streams where food is plentiful. This is where they should be hunted. Remember that these birds are small—usually less than a pound—and fast, and that they will sometimes appear closer than they are. It pays to keep the weather in mind when hunting them, as they will be among the first waterfowl to leave an area when a cold front is coming in.

Field dressing instructions and recipes can be found on pages 241-251.

GREEN-WINGED TEAL

The green-winged teal's breeding grounds lie from California eastward to Iowa, north to the arctic regions of Canada, and west to Alaska. It winters from Washington down the Pacific Coast to Mexico, as well as in Montana, Wyoming, Kansas, Oklahoma, Arkansas, Mississippi, Alabama, and the Atlantic coastal states of Georgia, the Carolinas and Virginia.

The smallest of the ducks classified as puddlers,

the green-winged teal ranges in length from 12 to 15 inches. The speculum, which is quite small, is green and black. The male also has an iridescent green stripe on its head, starting at the front of the eye and going to the nape of the neck. His neck and head are cinnamon brown or chestnut colored. There is an edging of white feathers under the green on his wing, and the rest of his body is grayish-brown. The female, which is slightly smaller than the male, is a brownish-colored bird with a white lower breast and belly and green speculum.

Like other members of the teal family, the greenwing is a very quiet bird. The male chirps and emits a high-pitched whistle when he does decide to talk, while the female usually quacks softly.

The birds pair up before they reach their breeding grounds in early spring. During courtship, one male will follow another and swim slowly around the female. Much peeping, head bobbing and splashing occurs until the female finally chooses a mate. After courtship, the female may lay anywhere from six to 15 eggs in a grassy nest built in a hollow near water. The male departs at the beginning of the incubation period, which lasts from 21 to 23 days.

From the time of hatching, it takes most green-winged teal ducklings about six weeks to learn how to fly. By adulthood they will be able to hit speeds of 50 miles per hour, which can increase with favorable tail winds. The birds travel in tight formations, twisting and turning as they go.

The green-winged teal is a hardy bird and can withstand the cold weather very well, returning to its wintering grounds only when the ponds and streams it inhabits are totally frozen over. In spring, it will be back on the nesting grounds before the ice has completely melted.

Vegetable matter accounts for most of the bird's diet, although it does supplement the menu with insects and mollusks and, occasionally the flesh of decaying salmon that have traveled upstream to spawn and die.

The life expectancy of the green-winged teal is approximately seven years. Its chief enemy is the crow, which eats both the eggs and the ducklings. Coyotes, raccoons, foxes, opossums and skunks will also eat the eggs, while hawks, owls and eagles will attack the adults.

Hunting Tips/green-winged teal

Due to its erratic flight patterns, the green-winged teal is one of the most difficult ducks to shoot while in the air. The hunter may spot many teal basking in the sun on sandy flats and bogs. Such times can provide

fast and furious sport, although those instances are rare, as the birds usually stay hidden in high grasses and reeds near a watering hole until dusk, when they emerge to feed. Incidentally, they are strictly freshwater creatures. Using a good blind and caller is probably your best bet at getting a fast-flying teal. Or try lying flat on your back in a skull boat and letting the boat drift toward a marsh or sand bar where the birds have been spotted. When you get within range, the excitement takes place in a matter of seconds.

Pages 241-251 contain steps for field dressing and recipes.

GADWALL

Although once common across most of North America, the gadwall has dwindled in numbers in recent years and you do not find it in large flocks anymore. During breeding season the birds congregate in the central Canadian provinces. In winter the gadwall may be found in all the Pacific coast states, in the Gulf States, and the Atlantic coastal states as far north as New Jersey. Most winter in Mexico, however.

The male gadwall is about 20 inches long and weighs about 2 pounds. The neck and head are dark brown with a very dark bill. The belly is white, and the chest and breast have gray-black scale-like markings. The light brown side feathers are interestingly patterned to look almost like a herring bone tweed, while the back and wings are solid dark brown. The somewhat smaller female is mottled brown, darker than the male, although her bill is lighter.

When they decide to sound off, which is fairly often, the female carries the louder call. She sounds much like a female mallard, while the male makes a *cack-cack* sound in addition to the whistles he makes during mating season.

The female normally chooses her mate from two drakes that pursue her. During courtship, the male face-to-face with the female extends his neck and makes a burping sound. The female then quacks loudly, cheering him on. Both of them bob their heads, and then the male bows and swims away. If the female is interested, she follows him, after which they take to the air and fly erratically until the female definitely chooses one partner. They eventually return to the water, where mating takes place.

The nest is most often built close to a grassy inlet, and is filled with down. The clutch consists of 10 to 12 cream-colored eggs, which require four weeks of incubation. However, it is very possible that the female will abandon her nest if it is disturbed. Meanwhile, having lost interest in the female, the male will abandon his mate and begin his molt, losing all flight feathers.

The ducklings feed on insects when first hatched, but eventually switch to a vegetarian diet. It is 50 to 60 days before they are able to fly. When they are finally able to, they can hit speeds of up to 45 miles per hour. Migration to the south occurs early, while the return flight north for breeding is quite late.

Since the gadwall's diet—more than any other surface feeder's—is almost totally vegetarian, with pond weeds the main staple, its flesh is found by many to be of gourmet fare. Many hunters have a tough time finding the bird, though, as it is very shy and often hides in tall foliage during the day. It generally feeds only after the sun has gone down.

The bird's average life expectancy is seven to eight years. Since they nest so close to farm land and search the farm lands for their food, however, many never reach this age as they are often destroyed by farm machinery.

Hunting Tips/gadwall

One excellent way to hunt for this bird is to stalk close to the edges of the water areas they inhabit. They are less disturbed by natural sounds than those of a man-made nature.

For field dressing techniques and recipes, please turn to page 241.

MALLARD

From urban ponds to country swimming holes, the mallard is the most well-known and easiest found of the surface feeders. A "typical" puddle duck, it thrives throughout North America—in the U.S. (including Alaska) and Canada—inhabiting shallow-water areas such as marshlands, ponds, lakes and streams where vegetation grows above the waterline. The mallard is capable of withstanding extremely cold temperatures but is a migratory bird due to its need for open water.

The mallard drake ranges in length from 23 to almost 30 inches and generally weighs 2½ to 3 pounds. The female is somewhat smaller, with a maximum length of 23 inches. The drake's coloration is quite beautiful. His head is an iridescent green, separated from the lower body by a white band that circles the neck. The breast feathers are brown with a purplish cast, while the belly and underwings are white. The tail end is black, edged with white feathers. Colored

primarily in mottled browns, the female pales in comparison.

However, when it comes to being heard, the female excels. She is the noisier bird, quacking loudly at the slightest provocation. As ducks go, mallards are a vociferous group and it is the female's calling that hunters imitate to attract their autumn quarry.

Both birds become quite aggressive during the mating season, with the female not allowing any other hen near her mate. Fighting between males usually takes place after pairing, with each male protecting his territory and the female from potential rivals.

Even though pairing takes place in the fall, mallards still go through the courtship ritual in the spring, normally in February and March. The male raises his head high, bows, shows his tail, preens himself, dips his bill in the water and pulls his head back sharply. Even though some courting may also take place in the air, with the male flying after the female, the courtship is completed when the female swims up to the male and touches his bill with hers.

The female will lay 8 to 12 eggs in a well hidden nest constructed of grasses, reeds and rushes. The male is quite aggressive during the time of nest construction, and defends the territory against all intruders. Once incubation begins, however, the drake leaves the area and begins his molt, which makes him incapable of flying.

After an incubation period of approximately 26 days, the ducklings are hatched. The young will remain in the nest for a few hours, and then immediately follow their mother to water. She watches her young carefully at this time, and will scatter the ducklings to shelter at the first sign of danger. This is a hazardous trip for the ducklings, and some are always lost to predators or fatigue. Those that do reach the water begin to feed on mosquito larvae and other small items. Later, they will convert their diet to seeds and vegetable matter.

The ducklings begin to fly after about two months. By this time, the drakes have grown new, mottled-brown feathers and are beginning to fly again.

The mallard starts migrating to the breeding grounds during late March. The trip southward for winter usually takes place in September and continues until about the middle of October. Some mallards do not migrate at all, however, having found year-round homes in waters that do not freeze over and where food is plentiful. Local parks, both urban and suburban, are frequent homes to these nonmigratory birds.

While mallards can reach an age of seven to nine years, many of them are killed either by predators or

Mallards

hunters before they reach their second year. The crow is the main enemy of these ducks, although they are also prey to skunks, raccoons, opossums, foxes and snakes. Turtles, bass, pike, pickerel and muskellunge will also eat them, especially the young since they are so vulnerable and inexperienced in the water.

Hunting Tips/mallard

A mallard on the wing is a most difficult duck to shoot, as adult birds can fly 60 to 70 miles per hour without difficulty. The best time to hunt them is in the early morning, as the duck's fine eyesight can easily detect a hunter in broad daylight. Try cornfields, rice fields, marshes, pond and lakes for best results. They are also quite wary, as hunters seek them out due to their good-tasting flesh. Despite this, they are extremely inquisitive and can be attracted to even drab-colored female decoys. They also respond to a caller quite well.

Speaking of decoys, one fall a friend and I were duck hunting in Connecticut, within view of Long Island Sound. Frank and I were in a blind with our decoys out. It wasn't very cold and even though we saw a few small flocks of mallards pass over, nothing ventured in. We had plenty of good decoys and Frank was working his caller to death.

At this point a strange thing happened. The ducks began to circle a point on a small island not far away. Then as they came in, the shooting began. It was about noon and very hot, and we hadn't even raised our guns. The island, though, was getting its limit. Soon after, we saw a small boat coming in with two young boys perched in it. The boys were about 15 or 16, but they said that they were older; and they had their limit. Their decoys were white plastic bleach bottles. They had crudely painted the necks of the bottles with either red or green stripes. A few of them even had yellow circles painted on them like eyes. Never before had I seen such decoys. I've seen similar bottles with white cloths used in cornfields as a lure for geese. I asked them how decoys that bright could ever work. They just laughed and said, "Well, we got our limit! What did you get?"

We parted, with Frank and I both convinced that they must've been just plain lucky. Obviously, the ducks had just decided to "drop in."

The next day was great—if you can call cold weather, no sun and all the other elements of a good duck hunting day "great." We were all ready to leave when all of a sudden we heard shots about a quarter of a mile away in a small cove. We did manage to get a few passes then when a few ducks came in. By noon we had bagged two birds apiece.

Soon I heard a small motorboat coming toward us and, sure enough, it was those two young kids and their grandfather. They all had their limit and were using those same white jugs! Frank and I just looked at each other and, after a few minutes of chatting with the grandfather, he wanted to sell us the rights to his decoys. He told us that *all* ducks are inquisitive and unless you understand this, you'll never get your limit. I told him that I had gotten my fill all over the United States, but this was a first for me, seeing such crazy-looking decoys! Frank agreed with me, too. The old man just smiled and said, "Well, maybe you like freezing and going home skunked. You won't, though, if you use my decoys." We thanked him for the information and they left.

We hit our limit later that afternoon, but we worked hard, like most normal waterfowlers. I can't help but wonder what a decoy like that would do to the commercial decoy business! Neither Frank nor I ever did try the bottles, but there have been plenty of times when I have frozen my feet and nose and sat so many hours waiting, only to have to pick up my decoys and put them away without getting a thing!

To this day I wonder if that old man knew something about ducks that we didn't.

Dressing out instructions and recipes can be found on pages 241-251.

PINTAIL

The most widespread duck of North America, the pintail will travel even farther into the arctic regions than the mallard. While common in the eastern half of the continent, it is even more abundant in the western section. It winters in the lower two-thirds of the continental United States, from the Atlantic to Pacific coasts, as well as in Central America and parts of South America, and breeds from the upper third of the United States to the Arctic Ocean. Its population is extremely large in Canada and on the tundra, particularly in western Alaska.

The male pintail is 25 to 30 inches long and weighs approximately 2 pounds plus. He has a blue-gray bill, a deep brown head, and a throat that is part brown and part white. The neck, breast and belly are white, the tail is black, and the back and sidefeathers are grayish and vermiculated in a darker color. The wings are grayish-brown, while the speculum is green with a brown border. The female's speculum, on the other hand, is a light brown, and her basic coloration is a mottled brown. Her overall length is about 23 inches. Both male and female bear long, slender necks that enable them to surface feed much easier than other members of the duck family. The name "pintail" is of course derived from the two long central feathers that adorn their tails.

The drake emits a soft whistle during mating season, but quacks when threatened or in flight. The female's quack is rough thoughout the year except during mating season, when she makes a soft call.

Pintails pair up after arriving at the breeding grounds. Courtships can be very elaborate, with as many as five or six males vying for one female's attention. The males circle around and put on displays, each trying to outdo the other for a prospective mate. One may do a water ballet by lowering his neck and scooping up water which he splashes up into the air, while another may lift his head erect, proudly raise his wings, then fan his tail. If attracted to a male, the female will eventually swim after him.

Nests are usually made on the ground above water level. After they are filled with grasses, straw and down, six to 10 light olive-colored eggs are laid, which the female incubates for about a three-week period. The male remains in the area and assists with rearing the young.

After hatching, it takes about two months for the ducklings to learn how to fly. The female will lose her flight feathers at about the same time, and it will be three weeks before she is able to fly again. The fastest flier of any of the ducks of North America, the adult pintail has been clocked at speeds in excess of 65 miles per hour. Should favorable tail winds prevail, they can achieve speeds of 90 miles per hour!

Toward the end of August or the beginning of September, the birds begin to flock on lake shores for the migration trip south. This migration at high elevations is led by the adult males, with the teenage ducklings and females following. The flights back north will normally begin in mid-February.

Since the pintail is primarily a vegetarian—it feeds on bulrush, smartweed, pondweed, millet, wild rice and such—its flesh is considered to be tasty. Cultivated grains are also high on its menu.

The life expectancy of the pintail is seven to eight years, although most of them do not survive beyond the age of five. The eggs are subject to predation by ravens, while jaegers will take the chicks. Hawks, owls and eagles will attack the adults.

Hunting Tips/pintail

Because the pintail is another surface-feeding "groupie," you can often spot it swimming alongside mallards, various teal, and the like. It is not a particularly curious bird, however, so it is not often fooled by hunters using decoys, although decoys employed with good mallard calling have proven successful. Also, at the first sign of any danger, the birds become very noisy. When they do hear gunshot, however, they'll frequently leave the water and fly straight into the air in a flock, giving the gunner a good chance to knock down a few birds.

For field dressing instructions and recipes, please refer to pages 241-251.

SHOVELER

The shoveler is a pond duck whose name is derived from its large, uniquely shovel-shaped bill. A ubiquitous bird, it is found in both North and South America as well as in other parts of the world such as Africa and Australia. In the United States, this hardy duck may be observed in all 50 states (including Hawaii) at some point during the year. Its wintering grounds include the coastline of the Pacific from Washington south and into Arizona, New Mexico, Texas and throughout the Gulf Coast States. To the East, it winters in the southern interior states and the Atlantic Coast from South Carolina south. The breeding range of the shoveler extends from California eastward to Wyoming, Nebraska, Iowa and Wisconsin, and northward to the northern tiers of Canada and Alaska. In recent years it has been making a comeback in the East as well.

The most unusual part of the shoveler is its large spoon-shaped bill, which is longer than its head and is larger at its tip than at the base. The bird uses this bill to scoop food out of the water. To get rid of the mud and water, it then sifts seeds, insects, small fish, mollusks and tadpoles through comb-like teeth.

The drake measures approximately 20 inches in length and weighs close to 1½ pounds. Coloration is dark green, almost black, with purple iridescence on the head and neck. His breast is white, while the back feathers are bluish-brown fading to lighter shades at the tips. The wings range from blue to green-edged-in-white on the speculum to gray-brown on the primaries. The belly and sides are warm brown. The rump and tail again return to the dark green-black color of the head. The female is almost the same size as the male, but overall appears brown, except for some blues and greens on the wings. Like the teals, both sexes are extremely quiet.

Shovelers fly to their breeding grounds in small flocks and pair after they have arrived. There is little courtship display, and the birds seem to pair off without fanfare or difficulty. One interesting note is that older drakes occasionally share their mates with younger males, probably because the female shoveler reaches sexual maturity later than the male. In short, shovelers are polyandrous, which is a rare phenomenon in the avian world. It probably also accounts for their non-demonstrative courtship, since the males are not fierce competitors.

Nesting spots seem to be chosen indiscriminately, with some being close to water and others being far away. No matter where they are built, however, they are well-concealed—usually in tall grasses—and lined with grasses, weeds and down.

After breeding, the female will lay 10 to 12 greenish eggs. Once all the eggs are laid, the male departs and leaves all the incubation and rearing responsibilities to the female. The ducklings hatch after about three weeks, and are immediately led to water so they may begin feeding on insects. The young birds do

not exhibit the spoon-shaped bills until they are two weeks old, and they do not begin flying until two months have passed. During this period, the male has gone through his molting stage and is capable of flying again. The female starts molting after the ducklings are capable of flight, and is able to start flying again in September. The shoveler is a fast flier, attaining speeds of 50 miles per hour and more with little difficulty. The bird is also an excellent swimmer and walker.

The shoveler begins its migratory flights from the wintering grounds in October, and doesn't return to the North until late March. The ducks are usually in transit for about six weeks during this period, and generally fly low and steady in small flocks.

A sociable bird with a diet that is 65 percent vegetable matter and 35 percent animal matter, the shoveler lives to about seven years of age. Its enemies are the same as those of other members of the duck family, particularly those that spend a good deal of time near water.

Although the shoveler is classified as a game bird, its flesh is often barely edible or not edible at all,

SPECIAL TIPS FOR WATERFOWLERS

Here are some tips that waterfowlers, veteran and novice alike, should keep in mind to ensure an enjoyable and successful hunt.

1. Plan your hunt before, not after you arrive at the hunting site.

2. Know the extent of the hunting season and the bag limit in the area you will be hunting.

3. Become familiar with the hunting area by studying a map (make sure you bring it with you). Also, if possible, scout the area beforehand. If you can't, at least hunt with someone who knows the territory.

4. Be aware of the weather forecast for the days you will be waterfowling; a cold front, fog, rain, snow, high winds or a blizzard will all affect the movement or non-movement of ducks and geese and will determine what you will wear as well as the equipment you'll have to bring.

5. Be able to identify the birds you hunt—in flight, on the ground and in the water.

6. *Decoys.* Know the rules, if any, concerning decoys in the area you will be hunting. Know how and where to place your blocks, decoys, etc. Know how to handle all your decoys, how to clean them, transport them and care for them.

7. *Blinds.* All blinds should be designed to conceal you from keen-sighted ducks and geese. There are many types of blinds—temporary, permanent, floating, etc. What you are hunting, and where, will largely determine

the kind you need. So seek out an expert's advice to assist you, especially if you are planning to make your own.

Also, remember that when constructing a blind, position it so that you never shoot over someone else's head. In a given locale, know who is in which blind; do not overcrowd; make sure you place your gun so it will not fall inside a blind; and leave a "borrowed" blind cleaner than you found it.

8. The appropriate gun and the right-sized shells will depend on the species you are waterfowling; do not be afraid to ask the locals or the experts for their recommendations.

9. Your dog is your best friend and helper, so treat him as your partner.

10. Practice and practice with your caller, both hard and soft. This is the only way to become a proficient caller. Just practice and listen to the actual birds under different conditions.

11. Do not overhunt an area at any time or your birds will leave. Hunt until noon the latest, because the birds will settle down, and your hunting will last longer and will be more enjoyable and fruitful.

12. Finally, especially if it is warm, dress out your birds quickly or at least open them and hang them. Never place one duck on top of another, as the heat from their bodies will lead to rapid spoilage. Keep them apart and your efforts will be rewarded.

depending upon the time of year it is bagged and what it has been eating. Unlike many other waterfowl that are primarily vegetarians, the shoveler tends to consume more than its share of animal matter. However, for those of you who do go after it, the dressing out steps are the same as for other ducks and can be found on pages 241-251. And for you waterfowlers who would seek this duck as a mount, review the tips on "Mounting Your Bird," page 191.

WOOD DUCK

Last, but certainly one of the most interesting and beautiful of the surface feeders, is the wood duck. Although it may be found in all the states of the Union at some time during the year, it is primarily an eastern bird, breeding from Nova Scotia and New Brunswick west to the Great Lakes and south as far as the Gulf States. During the cold months, heavy concentrations are found in the Carolinas and the states along the Gulf of Mexico, and some have been known to migrate as far as Jamaica and central Mexico.

The woody is to waterfowl what the ring-necked pheasant is to upland birds: positively alluring because of its appearance. The colorful drake ranges in length from 17 to 20 inches and in weight from about 1 to 1½ pounds. Overall, this duck is graced with bold aquatic colors contrasted with bars of white. His short bill is tomato red with a black tip. His head has two thin white stripes that accent a long, metallic-green crest whose sides are shaded in purple and blue. Don't mistake his eyes as being bloodshot, for they are pure red. The throat has a patch of white, the belly is white, and the breast is white stippled on a generally brownish-purple background. A black-and-white stripe divides the breast from the side feathers, which are buff. Although the wing primaries are gray, the coverts and secondaries are dynamic shades of purple, blue and green. The final touch is its long, dark tail.

Though not nearly as colorful as the male, the smaller female possesses much more in terms of looks than other hens in the duck family. Her gray-green crest is shorter than the male's; the eye ring, throat and belly are white, while the rest of the body is generally grayish-brown. Her breast and sides, though, are white flecks against brown like the male's.

Both male and female make whistling and guttural noises.

Wood ducks arrive at their breeding grounds in March, traveling in small flocks. Once at the northern grounds, they soon pair off and mate. The female usually initiates the courtship ritual by pointing her bill at the water and whistling softly. She then caresses his white throat patch with her bill, while her suitor displays his colors for her. He will also erect his crest and tail to impress her. Once paired, the two birds show an affection toward one another that is rarely found among other wildfowl.

Not long after courtship, the male and female go either to the place where the female was hatched or where she nested the previous year. The nesting spot usually consists of a tree hollow or even an abandoned woodpecker's hole high in a tree. The opening must be at least three inches in diameter and must contain a minimum of 50 square inches of floor space. Interestingly, the male inspects the prospective home as carefully as the female.

Once the nest has been chosen, the female settles in and lays between 10 and 15 shiny, white eggs. Incubation, which is the sole responsibility of the female, requires about four weeks, during which time the male does remain in the immediate vicinity.

After the young are hatched, the ducklings make their way down to the ground within a 24-hour period. Some experts say they jump from the nest, while others say that the female carries them down in her bill. Either way, the mother soon leads them to the water so they can begin feeding on insects and small aquatic animals.

The ducklings become capable of flight after about two months. During this time, the male loses his colorful plumage and flight feathers. And once the young are no longer dependent on their mother will she begin her own molt. When all the ducks can take to the skies again, the birds begin to migrate south for the winter, usually before late October. They start their return migration to the breeding grounds around mid-March.

Because of its sturdy legs and "sure-webbedness," the woody can climb to and perch on low branches, which facilitates its search for such foods as acorns, seeds and nuts. Add to these its regular staples of wild rice, smartweed, duckweed and water lilies, and the wood duck boasts quite a varied diet. This makes the bird's flesh extremely tasty—so much so that it was almost hunted into extinction in the early 1900's. Strict hunting regulations as well as the duck's responsiveness to nurturing in specified areas have enabled it to make a remarkable regeneration since that time, however.

The wood duck's average age is four years old. Since it isn't a land-nesting duck, the bird is safe from the enemies of most ducks. Tree-climbing snakes, on the other hand, take a heavy toll, as do winged birds of prey, such as the hawk and owl. The raccoon is the biggest robber of the nest.

Hunting Tips/wood duck

Many successful wood duck hunters are afield in the early morning and late afternoon hours. Most states allow gunners to take only one or two woodies a day, but the bird is so beautiful and good tasting that a small bag limit is more than enough enticement to keep hunters interested. Jump shooting, which involves walking along a stream or hunting a number of different ponds and potholes during the day, can be quite effective on woodies. The birds can also be decoyed effectively, but keep in mind that they are fast fliers and usually don't circle a decoy spread like mallards or other ducks do. Be ready, because you'll get but one chance at a given flock.

Dressing out techniques and recipes are detailed on pages 241-251.

Diving Ducks

CANVASBACK

Of the diving ducks, the canvasback is one of the largest and most sought after. Weighing about 3 pounds and measuring 21 to 23 inches, the canvasback breeds primarily in the Canadian provinces of Alberta, Manitoba, Saskatchewan, British Columbia and the Northwest Territories. The birds also breed in the Yukon River drainage of the Yukon and Alaska, as well as in parts of Washington, Oregon, Utah, Idaho, Montana, Wyoming, the Dakotas, Nebraska and Minnesota. Winter territories range from southern British Columbia south along the Pacific Coast to Mexico, and from northwestern Montana, northern Colorado, northeastern Arkansas, southern Illinois and Chesapeake Bay south to Florida and the Gulf coasts of Louisiana, Texas and central Mexico.

While similar in appearance to the redhead duck, the canvasback boasts a bit more distinctive coloring. The male's breast, wing primaries, rump, tail and under tail coverts are black, while his secondary and wing covert feathers and his back are finely etched striations of gray and white, resembling a woven swatch of canvas. His head is a muted red color, while his flank feathers go from gray to white on the belly. The female is colored much like the male, although several shades lighter, and she has a light brown head.

The canvasback has a fairly good vocabulary. The male peeps, growls, croaks and coos during the breeding, while the female quacks and *cuck-cucks,* and gives out a shrill-sounding call when alarmed.

Traveling in large flocks, often in V formations, canvasbacks begin to return to their breeding grounds in early spring. They pair up only after they have reached those grounds, and only after the courtship ceremonies have taken place. Courtship begins when the male throws back his head until it touches his back, and then utters a cooing sound as he returns to normal position. The female will then *cuck-cuck* in response. She may take off in flight if pursued by several males, but she will eventually select a mate and fly off with him alone.

The nest, which is extremely well-camouflaged by tall reeds in the water, is normally built near the shore of a pond, lake or slough. It is 18 inches in diameter, with the inside containing dead reeds and little down. Once the nest is completed, the female will lay from 7 to 10 eggs that must be incubated for 28 days or so.

Canvasback

The male leaves the female at this time, preferring instead to join other male canvasbacks and molt on a nearby body of water.

After hatching, the ducklings are capable of flight anywhere from 9 to 10 weeks later. Once they learn how to fly, however, they will exhibit extremely fast flights, reaching speeds of up to 75 miles per hour. The young ducks also grow protective feather cover that enables them to dive into deep water.

The canvasback loves the northern climes and won't leave the breeding grounds until the waters start to freeze over. The migration back north will begin as early as possible in the spring.

Since the bird's nest is usually built in reeds that are slightly offshore, the canvasback has little to fear from many land-based predators. Crows will steal the eggs, however, and minks, otters, fish, turtles, hawks, owls and eagles will attempt to take both young and adult birds. Due to their great speeds, canvasbacks are usually able to elude most winged predators.

An excellent swimmer and diver, the canvasback spends much of its daytime hours rafted out on big bays, river mouths or the ocean, returning closer to shore to feed at night. The bird will dive as deep as 30 feet to obtain food. About 80 percent of its diet is made up of vegetable matter, especially wild celery. The animal portion of its diet includes insects, larvae, mollusks, crustaceans and fish. Thanks to such a varied, primarily vegetable diet, the canvasback's flesh is considered gourmet fare by diners in the know.

Hunting Tips/canvasback

As well as being a shy bird, the canvasback is extraordinarily wary of the hunter. Gunners who use blinds and decoys often have a tough time getting their quarry. Better to use a skull boat, painted with dark, camouflaged colors, to reach the canvasback concentrations. Cover the boat with mud and clay, and even put a couple of decoys on the bow to make it look like a floating log. These birds move in bad weather, so if you can endure the cold and wet, your chances of success are greatly increased. Some of the best canvasback hunting takes place in the Chesapeake Bay area during the early fall.

For field dressing techniques and recipes, please refer to pages 241-251.

GREATER SCAUP

The greater scaup has a broad range, and in summer may be found in areas such as arctic Asia and Europe, northern Scotland, the Outer Hebrides and Iceland. In winter, large concentrations converge along the shores of the Mediterranean, Black and Caspian seas. The North American population, whose range is more limited than the lesser scaup, winters from Alaska to southern California on the Pacific side and from Texas along the Gulf Coast around Florida and northward to Maine on the Atlantic side. It breeds in the tundra areas of Hudson Bay, the Northwest Territories, the Yukon and Alaska. While not a saltwater breeder, it prefers to winter in saltwater areas.

Scaup, in general, are another group of beautiful birds. The greater scaup measures anywhere from 17 to 20 inches in length, with a weight of about 2 pounds. The male has a lustrous, dark metallic-green head and neck. His breast and rump are black, his flanks and belly are white, and his back is white with narrow, dark vermicular crossings. His upper wings, tail and under tail coverts are deep brown, while the secondary feathers are white edged with brown. Both the male and female have bright, blue-colored bills, and they are called "bluebills" in some areas. The female is generally lighter in color, however, and wears a white patch on the front of her face.

The bird's name is derived, many believe, from the sound it makes, which sounds more like a *scaup* then a quack. The greater scaup is a quiet bird when compared with other diving ducks.

The courtship display, which occurs at the breeding ground, is not very impressive. The male initiates the ritual by coughing, flicking his wings and tail, throwing his bill back until it touches his rump, and then snapping his head back to an upright position. If the female is interested, she will call softly to him. The birds dip their bills in the water several times before mating.

After mating has taken place, the female will build a nest that resembles a cradle in tall grasses that serve as protection. The nest will measure six to eight inches in diameter and two to four inches in depth. It will be sparsely lined, and will usually be located within a few feet of another pair's nest.

When she is ready, the female will lay six to 10 eggs. As is usual with most ducks, the male leaves when the female begins incubating. He heads either to sea or to a large lake, where he joins other males and starts to molt.

The young ducklings are able to fly after about seven weeks, at which time the female loses her flight feathers. While the scaup's takeoffs are very clumsy, once it is aloft it reaches speeds of approximately 60 miles per hour. The birds fly at very high altitudes during migration.

Most greater scaup begin their migration from the breeding grounds in the middle of September. They usually migrate northward to their breeding grounds around the middle of March, unless a harsh winter in the North delays them. The greater scaup is a flocking bird, and will travel, nest and fly together in great numbers.

Primarily an animal feeder, the bird dives for and eats mussels, clams, oysters, barnacles, crabs, fish and snails. It also will eat vegetables such as stems, leaves, roots and seeds.

The lifespan of the greater scaup is seven to nine years. Crows, hawks, gulls, owls, eagles, foxes, minks, turtles and fish are some of the predators that threaten it. The bird is also taken by hunters, although its flesh is not considered to be good table fare due to the bird's diet.

Hunting Tips/greater scaup

Most scaup hunting takes place along the Atlantic coastline of Long Island and in the Chesapeake Bay area. The greater scaup is a rather wary bird, particularly during the hunting season when it remains at sea during the daytime and feeds at night, thus avoiding most gunners. When alarmed, it often dives underwater, and is capable of staying beneath the surface for a full minute.

For dressing out instructions and recipes, turn to page 241.

LESSER SCAUP

The lesser scaup is so similar to the greater scaup that it is difficult to tell them apart. The difference in size between the two is only about one-half inch, and the coloration is almost the same. Except for being slightly smaller, the female lesser scaup is practically the twin of the female greater scaup.

The lesser scaup is not a vocal bird. Its call is very similar to that of the greater scaup, but not quite as clear. The male will also coo, while the female emits a harsh sound.

Unlike its slightly bigger cousin, the lesser scaup prefers freshwater to saltwater. The bird winters from the state of Washington around the perimeter of the United States, all the way to Connecticut. Lesser scaup also travel as far north along the Mississippi River as southern Illinois. In spring the birds fly in great numbers to breeding grounds that range from the north-central states and southeastern Ontario north through the prairie provinces of Canada and southern

British Columbia, to the west coast of Hudson Bay across to eastern Alaska and the Mackenzie Delta.

The lesser scaup doesn't return to the breeding grounds as early as the greater scaup does, primarily because the lessers go to more southerly areas. There is no ice when the birds arrive.

Pairing takes place before the birds leave their winter territories. During courtship, the male will bow to the female and make his *scaup* sound. The female may swim around the male, lifting her bill with a jerky motion. The two may also nip at each other somewhat, and preen to display their white feathers. The courtship display is quite similar to that of the greater scaup—in other words, not very elaborate. Lesser scaup prefer to build their nests near small ponds and sloughs. Most nests are built on dry land, either in high grass, under brush, protected by large rocks and at times out in the open. The female fills the cradle-like structure with grass and down.

Most clutches consist of nine to 12 eggs, which require a little less than four weeks to hatch. The young ducklings tend to stay together, flocklike, rather than scattering when predators are nearby. If the ducklings feel they cannot escape the danger by swimming away, they will dive. When they return to the surface, though, the young birds will immediately band together again. This safety-in-numbers approach works quite well for lesser scaup.

While the ducklings are gaining their bearings, papa duck, meanwhile, has left and gone into his molting, flightless period. In two and a half months, when the young are able to fly, the mama then goes into her molt. When grown, the ducklings eventually will be able to fly at 50 miles per hour.

The birds generally migrate farther south than the greater scaup, and consequently don't reach their winter grounds until November through early January. Interestingly, they fly almost non-stop in their quest to reach the warmer climes, perhaps only stopping for very brief rest and feeding periods. They begin their return to the breeding grounds in mid-March.

Since the lesser scaup consumes more vegetable matter than the greater scaup, its flesh is unquestionably more edible. About 60 percent of its diet consists of pondweeds, grasses (including wild rice), sedges, wild celery and smartweeds, while the rest includes animal matter such as mollusks and crustaceans.

The average lifespan is from seven to nine years, although, as with all ducks, many birds don't live that long. They are subject to virtually the same predators as most members of the duck family.

Hunting Tips/lesser scaup

The bird is not greatly hunted in the United States, and is not quite as wary as the more widely hunted and popular ducks. It will feed at night during hunting season, however, staying on large bodies of water during daylight hours. One excellent time to hunt these birds is when they first arrive in an area. They are hungry and not familiar with the territory at that time, and can offer good sport for a limited time. Once they learn which areas are dangerous, they become much more difficult to find.

Field dressing techniques and recipes may be found on pages 241-251.

REDHEAD

The redhead is an average-sized duck that many people can't distinguish from the canvasback. The redhead has a breeding range that includes parts of Nebraska, Iowa, the Dakotas, Minnesota, Montana, Idaho, Washington, California, Nevada, Oregon and Utah. It breeds as far east as western Pennsylvania and as far north as southern British Columbia, northern Alberta, central Saskatchewan and central Manitoba. Its winter range on the Pacific Coast runs from Washington south to Mexico and east to Louisiana, and on the Atlantic Coast from New Jersey south to North Carolina.

The redhead has a length of about 20 inches and weighs approximately 2½ pounds. The head and neck areas of the drake glisten with a rusty russet color. His breast, lower neck, upper back, rump and upper and lower tail coverts are black. The back, sides and flanks are white with black barring, while the belly itself is white. The wing coverts are gray, with the speculum pale gray with white edging. The female closely resembles the male, except her head lacks the reddish cast.

The redhead is a noisy bird as well. The male's call sounds quite similar to the meow of a cat, while the female makes a high-pitched squeak. She also emits a rattle-like *queek* during mating season.

Migration to the breeding grounds occurs early, and it is presumed that the birds pair off once they reach their destination. The female initiates the courting by emitting a soft note and pecking the feathers of the male she is interested in. In response he throws back his head, touches his tail, then slowly brings his head forward again. At this time he also calls softly to the female, and makes a pretense of preening behind his wing. Before mating, both male and female dip their bills in the water.

The nest, which measures about 16 inches in diameter, is usually made on a platform of dead reeds and rushes that are 10 to 12 inches above water. It is quite deep and lined with a large amount of down. A point of interest here is that both canvasback and redhead females will make their nests close together or even share the same nest. Two or more redheads also may lay their eggs in the same nest. Most females lay their eggs in a nest they have built themselves, however.

The normal clutch consists of 10 to 15 eggs, which are hatched in a little less than four weeks. Survival of the young ducklings seems more secure since they are hatched over water and do not have to make a perilous journey over dry land. The ducklings immediately take to the water and begin to feed on insects, although they soon switch to a vegetarian diet consisting of wild celery and grasses.

The young ducklings become capable of flight after about nine weeks. Unlike other members of the duck family, the male and female go into their molt during this time, meaning that all members of the family are incapable of flying at the same time. Once they regain their abilities to fly, they are able to hit 60 miles per hour with ease.

Redheads fly fairly long distances during migration, traveling in large, V-shaped flocks at extremely high altitudes. They begin their migratory flights to the winter territories in mid-September and usually reach their destinations by the first week of November. The flights to the breeding grounds begin the first of March, with the last of the ducks reaching the north by the middle of April.

With a life expectancy of seven to nine years, the redhead is safe from many of the natural predators of ducks since its nest is built on water. Raccoons do pose a threat, however, and crows will steal the redhead's eggs with impunity.

The redhead will frequently feed throughout the entire night, especially during hunting season and especially during times of the full moon. When found along the coasts its flesh is not as delicate as usual, due to a larger-than-normal intake of snails, mollusks, insects and other animal matter. The bird prefers vegetables such as wild rice, wild celery, bulrush, widgeon grass and musk grass, and when found inland its flesh can be exquisite.

Hunting Tips/redhead

Once a flock of redhead ducks has been spotted and shot at by a hunter, the birds will quickly depart the area at high speeds, reach watering places and then dive as deep as 10 feet, making it impossible for the gunner to get at his quarry. Redheads ideally should be hunted with a good caller, blind and decoys. Make sure that you space the decoys father apart than you would with mallard decoys, as diving ducks need greater space to feed. They move around a lot and frequently dive to great depths, as compared to surface ducks which usually put their heads only a few inches underwater to feed.

Pages 241-251 contain field dressing instructions and recipes.

Wild Geese

CANADA GOOSE

Its haunting cries symbolize the fall season more than any other sound made by a wild creature. Flying south at high altitudes in huge V-shaped flocks, the majestic Canada goose epitomizes wildlife and somehow stirs up our own deep-seated feelings to be free on the wind.

The Canada itself is probably the best-known and most-hunted member of the goose family. (There are five subspecies, the only difference being subtle color, size and voice variations.) Its range is all of the United States and most of Canada. It winters in almost every one of the lower 48 states, and breeds throughout the northern tier of states and Canada. The western coast of Hudson Bay across to Labrador and Newfoundland is a particularly popular breeding area. But if you include the growing population of resident, or non-migratory, geese, then many of the lower 48 states may also be considered as having breeding Canada populations.

Ranging in length from 22 to 42 inches, and with a weight range of 8 to 14 pounds, the Canada goose is brownish-gray in coloration. The head and neck of both male and female are ink-black, with the exception of white cheeks and chin straps. The upper part of the body is grayish-brown, although the feathers there are slightly edged. There is also barring on the lighter-colored flanks. The breast and belly are a lighter shade of brown-gray, with very faint bars. The primary wing feathers are black, with the secondaries a darker brown and the coverts a lighter brown. The tail is black, and the tail and under-tail coverts pure white. The bird's wingspan can stretch up to six feet across.

A noisy bird, the Canada can *honk* quite loudly, especially when it is searching for its mate. When large flocks assemble, the honking noises can often be heard up to a mile away. The birds also hiss when threatened.

Canada geese always return to the identical breeding grounds where they were hatched, stopping to rest at the same spots along the way. When they do reach the breeding grounds, the males will engage in vicious fights for the opportunity to woo any available females. The neck is used quite extensively in the courtship ritual, with the male and female rubbing their necks against each other and then passing them over each other's body. They also go through the bill-dipping ceremony before mating. Once a mate is chosen, the male and female will then stay together and mate for life. Contrary to popular belief, however, if one of the pair should die, the other will not lead a

Canada goose

solitary existence for the rest of its life. While it may spend one spring alone, it will eventually seek another mate.

After mating, the female will lay five to seven whitish eggs in a bulky nest that she has constructed of whatever materials happen to be nearby. The nest may be built on top of a muskrat house, on the bank of a stream or pothole, on top of rocks or boulders, or in a tree. Some hens even take advantage of man-made structures and abandoned osprey or eagle nests. Regardless of how the outer structure appears, it is well-lined with down to provide a warm, cushiony home for her eggs and goslings. In fact, since the nests are usually left exposed, the thick down is the only available camouflage.

The eggs hatch after being incubated by the female for approximately four weeks. The gander keeps a constant watch of the nest during this period, and will put up a fierce fight to keep anything and everything away from the female and nest. About two days after the eggs have hatched, the father will lead the goslings to water with the mother following. Both the female and male molt immediately after nesting, and since the young have not yet grown flight feathers, the entire family cannot fly for at least a month. They will sleep on the water during the night, and return at almost the same hour in the mornings and evenings to feed on shore.

Once the birds have regained their flight feathers, they begin to mass in large flocks preparatory to their migration to the winter grounds in autumn. While migrating, Canada geese fly in flocks in the familiar V formation, honking as they go. The flight leader is usually an older male, who will drop back and let another male take over the lead when he tires. The birds return to the North in April and May, flying day and night and stopping when they become fatigued or hungry. With a good wind behind them, the birds can hit 65 miles per hour with little difficulty.

Innately intelligent birds, Canada geese seem to have a sixth sense as to where protected areas with good food sources are located. They will even change their feeding habits—spending the nights feeding and the days resting in sanctuaries—if they find an area that suits their dietary needs. The Canada is basically a grazing bird and will eat a variety of grasses. It also likes food produced on cultivated lands, much to the consternation of farmers who live near refuges.

If not taken by hunters, the Canada can expect to live from 15 to 20 years. While the young and the eggs of the Canada goose are subject to predation from skunks, raccoons, foxes, coyotes, hawks, eagles, owls

and turtles, the adult is safe from most predators due to its size. Thanks to its very rich diet, however, the Canada makes for superb table fare and is consequently sought after by a large number of hunters.

Hunting Tips/canada goose

Depending upon which area of the country you live in, the best way to hunt geese is: field hunting, which involves hiding in a blind and attempting to call the birds into range through the use of silhouette decoys and calls; firing line or pass shooting, where you study the flight patterns of birds coming in and out of a refuge and set up along those routes; and hunting over open water, where you hide in a blind and use calls and floating decoys to lure the birds into range.

For dressing out procedures and recipes, please see pages 241-251.

SNOW GOOSE

Scientists recognize two species of snow goose— the greater snow goose and the lesser snow goose— with the primary difference being that the greater snow goose is a larger counterpart of the lesser variety. The smaller bird seldom finds its way to the Atlantic Coast, while the greater snow goose is strictly an eastern migrant. In general, snow geese breed along the Arctic Coast from Point Barrow to Southampton Island and Baffin Island. In winter they can be found from the West Coast to the Mississippi Valley and from southern British Columbia through Oregon, Colorado and parts of Illinois down to the Gulf Coast from Texas to Florida. The greater snow goose may be found wintering along the Atlantic Coast from Maryland to South Carolina.

Male and female snow geese are similar in appearance. Each bird has a body length of about 30 inches and each weighs 5 to 6 pounds. The snow goose is completely white with the exception of the black primaries and wing tips. Its head is often stained rust-colored from bobbing for food in mineral-rich waters. When its wing tips are not visible, many people mistake the snow goose for a small swan.

The snow goose communicates with a shrill *honk* or gabbling.

Like other members of the goose family, it is believed that snow geese mate for life. Due to the inaccessibility of their nesting grounds, however, the birds have not been studied as extensively as other geese, and much information is still missing on their habits. It is presumed that pairing up is done on the winter range, prior to leaving the wintering grounds. Though they will put on a good show to discourage other males, male snow geese do not get into vicious battles with other birds.

Breeding takes place after courtship, with the female then building a shallow ground nest and filling it with a sparse amount of vegetable matter and an extravagance of down. The nests are usually found in wetlands, as there is little dry ground in the parts of the world where snow geese breed. The female lays four to eight eggs that are incubated for four weeks, sometimes by both the male and the female. If the male does not help with the incubating, he will remain close at hand, alert for danger.

Once the eggs have hatched and the down has dried, the goslings leave the nest and begin feeding on insects. Since the goose is primarily a vegetarian, the young birds soon switch their diet to vegetation. The goslings attain their flight capabilities after about 50 days, and in mid-September are ready to join the rest of the flock on the trip to the winter grounds.

Snow geese are strong fliers, attaining speeds of 50 miles per hour. If they have a favorable wind behind them, their speeds can go much higher than that. They travel both day and night during migration, and stop for rest, food and water along the way. The flocks travel at high altitudes, up to 5,000 feet, in the standard V formation. Many times the birds are difficult to spot, as they fly so high that their coloring blends in with the clouds.

As is true with most members of the goose family, snow geese will stick to a pattern of feeding at the same time every day, and will usually land during migration at a stopover area where they have landed before. Although not much is known about their summer feeding habits, on the wintering grounds they eat aquatic plants as well as fresh sprouts of cereal and ordinary grasses. In autumn they frequent the stubble fields. Berries, wild rice, aquatic insects and small mollusks are also consumed.

The normal life span of the snow goose is a little more than 10 years. In their breeding grounds, they are the prey of such predators as gulls, jaegers, arctic foxes and ravens. In their winter grounds, one of their greatest enemies is the hunter. Their flesh is not nearly as delicate as that of the Canada goose, but it is still quite edible. Most gunners use the same hunting tactics that they use for Canada and white-fronted geese.

Dressing out instructions and recipes begin on page 241.

WHITE-FRONTED GOOSE

A widespread bird, the white-fronted goose breeds in the arctic regions of northeastern Europe, Asia and North America. On this continent, it breeds in the northern half of Alaska, the Yukon and the Northwest Territories. It also breeds along the southern coast of Greenland. It winters in the southern parts of Europe, Asia and in North America from southern British Columbia and southern Illinois south to the Gulf Coast states and Mexico.

The bird itself is about 30 inches long and weighs around 5½ pounds. Its head, neck, back, rump and wings are gray-brown in coloration. The tail is dark brown with white edging, and the upper and under tail coverts are white. The breast and belly are grayish-white splotched with blackish-brown. A broad white streak reaches from the pink bill into the forehead. The male and female look alike, although the female is somewhat smaller in size.

Like all geese, the whitefront is a noisy bird, emitting a *wa-wa* sound when it talks and gabbling constantly when it feeds.

As with other geese, white-fronted geese also mate for life. The courtship ritual is quite similar to that of the Canada, although the white-fronted male is extremely protective of the female even after the two have paired. He'll make threatening gestures to any other male he feels is approaching too close to his mate.

After breeding, the female hollows out a nest in the ground and fills it with grass, moss and a large amount of down. Most nests are built near the edges of pools or lakes. Once she has completed the nest, the female will settle in and lay one egg per day for five to seven days. The pale pinkish eggs take about a month to hatch.

The male, who has stayed nearby in the event of danger during this period, now assists in the care of the goslings. It will take about two months before they are able to fly. During this time, both adults lose their feathers. Once the family members have all regained their flying abilities, they can reach 50 miles per hour with little trouble. As with most geese, the white-fronted goose must run on the water before it gains enough momentum to take off.

White-fronted geese are hardy birds that seem to withstand the cold weather better than other birds do. The birds will stay at their breeding grounds until they are forced to leave by ice covering the lakes, ponds and streams, usually in mid-September in the far north. The birds then don't return to the breeding grounds until late April or early May. As with other geese, this species also fly in a V formation, with an experienced gander in the lead for much of the way. During migration, they fly so high that they are difficult to spot.

The bird's diet includes wild grains, grasses, berries and buds as well as cultivated grain from farms. Feeding takes place twice a day at set times in the morning and later in the afternoon. Thanks to such a vegetation-filled diet, the white-fronted goose is the best-tasting of all members of the goose family.

The average life span of the white-fronted goose is 12 years. Jaegers, gulls, ravens, foxes and even bears will prey on it, although probably its greatest enemy is the hunter intent upon putting food on the table. Hunting tactics are basically the same as those employed for Canada geese.

Field dressing techniques and recipes follow.

Dressing Out Ducks and Geese

Anyone who has ever hunted waterfowl will agree that there are many ways to dress out a duck or goose. And what you do—and how—is largely determined by the weather conditions.

If the temperature is below 40° F. (4° C.), you can opt to wait until you get back to camp or home to dress out your bird. It's a good idea, however, at least to dry-pluck the breast feathers and expose the breast to the cool air, letting some of the body heat out. Simply rub your thumb and forefingers together with the feathers that cover the breast area and they will come off very easily, especially since the bird is still warm. Remember that if you do wait to eviscerate, the bigger the bird, the more body heat it contains and the greater the possibility of spoilage. So if you've bagged a big one, I would suggest that you open the bird as well as dry-pluck the breast feathers. Make an incision just under the breast and cut straight down to the vent, or cut horizontally across the bird under the breast. The key thing is to open the bird to start the cooling process.

To many hunters the breast of the duck is the most important part. They want to save only that and discard the rest. After you have plucked the feathers off the breast of the duck, you can use a pair of shears to cut into the soft area and cut the breast completely out while you throw the rest of the bird away.

If it is warmer than 40° F. (4° C.), you will immediately want to remove the entrails to let some of the body heat out of the bird. This will prevent the bird from spoiling and help it taste a lot better than if it had begun to sour, or turn green. This could ruin a good bird and make it unfit for the table. As with other birds, to field dress, begin by making a straight cut from the edge of the breastbone to the vent (or from the vent, up; either way accomplishes the job), or make a curved incision (*See Figure 4-1*). Open up this area with your hands, pull out the innards and detach the intestines as close to the anus as possible. Then take your knife and slit the throat as shown in *Figure 4-1* and pull out the crop and windpipe and cut them off.

You should be able to reach in with your fingers and get out everything with the exception of the lungs. Make sure you keep the liver, gizzard or giblets, because they are very tasty. Keep them in a small plastic bag or put them back into the cavity after you have wiped it out with a few dry cloths. Use dry leaves or grass instead if you have nothing else to use. Do not use water, as it will attract bacteria, especially if it is warm.

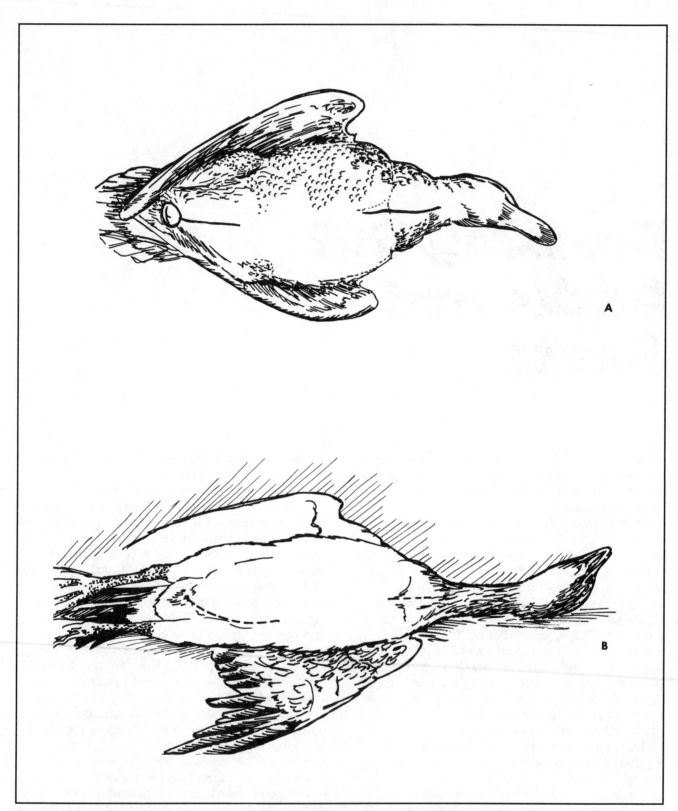

4-1. In dressing out ducks and geese, you can make either (A) a straight cut from the breastbone to the vent, or (B) a curved incision, starting at the vent and working around. Proceed as with other birds, making sure to remove the crop and windpipe by slitting in the throat area.

After gutting, prop the cavity open with sticks and hang the bird as high as you can so it will cool and so the dogs you've been hunting with cannot reach it. If you hang it on the edge of a blind or a tree, for example, it will also act as a decoy. So it will serve a dual purpose: good meat and a realistic lure. Goose hunters are always propping their dead geese up along with their own blocks or white squares as extra decoys in large fields where they are hunting. Do not, however, hang your catch in direct sunlight.

If you brought along an ice chest because you thought the weather was going to be warm, forget about the decoy and immediately place your ducks or geese in the chest for best results. This will cool the birds quickly.

Whether you should dry-pluck your birds or use the hot water dipping method depends on several factors: how much time you have; where you are; how many birds you've shot; and sometimes how much success you've previously experienced with a particular method. Many hunters use both techniques and I'll describe each one at this time, and you can take your pick.

As mentioned above with depluming the breast, dry-plucking, or picking, is simply to rub the feathers between your thumb and forefingers. You can pull the feathers with the grain of the skin, but at an angle is preferred by many, as you might tear some of the skin and end up with a bird that does not look very appetizing. Dry-plucking the bird is easier with the innards still in the bird, but the weather and time of course will dictate this. Do not pull too fast or too hard.

Waxing. Some hunters like to hang certain types of birds, including ducks and geese, for several days with the idea that they will taste better. Some even age them for eight to 10 days to give them a distinct flavor. By this time, in order to pluck their birds, they would require a good dipping. The waxing method, which I prefer, is just one step beyond the scalding process described in the turkey chapter. With the waxing operation, you simply take the bird and plunge it in a pail of hot (about 180° F., 82° C.) water to which some paraffin wax has been added. Use one cake of paraffin to two quarts of water. Hold the bird by the legs and slowly dip it into the water maybe two times, coating the plumage with the wax. Make sure you do not overdip the bird. You can check this by pulling at the feathers to see if they come out easily. You do not want to cook the fat on the skin of the bird. If you leave the bird in water too long, the skin will peel off in large areas, so take your time, test the water and keep the

temperature at 180° F. (82° C.). When the feathers are ready to come off, allow the wax to cool and dry and you can lift the feathers off rather easily.

After plucking the feathers, there will still be some small pinheads and plume on the bird. Use a dull knife or tweezers for these and singe off the filoplumes, or fuzz-like feathers. Do this by holding the bird in a horizontal position in one hand and a rolled newspaper in the other. Light the newspaper and, holding it at arm's length, let the flame singe off the feathers that are remaining. *Do not* face upwind if you are outside doing this; the flames could burn you by blowing back on you. A candle, cigarette lighter or propane torch are also effective and probably safer.

I find that whether I've aged a bird or not, the wet-dipping process with waterfowl is by far the most efficient. Many duck hunting clubs own their own plucking machines, which you can use, but for do-it-yourselfers, keep the above instructions in mind, and you can't go wrong.

Now, finish preparing the bird for eating. After you have completely gutted your bird and removed the feathers, cut the preen gland out by cutting around the button-like nodule found at the base of the tail (*See Figure 4-2*). Be careful not to cut into the gland itself, since it contains the oil that the bird uses to waterproof its feathers. Without this oil, the bird could not live very long unprotected from wetness.

You then want to cut off the feet at the first joints, the wings, if you don't want them, and the head. You should have a fine looking bird. Run cold, salted water through the bird to clean it further and start the chilling process. You really do not want to put the bird in a freezer at this point, because some body heat still remains. By freezing it quickly, you can cause a different taste in the bird, as fiber and crystals will react differently with warm birds as opposed to chilled ones. A good idea is to place the bird in an ice chest or refrigerator for about three hours or so if you are going to freeze it and not eat it right away. Also, if your duck is freezer-bound, be sure to review the basic freezing instructions found on pages 154 and 175.

Boning a Duck. If you really want to get something extra out of your hard work of duck hunting, try boning your bird.

Lay the duck on a good cutting board or flat wooden surface breast side down. Take a sharp knife, preferably a boning knife, that will not dull easily. If you need a whetstone, place it nearby, because you are about to carve the meat away as close to the bone as possible. As shown in *Figure 4-3*, start at about the center of the neck or as close to the front of the bird as

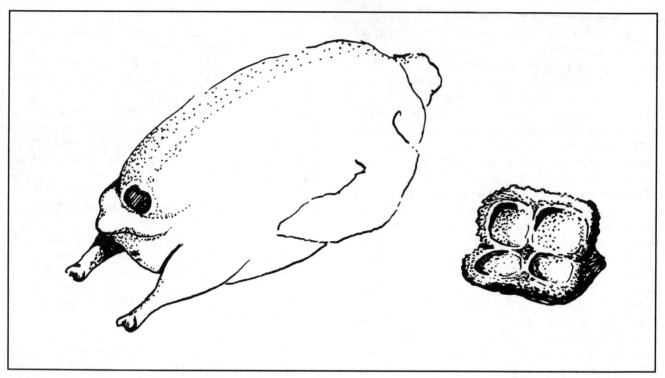

4-2. This will give you a good idea of what you'll find when you remove the preen gland on the underside of the bird. When cutting it out, be sure to leave yourself plenty of room around it so as not to puncture it in any way.

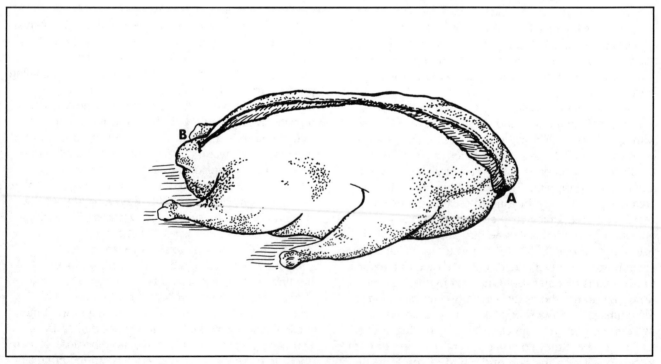

4-3. Boning a duck is not as difficult as you may think. Begin by placing your bird breast side down on a flat surface or a wooden cutting board. With a sharp boning knife, start at the neck (A) and cut down to the high rise in the pelvic region (B), making sure you cut through the skin and cartilage to open up the area.

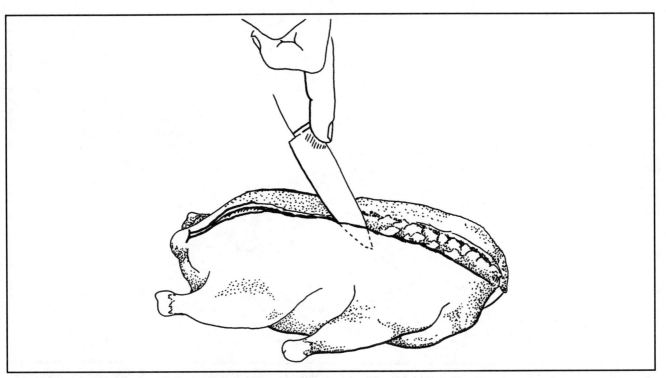

4-4. Cut along either side of the backbone until you reach the thighbone, peeling away skin and flesh as you go.

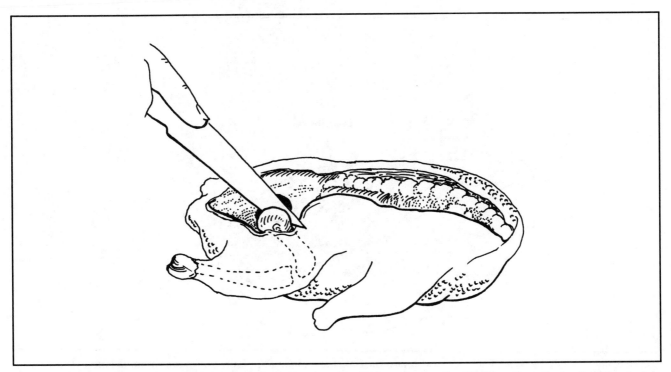

4-5. At the thigh joint, insert the knife between the ball and socket. Twist and sever the thighbone from the body of the duck; do the same on the other side of the bird.

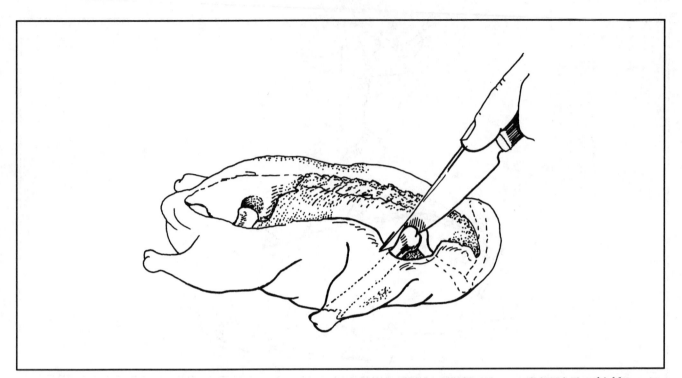

4-6. At the other end of the duck, wedge your knife down into the shoulder bone. Cut it free as you did with the thighbone; be sure to do both sides.

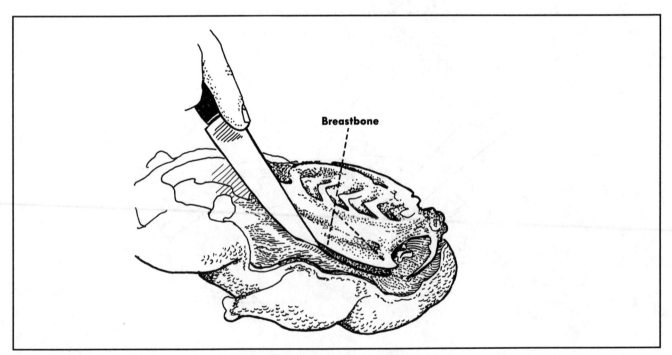

Breastbone

4-7. Now cut through the wing joints and back toward the breastbone, trying to lift the bones away from the meat as much as possible.

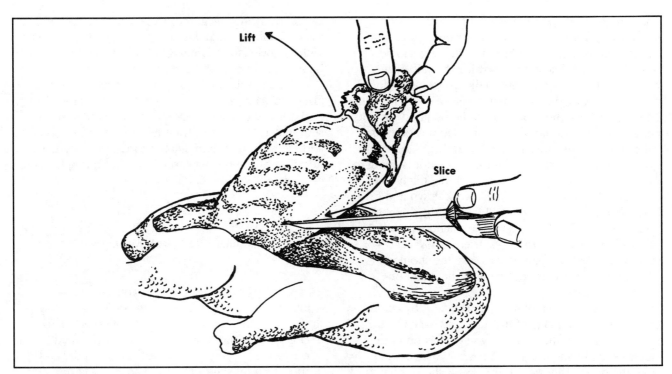

4-8. With one hand, lift up the entire skeleton while cutting away with the other hand any meat that's still attached. Be very careful not to cut into the breast of the duck.

4-9. Gently cut around the pelvic region to free the entire set of bones and extract them in one piece.

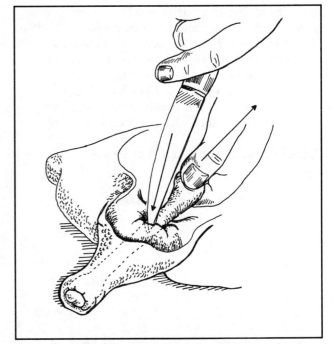

4-10. Finally, remove the leg and wing bones by pushing back the flesh around the bones and cutting away any tendons that still adhere. You now have a completely boned bird, ready to stuff with your favorite dressing.

you can get. Staying in the center of the bird, cut a straight line from front to back as deeply as you can, but be sure to stop at the high area in the back, which is at about the pelvic arch. Following the side of the backbone, cut from the front to the back where the thighbone is located, as shown in *Figure 4-4*. With your hands, peel back the meat next to the backbone as you cut along the sides of the backbone. Do this on both sides of that bone. Your bird will then begin to open up and you will start to see just how good it is going to be. Stop your cutting when you reach the thighbone.

With the point of your knife, work down and in between the socket and the ball joint of the thighbone until it breaks loose, then sever the thighbone itself. Do this on both sides (*Figure 4-5*). Then as in *Figure 4-6*, cut toward the front until you expose the shoulder bone and cut it free as you did with the thighbone; do this on both sides.

Remove the large bones from the flesh by cutting through the wing joints of the duck and back toward the breast. Lift up the bones as you do this on both sides, remembering to cut all the meat you can away from the bone (*Figure 4-7*). *Figure 4-8* shows how to lift up the bone with one hand, while using the knife with the other. Make sure that you do not cut into or take away from any of the breast. Look at *Figure 4-9*. This is almost the finale, so take your time, cut and pull at the same time all around the tail end or the pelvic area until you can remove the large portion of bone. As shown in *Figure 4-10,* push down on the meat attached to the leg bone and cut away the meat as you lift the bone out. Do the same with the wing bone.

There you have it. You've just boned your own duck. Now you can stuff it with your favorite stuffing. Try bread stuffing and seedless grapes as a starter.

Cooking/ducks and geese

Leftover Wild Duck
(Serves 2)

1 or 2 cold leftover ducks with bones	2 tablespoons soy sauce
1 small onion stuck with 2 cloves	4 cups beef stock
	5 tablespoons butter
1 teaspoon dried thyme	5 tablespoons flour
1 teaspoon salt	2 cups duck or chicken stock
½ teaspoon freshly ground black pepper	½ cup red wine
1 tablespoon Worcestershire sauce	1 tablespoon grated orange rind

Cut leftover duck meat into large serving pieces and set aside. Combine the bones and the next six ingredients with the beef stock. Bring to a boil and simmer for two hours. Strain broth and correct seasonings.

In large skillet over medium heat melt butter, add flour and cook, stirring, 5 to 6 minutes to color slightly. Add duck or chicken stock and cook until thickened, stirring constantly to prevent lumps. Correct seasoning, add pieces of duck and simmer for 25 to 30 minutes. Add the wine and orange rind and heat through. Serve on a bed of boiled white rice.

Creamed Duck with Mushrooms
(Serves 4 to 5)

2 cups leftover duck, cut into pieces	1 10-ounce package frozen peas
flour	2 tablespoons fresh parsley, chopped
4 tablespoons butter or margarine	salt, black pepper and paprika to taste
2 cups fresh mushrooms, sliced	½ cup sour cream
¼ cup onion, chopped	2 tablespoons sherry (optional)
1 10¾-ounce can chicken broth	
1 10¾-ounce can cream of chicken or cream of mushroom soup	

Dredge meat in flour. Melt butter or margarine in a large skillet; add meat, mushrooms and onion and brown over medium heat until onions are tender. Add chicken broth slowly, stirring constantly, then add cream of chicken or mushroom soup and blend well. Mix in peas, parsley, salt, pepper and paprika and simmer over low heat until peas are cooked, about 10 to 15 minutes. Add sour cream and sherry, if desired, and stir well. Serve over rice, noodles or biscuits.

Special Wild Duck
(Serves 4 to 6)

4 wild ducks	salt and freshly ground pepper to taste
4 apples	¾ cup currant jelly
3 large onions	⅓ cup brandy
4 celery ribs with tops	
4 tablespoons butter, softened	

Clean ducks and dry them thoroughly, inside and out. Stuff each duck with a piece or two of apple, a piece of onion and celery, all brushed with softened butter. Rub the ducks well with butter and season with salt and pepper. Melt the currant jelly, combine with brandy and baste ducks.

Place ducks in a large roasting pan on a rack and roast at 400° F., basting with currant jelly mixture every 10 minutes. Cook 35 to 40 minutes for rare duck, 45 minutes for medium-rare. Transfer to serving plate and pour over the pan juices.

Duck with Wild Rice

(Serves 5 to 6)

2 ducks, cleaned and cut into serving pieces	1 10¾-ounce can cream of celery soup
6 cups water	¾ cup wild rice, uncooked
salt and pepper to taste	¾ cup long grain rice
1 package onion soup mix	

Place ducks in a large Dutch oven with water and salt and pepper. Bring to boil and simmer until meat is tender, approximately 1½ hours.

Transfer the meat to a platter and add the soup mix and canned soup and rice to the liquid. Stir well and cook for an additional ¾ hour, or until rice is tender. Return duck to Dutch oven. A little more water may be added if necessary. Cook for 5 to 10 more minutes to heat duck thoroughly.

Duck a l'Orange with Orange Stuffing

(Serves 3 to 4)

1 large duck, cleaned	2 cups orange juice
1 medium onion, sliced	1 cup sherry
1 stalk celery, chopped	salt and black pepper to taste
1 large unpeeled orange, sliced	

Orange Stuffing:

3 cups stale bread, broken in pieces	½ cup pecans or almonds, chopped
1 cup milk	½ cup butter or margarine
½ cup orange juice	2 cups celery, chopped
salt to taste	3 eggs, beaten

Wash duck and dry the night before cooking.

Place onion, celery and orange slices in a large roasting pan. Lightly salt cavity of duck and place bird on top of vegetables and fruit. Mix together the orange juice and sherry and pour over duck. Cover and refrigerate, basting occasionally. Prepare Orange Stuffing.

Orange Stuffing: Place bread in large mixing bowl with milk, orange juice, salt and nuts. Let stand.

In a medium skillet, melt butter or margarine over low heat. Add celery and cook until it begins to become transparent. Combine butter and celery with bread mixture, add the beaten eggs and mix well.

Remove duck from refrigerator, stuff, and salt and pepper the breast. Roast at 350° F. for approximately 2 hours or until the duck is tender. Baste several times during cooking.

Roast Duck with Sweet Potatoes

(Serves 2)

2 cups apples, sliced	1 duck, cleaned
½ cup dark seedless raisins	3 or 4 fresh sweet potatoes, peeled and halved lengthwise
1 cup chopped walnuts (optional)	1 cup orange juice
1 cup dark brown sugar	

Combine apples, raisins and nuts, if desired, with half the brown sugar and mix well. Fill cavity of duck with this mixture and place in roasting pan. Put sweet potatoes around duck and sprinkle them with the remaining sugar. Pour orange juice over duck and sweet potatoes and tent with aluminum foil. Roast at 325° F. about 2 hours, basting occasionally.

Dutch Duck and Sauerkraut

(Serves 3 to 4)

1 duck, cleaned and dry	1 cup onion, diced
salt and black pepper to taste	1 cup celery, diced
	1 cup water
2 quarts sauerkraut	2 tablespoons sugar

Place duck in a roasting pan, lightly salt the cavity, and salt and pepper the flesh. Place sauerkraut around the bird. Add water to the pan and sprinkle onion and celery over the sauerkraut.

Cover duck and cook in oven at 350° F. for about 1½ hours or until tender. Uncover for the last 20 minutes of cooking to allow duck to brown.

Stuffed Roast Duck
(Serves 4 to 6)

4 wild ducks

4 slices barding pork

Stuffing:

1 cup onion, chopped
1 cup parsley, finely chopped
1 teaspoon dried thyme
½ teaspoon sage

2 cups bread crumbs
1 teaspoon salt
1 teaspoon black pepper, freshly ground
1 cup butter, melted

In a large mixing bowl, thoroughly combine the first 7 stuffing ingredients. Add just enough melted butter to make the mixture moist. Stuff the ducks and tie a piece of barding pork over each breast.

Place on a rack in roasting pan and cook at 350° F. for 45 minutes to an hour. Baste frequently with melted butter.

Breast of Goose with White Wine Sauce
(Serves 4)

1 goose breast, skin removed
salt and pepper to taste
flour

4 tablespoons vegetable oil
1 small onion, minced
2 cloves garlic, minced

Season the breast and dredge in flour. Heat oil in a medium-hot skillet and brown breast on both sides. Add the onion and garlic and cook until tender. Add the cream sauce, cover and reduce heat to low. Cook for approximately 45 minutes or until tender.

White Wine Cream Sauce:

2 cups chicken broth
½ cup butter or margarine
1 cup evaporated milk
3 tablespoons cornstarch plus water

¼ cup sour cream
¼ cup dry white wine
salt to taste

White Wine Cream Sauce: Over medium heat, warm chicken broth in saucepan. Add butter in chunks and stir until it is melted. Add evaporated milk; stir and heat until hot. In a separate bowl or cup, mix enough water with the cornstarch to cover it and make it liquefy; then slowly add it to the broth, stirring constantly until the mixture thickens. Add sour cream, wine and salt to taste. Pour over breast of goose. This is also excellent served with other birds or chicken.

Cheddar Creamed Goose
(Serves 4)

1½ to 2 cups leftover goose meat, cut into one-inch cubes
2 to 3 tablespoons flour
4 tablespoons butter
2 tablespoons vegetable oil
1 small onion, diced
1 10¾-ounce can cream of mushroom soup

1 10¾-ounce can cheddar cheese soup
1 10¾-ounce can chicken broth or 1 cup broth from the baked goose
salt and pepper to taste
1 10-ounce package frozen peas and carrots

Dredge goose cubes in flour. In a large skillet melt butter with oil over medium heat. Brown cubes on all sides in skillet. Add onion and continue to cook for about 10 minutes, until onion is tender. Add soups and broth, stirring well. Sprinkle with seasoning to taste and add peas and carrots. Cover and simmer for about 10 to 15 minutes, stirring occasionally. Serve over rice, toast points or your favorite biscuits.

Smoked Goose
(Serves 4 to 6)

salt and freshly ground black pepper
⅔ cup salt
1 tablespoon sugar

1 teaspoon saltpeter
1 clove garlic, sliced
1 large, whole goose, cleaned

Rinse goose in cold water and pat dry. Sprinkle inside of cavity with salt and pepper. Combine ⅔ cup salt, sugar and saltpeter. Rub outside of goose with garlic clove; then rub the entire goose with the salt mixture.

Place the goose in a crock and cover with a cloth, then the lid. Set in a cool place for 7 days, turning occasionally. Drain any juices off the goose and cover the entire goose with cheesecloth. Smoke as you would any meat. Chill and slice very thinly to serve.

Roast Goose with Cherry Sauce
(Serves 4 to 6)

1 large goose, cleaned
salt and pepper to taste

paprika
½ cup butter or
    margarine

Cherry Sauce:

⅓ cup white sugar
⅓ cup brown sugar
2 tablespoons cornstarch
½ teaspoon cinnamon
1 cup cherry juice plus ½
    cup water

2 cups sour cherries,
    pitted and drained
2 tablespoons lemon juice
2 tablespoons brandy
    (optional)
2 tablespoons butter or
    margarine

Preheat oven to 425° F. Place the well-cleaned goose in a large roasting pan. Season the bird with salt, pepper and paprika. Melt butter in a saucepan and pour over the goose. Place a cover on the roaster or use a foil-type tent. Place the bird in the oven and immediately reduce the heat to 325° F. Roast for about 2 to 2½ hours until the thigh meat is tender.

Uncover goose and spoon off the accumulated juices. These may be used for gravy or for soup stock. Use about one-half of the cherry sauce and baste the goose with it. Continue to bake for about a half-hour more to let brown. Baste once more in about 15 minutes. Keep remaining sauce warm in the saucepan and serve with goose at the table.

Cherry Sauce: Blend white and brown sugars in a saucepan. Add cornstarch and cinnamon; mix. Slowly add cherry juice and water, stirring well. Bring to a boil over medium heat, stirring constantly. Remove from heat; add cherries, lemon juice, brandy and butter. Keep sauce warm until ready to use.

Index